To Steve

Best Wishes

Keith

CONSULTING
MASTERY

KEITH MERRON

CONSULTING
MASTERY

How the best make the biggest difference

BERRETT-KOEHLER PUBLISHERS, INC.
San Francisco

Berrett-Koehler Publishers, Inc.
235 Montgomery Street, Suite 650
San Francisco, CA 94104-2916
Tel: (415) 288-0260 Fax: (415) 362-2512 www.bkconnection.com

Ordering Information
Quantity sales. Special discounts are available on quantity purchases by corporations,
associations, and others. For details, contact the "Special Sales Department" at the
Berrett-Koehler address above.
Individual sales. Berrett-Koehler publications are available through most bookstores.
They can also be ordered direct from Berrett-Koehler: Tel: (800) 929-2929;
Fax: (802) 864-7626; www.bkconnection.com
Orders for college textbook/course adoption use. Please contact Berrett-Koehler:
Tel: (800) 929-2929; Fax: (802) 864-7626.
Orders by U.S. trade bookstores and wholesalers. Please contact Publishers Group West,
1700 Fourth Street, Berkeley, CA 94710. Tel: (510) 528-1444; Fax (510) 528-3444.
Berrett-Koehler and the BK logo are registered trademarks of Berrett-Koehler Publishers, Inc.

Printed in the United States of America

Berrett-Koehler books are printed on long-lasting acid-free paper. When it is available, we choose
paper that has been manufactured by environmentally responsible processes. These may include
using trees grown in sustainable forests, incorporating recycled paper, minimizing chlorine in
bleaching, or recycling the energy produced at the paper mill.

Library of Congress Cataloging-in-Publication Data
Merron, Keith.
    Consulting mastery : how the best make the biggest difference / by Keith Merron.
        p.   cm.
    Includes index.
    ISBN-13: 978-1-57675-320-0
    1. Business consultants. 2. Consultants. I. Title.
HD69.C6M454   2005
001—dc22   2004062317
FIRST EDITION
10 09 08 07 06 05   10 9 8 7 6 5 4 3 2 1

Text design by Detta Penna
Copyedit by Pat Brewer
Index by Joan Dickey

CONTENTS

PREFACE

WHEN I WAS A YOUNG CONSULTANT, a trusted, senior advisor of mine sometimes said to me: "Keith, that piece of work you just did was helpful, but not powerful." I was adding value, he was telling me, but not truly making a difference. That feedback stuck in my craw, and many years later, there it remains. For me, "good enough" is never good enough.

This book aims to answer one fundamental question: How do I make a big difference as a consultant? Many consultants want to make a difference, yet few manage to be more than "helpful." They solve problems and plug holes for the client, often unaware that the process they are engaging in does little to alter the very dynamics that created the problems in the first place. Moreover, most consultants cannot see the limiting features of their own approach because they follow a model of consulting that is rarely discussed, challenged, or examined. After all, most consulting firms that make a lot of money utilize the same model, so it must be successful.

A DIFFERENCE IN PERSPECTIVE

This book shifts the perspective. The shift moves the consultant from being a savior and problem-solver to being an empowering partner. Picture on the one hand a consultant who follows the conventional problem-solving model that most consultants follow and indeed solves the problem for the client. Contrast that with a consultant who engages the client organization in a process of inquiry that results in a set of insights that over time alters the culture itself—the way the organization thinks. This first consultant is "helpful." But the second consultant is extraordinary because his work catalyzes insight, awareness, and deep change. That kind of consulting rocks the client's world.

The difference between the two consultants isn't just a difference in behavior. Nor does it involve adopting new tools and techniques. No, the difference is in the consultant's attitude, a difference in the consultant's mindset, a difference in the consultant's definition of who he is as a consultant. In short, to move from being a problem solver to an empowering partner requires a fundamental shift in one's *inner stance* as a consultant.

THE AUDIENCE FOR THE BOOK

This book is directly aimed for serious consultants committed to improving their craft. In particular, it's written for those consultants whose goal is to change or enhance the growth of the client organization in some appreciable way. This includes—but is by no means limited to—consultants who help reorganize organizations, create strategic direction, craft marketing approaches that significantly reshape a company's definition of its business, and seek to positively influence an organization's culture. It includes external and internal consultants alike.

While aimed at consultants in general, this book is also extremely relevant for anyone engaged in a helping relationship with others. Anyone who is explicitly or implicitly helping another person, group, or organization improve in some way would benefit from the insights and perspectives this book offers. This audience includes Human Resources professionals, people who coach others, clergy members, psychologists, counselors, health caregivers, and many others.

Regardless of your orientation, this book asserts that in order to be masterful, you must attend to the dynamics of change. Mastery requires that consultants understand the forces promoting or inhibiting change, and know how to mobilize them in a positive direction. It requires them to pay attention to their own state of being and to cultivate that state as an important force in the change process. Mastery also requires consultants to enable the client to "own" the outcome of their joint efforts and to continue to receive benefits from their work long after the consultant leaves. Too many consultants are hindered by their inattention to their *inner stance.* They fail to see their "self" as a crucial force for change. As a result, they follow the structure and rules of consulting and fail in its art. It is artistry that differentiates the best consultants, and the artistic nature of consulting is our focus here.

Through the insights offered in this book, you are encouraged to reflect on your own inner stance and create the potential for even greater success as a consultant.

THE INTERVIEWS

When I began to formulate ideas for this book, I sought to deepen my understanding of those qualities of being that make the biggest difference. I conducted lengthy interviews with 14 contemporary masters of the consulting craft. They are, in alphabetical order: Linda Ackerman Anderson, Bill Belgard, Geoffrey Bellman, David Bradford, John Carter, Stephen Dichter, Brenda Jones, Jack Knight, Anthony Reilly, Charlie Seashore, Edie Seashore, Ron Tilden, Meg Wheatley, and Chris Worley. I transcribed all the interviews and then did a content analysis of their thoughts to identify shared themes in their views about consulting mastery.

Along with my own perspective on consulting, this book offers those themes, and the wisdom underlying them. Instead of focusing on skill and technique, these masters will help us learn about the importance of the *inner stance* of the consultant in the process of change. Examples throughout the book are drawn from my own experience and observations of others. In all cases, the examples are real or composites of real situations, unless otherwise indicated. The actual names are removed to protect confidentiality.

In addition to my discussions with the master consultants, I sought the perspective of ten executives in client organizations who have worked extensively with change consultants, and who hold extremely high standards. Their comparisons of consultants helped me better understand client expectations and see what they value most in a consulting relationship. [For more detail about the interview process, see Appendix A.]

While influenced by the interviews, most of the thoughts and expressions contained in this book are my own, built from 25 years of experience as a consultant and shaped by many mentors and guides along the way. At the same time, while I can claim ownership for much of the expression of the ideas, I am hardly the first person to have seized upon the concepts. Instead, they are my own way of thinking about so much of what I have learned from others along the way, including Chris Argyris, Bill Torbert, Terry Deal, Lee Bolman, David Bradford, Ron Tilden, and countless others I have had the privilege of knowing and to whom I feel deep gratitude for their wisdom and guidance.

THE STRUCTURE OF THE BOOK

This book is divided into five sections. Each section guides readers through a journey of exploration into their own inner stance as they learn from the experience of master consultants. The book follows a

A NOTE TO READERS

I am acutely aware of a particular paradox in writing this book. On the one hand, I contend that masterful consulting has much more to do with inquiry than giving answers. In one of the chapters, for example, I make an important distinction between advice giving and guidance. Advice giving has to do with answers, while powerful guidance has to do with good questioning. And yet—here's the paradox—I use an undeniably "authoritative voice" throughout this book: I am clearly presenting a perspective rather than offering a process of inquiry. Hence there is a tension between the form of the book and the very attitude it recommends. I can only resolve this paradox with the thought that this book is essentially an extended, personal perspective on consulting, and it does not constitute consulting work in itself. If we were to meet in person, and I were to coach or consult for you, my approach would be more personal, and more inquiring.

Having said this, I share my perspective boldly, not because I believe I have THE ANSWER, but because I care deeply about the questions and challenges posed in the book. In offer-

natural flow of learning—from a conceptual understanding of consulting mastery, to a view of mastery in action, and finally to learning how to attain mastery in oneself. In laying a conceptual foundation, I offer a view of the way consultants typically practice consulting, paying particular attention to the underlying and rarely examined assumptions upon which most consulting practices are built. The remainder of the book focuses on an alternative way of looking at consulting; one that I believe has the potential for achieving far greater impact and positive outcomes than the typical approaches.

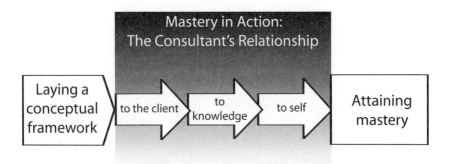

FIGURE 1: THE FLOW OF THE BOOK

ing the principles of consulting mastery, I hope you, the reader, will treat the contents as a catalyst toward inquiring into your own practice. Toward this end, as you read about the distinctions offered in the book, I encourage you to reflect deeply about what you do and how you are as a consultant. Imagine yourself in different client situations and feel what it might be like were your inner stance aligned with some of the principles offered here. Look deep for ways in which you may unconsciously not be practicing consistent with your goals, beliefs, and strategies. Similarly, seek to find ways in which your practice is already aligned and know that there are others on a similar path.

In the end, whether you agree with everything I write or not, what matters most is that you stay in the question: How can I lift my consultant practice to a new level? How do I act as a consultant so that my actions make a bigger difference? It is the question that gave rise to the book, and it is by keeping the question alive that you will find greater mastery.

Acknowledgments

Rare is the book that is written alone, and this one is no exception. I am deeply grateful for the enormous support and encouragement I have received in the process of writing. First and foremost, I want to thank Steve Piersanti and the whole staff of Berrett-Koehler who believed in this work and who partnered beautifully with me at each step along the way in bringing this book to life. Steve in particular, demonstrated so effortlessly the many principles embedded in the book as he guided me and helped me clarify my own thoughts on the subject. I want to also thank Michael Finley, Doug Gorney, and Pat Brewer whose editing support took what would have been too many ponderous phrases and lengthy diatribes and helped make the text into something more palatable to the reader. I am deeply appreciative of my partners at Avista Consulting Group: Martha Borst, Marty Kaplan, and Jeri Mersky, whose wisdom and ability to "walk the talk" have been an inspiration to me. Many others played a significant role in helping shape the thinking of this book. To each of them, I am grateful, including Patricia Moore, Tim Kelley, Brad Margolis, Roland Sullivan, Bill Belgarde, Geoffrey Bellman, David Bradford, and Michael Lipson. I also want to express my deepest thanks to Andrea Markowitz, Kathleen Epperson, Marchelle Brain, and Frank Basler who read early versions of the manuscript and who gifted me with their thoughts, feedback, and encouragement. I am particularly thankful to Frank who went the extra distance and offered valuable suggestions that helped me tighten up the book's structure without losing any of its message.

Finally, I want to thank my wife and son, without whom this book could not have been written. To my wife, Tina Benson, for her enthusiastic encouragement, belief in me, and support of my early morning forays into my office without complaint as she took over a greater responsibility in our household. And to my son, Josh Benson-Merron, for joining me in learning how we can become better in our roles as father and son, and as good human beings in life. This book is dedicated to the wonderful young man that he is—and the wise man that he is becoming.

Seeking
Greatness in the
Consulting
Profession

The greatest discovery of my generation is
that a man can alter his life simply by
altering his attitude of mind.

—*William James*

SAM, AN EAGER YOUNG CONSULTANT, was leading his first client engagement. Bright and aggressive, with a fresh MBA under his belt, he had been under the tutelage of one of the best partners in his consulting firm for three years. Now, having received a set of important distinctions and a proprietary consulting process, he was ready to strut his stuff. He did everything his partner taught him, and it seemed to work. He showed the clients all the important and relevant research that pointed to the flaws in the client organization. He used a team of bright consultants to gather and analyze data about the client, its competitors, and key trends in the industry. He showed the client the changes it needed to make to get ahead of the industry in its market space. At each step along the way, the client seemed eager, interested, engaged, and impressed with Sam's know-how.

1

At the final meeting, Sam's report was well received and a team of leaders in the client organization almost instantly accepted the recommendations he made. They assured Sam of their commitment to implementing these changes and even adopted Sam's sensible timeline that balanced a high degree of urgency with awareness that these things take time. At the end of this meeting, Sam was one happy consultant.

Months later, he could not have been more disappointed. For the first few weeks, the client began making plans to implement the recommendations. However, an unexpected dip in sales, coupled with some missed product development deadlines, caused the client to shelve some of Sam's recommendations. They assured him it was a temporary problem, and they would get back on track as soon as this temporary setback was addressed. They never did.

It was obvious to Sam that the process and the expertise he provided were right on target. The fault, clearly, lay in the client's lack of ability to deliver on its end and to stick with the plan. In debriefing with the partner about the failed effort, the partner pointed out some things Sam could have done differently, offering clever tricks of the trade that might have made a difference. The partner also pointed out that these things happen and that it was part of the learning process. "You are destined to do great things," the partner said. "Don't let it get you down."

The partner's sage counsel was welcome, and Sam was eager to tackle the next client opportunity with renewed vigor. Little did he know that it was almost inevitably doomed to fail. It would make money, but it wouldn't make a difference. Nor did the partner have any inkling of this. No one else in the firm did either. They were making plenty of money, in fact, with enough financial success that this and other failures were easily shrugged off. The failure pattern was left unexamined while the consulting firm got to continue the game.

Sam's story is repeated time after time in consulting engagements all over the world. Many consultants have seen outcomes like Sam's many times yet find themselves in the same scenario. Caught in the same pattern that most of the consulting world is following, they cannot see an alternative. As a result, many, if not most clients are either cynical about consultants or angry about how intractable the whole system is. Yet they too continue to participate in the pattern, hoping that the next time they hire a consultant, the outcome will be different. It rarely is. I am reminded of the famous definition of insanity—doing the same thing over and over again and expecting a different outcome.

THE RULES OF CONSULTING

The rules for "successful" consulting were created a long time ago. Someone unknown, perhaps a trusted advisor of a king, first conceived them. About 100 years ago, they were reformed and applied to business by Frederick Taylor. Clarified and made universal by James O. McKinsey, Marvin Bower, and others in the middle of the 20th century, the rules were popularized in the late 20th century by a slew of consultants who used them to earn riches beyond belief. Few have written these rules down, yet almost everyone in the consulting profession knows them, follows them, and benefits from them. Almost always, the current rules of consulting are based on the claim that the consultant has specialized expertise, crucial to client success. They are as follows:

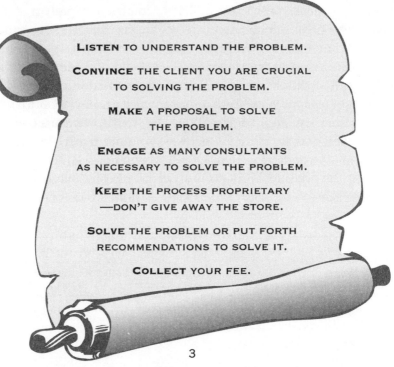

LISTEN TO UNDERSTAND THE PROBLEM.

CONVINCE THE CLIENT YOU ARE CRUCIAL
TO SOLVING THE PROBLEM.

MAKE A PROPOSAL TO SOLVE
THE PROBLEM.

ENGAGE AS MANY CONSULTANTS
AS NECESSARY TO SOLVE THE PROBLEM.

KEEP THE PROCESS PROPRIETARY
—DON'T GIVE AWAY THE STORE.

SOLVE THE PROBLEM OR PUT FORTH
RECOMMENDATIONS TO SOLVE IT.

COLLECT YOUR FEE.

On the face of it, these rules of consulting look just fine. But how much do these rules truly benefit clients? Most consulting firms claim the benefit is great. I am not so sure. What most consultants and firms only seem to pay attention to is the transaction between client and consultant, rarely recognizing the sizable residue or unintended consequences of the way the consulting game is played. Something is missing in the world of consulting, but few of the financially successful consultants can see it or if they do, would want clients to see it. Take a look at the record, they would say; you can't argue with success! What those consultants won't show you is their list of failures. It is extensive.

It's No Longer Working Well

Expert-based approaches* to consulting remain preeminent because they have worked well in the past, and continue to work well in certain situations, particularly those where there is a clear line between cause and effect and where the variables are definable and containable. Yet in so many other situations, I believe the structured, expert based approaches fail. The world is changing so rapidly and the challenges organizations face are so knotty that the structured methods rarely work. They try to impose a set of processes in conditions that no longer fit. Moreover, the validity of those approaches in so many situations goes almost entirely unquestioned in the consulting profession. Why? Perhaps for no other reason than that we as consultants, along with everybody else, tend toward the comfort of sameness and avoid the nether world of uncertainty. As a result, while there are indicators that the consulting profession is no longer meeting the needs of its clients well, we have been slow to heed the warning signs.

* I am making a distinction here between expert consulting and process consulting as made by Peter Block in his book *Flawless Consulting*. *Expert* consultants primarily sell their knowledge and expertise. By contrast, process consultants, while equipped with knowledge and expertise, are more interested in creating a process whereby clients can discover for themselves the knowledge necessary to take effective action. Process consultants also typically focus on the client's human dynamics—the processes of decision-making, teamwork, organizational behavior, etc.—and aim to help the client improve them. While no consultant falls exclusively into the expert or the process category, most lean in one direction or the other.

The signs are legion. They include:

1. Demand for consulting is declining, and as a result, consulting firms are being forced to downsize.

2. Many consulting firms are falling out of favor as their practices are subjected to deeper scrutiny. Witness the Andersen Consulting debacle with Enron.

3. More and more books have been published that debunk the sovereignty of the consulting profession.[1]

Indeed, as I write this book, I believe the consulting field is in disrepair. A recent article in *Consulting News* reported that consulting firms are bidding on more projects and winning far fewer, while simultaneously experiencing an increase in the length of their sales cycle and a decline in their average engagement size. The situation is expected to get worse. Leaders of large consulting firms report that many clients have gone for a long time without consultants and don't miss them. And without the "next big thing" to sell, consultants are having a hard time fighting the indifference. The article also reports that clients have been complaining they were routinely oversold in the late 1990s—sold things they didn't need.[2] Anecdotally, I see more senior consultants struggling for business now than I have seen in the 25 years I have been a consultant.

Since the profession does not have hard data on the success or failure of consulting efforts, it is hard to pin down the emerging downward trend. There are, however, some strong indications. For the first time in decades, for example, growth in the Gross National Product is outstripping growth in the consulting industry.[3] And revenue growth in the largest consulting businesses, while robust in the 80s (20–30% annually on average), has slowed to a snail's pace.

I believe these troubling trends are a direct outgrowth of the fundamental rules upon which most consulting firms base their practice. These rules form practices that are destined to continue to erode the confidence in and effectiveness of consultants. In particular, the causes of this erosion are two-fold: (1) The fundamental beliefs and assumptions that underlie the current rules, and (2) The rules behind the rules, often unseen by clients.

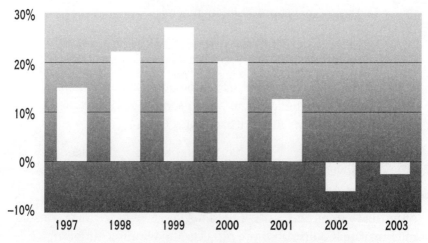

FIGURE 1: STEADY DECLINE IN THE CONSULTING INDUSTRY[4]

QUESTIONABLE ASSUMPTIONS

Many of the flawed assumptions underlying many of the consulting profession's practices have been known for a while. Ten years ago, for example, Nitin Nohria and J. D. Berkeley found that in the majority of cases, research shows that many of the fads, including TQM, Process Reengineering, MBO, and others "rarely produced the promised results."[5] And a myriad of articles in the early 90s showed how TQM efforts too often fell well short of their aims. Most of the research on the subject suggests that less than one-quarter of the TQM efforts produced tangible and enduring results.[6]

In spite of the apparent growing failure rate, the consulting profession continues to seek the next big thing that they can offer and consultants continue to blame clients for poor execution. In so doing, we are subject to the same tendency as other industries: We avoid examining the assumptions and biases that underlie the way we approach our work.

One fundamental assumption, for example, is that knowledge, and the structured transfer of knowledge, is the most appropriate thing a consultant can offer. Is it, though? It may in fact be the *least* essential thing we can offer. Perhaps it only provides the *illusion* of comfort. Perhaps we are only peddling the appearance of a useful methodology, as Harold Hill fraudulently peddled the "think theory" of music in Meredith Willson's *The Music Man*.

Another unquestioned assumption is that there is magic in tools and techniques. Consultants unfailingly cite them, and the authority from which they derive, rarely exploring whether these tools really make a difference. Clients and consultants alike jump on the next bandwagon of consulting ideas, hoping to find that elusive magic pill. Rarely do those who follow this path recognize that real solutions do not lie in magic pills. Clients often want easy answers, and many consulting firms are all too eager to send young consultants, still wet behind the ears, to dish them out. The results are too often disappointing to the client. One CEO I know, for example, refuses to hire consultants any more. He is tired of them trying to sell him their "approach." He knows that there is no one answer and is suspicious of anyone offering it. Another senior executive I know says her company is "consultant phobic." She says, "We are tired of consultants promising the world, and not delivering."

Too many consultants readily serve up tools, processes, and techniques while failing to appreciate the deep thinking and understanding that created them in the first place. Too often we fall back on tools and techniques to quell the natural anxiety associated with the consulting process or to avoid facing the fear that perhaps we are not adequate to the task at hand.

TOOLS AND TECHNIQUES GIVE US COMFORT; THEY HAVE NOTHING TO DO WITH CONSULTING MASTERY.

Perhaps the biggest assumption of all is the belief that the goal of consulting is to provide advice toward solving problems, failing to recognize that the real challenge most clients face is in producing the change itself. Robert Shaffer said it well when he said that the trouble is that most consultants "don't make client implementation a central focus of their consulting practices. Most are almost completely dedicated to providing managers with insights and ideas about change; they pay virtually no attention to helping the client *effect* change."[7]

THE RULES BEHIND THE RULES

If you were to peer behind the scenes of the consulting game as typically played, you would find a game behind a game. Few consultants and consulting firms want clients to know about what is behind the scenes, for if they did, many clients would not hire them. The rules of the game behind the game are designed to make the most money for the consultant or the consulting firm, often to the detriment of client outcomes. The game behind the game has the following rules:

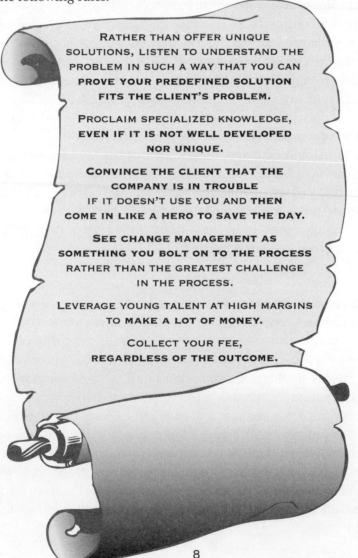

RATHER THAN OFFER UNIQUE SOLUTIONS, LISTEN TO UNDERSTAND THE PROBLEM IN SUCH A WAY THAT YOU CAN **PROVE YOUR PREDEFINED SOLUTION FITS THE CLIENT'S PROBLEM.**

PROCLAIM SPECIALIZED KNOWLEDGE, **EVEN IF IT IS NOT WELL DEVELOPED NOR UNIQUE.**

CONVINCE THE CLIENT THAT THE COMPANY IS IN TROUBLE IF IT DOESN'T USE YOU AND **THEN COME IN LIKE A HERO TO SAVE THE DAY.**

SEE CHANGE MANAGEMENT AS SOMETHING YOU BOLT ON TO THE PROCESS RATHER THAN THE GREATEST CHALLENGE IN THE PROCESS.

LEVERAGE YOUNG TALENT AT HIGH MARGINS **TO MAKE A LOT OF MONEY.**

COLLECT YOUR FEE, **REGARDLESS OF THE OUTCOME.**

Together, the assumptions described above and the behind the scenes rules cause consultants to operate in a way that has a high payoff for the consultants and a limited payoff for the client. They beckon consultants to read, research, and write about theories, tools, skills, and techniques, while simultaneously losing sight of a deeper phenomenon, one not so easily observed and tested: namely, the way consulting is typically practiced is the primary source of failure, or at best, limited success. These assumptions and underlying rules also cause consultants to ignore what masterful consultants know well—that the *inner stance* of the consultant is often a far greater determinant of client success than anything else. By ignoring these core truths, the profession has given itself over to fashion and fads.

WHAT DIFFERENTIATES GOOD CONSULTANTS FROM GREAT ONES?

In the field of organizational change consulting, little has been written about what differentiates good consultants from masterful ones.[8] Many dedicated practitioners in change-consulting fields are well armed with the tools of their craft, yet they often disappoint their clients. Why? Because of the commonly held belief that tools and techniques constitute the most essential aspects of consulting.

THROUGHOUT THIS BOOK, I REFER TO BOTH "CHANGE CONSULTING" AND "CONSULTING" INTERCHANGEABLY. I AM DEFINING CHANGE CONSULTANTS AS THOSE WHO AIM TO CHANGE ORGANIZATIONS AS A WHOLE IN SOME SIGNIFICANT WAY.

All consultants have a profusion of tools, techniques, models, and theories at their disposal and yet few are consistently effective. Even fewer are extraordinary. So a huge question is dying to be asked: What constitutes consulting mastery? Unfortunately, little research has been done on the question and few books speak to the issue.[9]

Most of what is written focuses on the surface elements of consulting and rarely looks at the deeper patterns that underlie the consulting experience. With so much focus on tools, techniques, processes, and specialized knowledge, the underlying dynamics of the consulting process often get short shrift. They include:

- The quality of the relationship between client and consultant

- The conduct and character of the consultant

- The definition of who the client is and the deeper purpose of the consulting engagement.

These hidden features of the consulting process are what masterful consulting is all about. They can't be "seen" in the conventional sense; they lie under the waterline. They can, however, be clearly felt. I cannot say it any clearer than the fox in Antoine de Saint-Exupéry's *The Little Prince,* who said ". . . and now here is my secret, a very simple secret: It is only with the heart that one can see rightly; what is essential is invisible to the eye."[10]

The source of mastery isn't found in one's outer actions, or in the effective use of the tools of the trade. It is found invisibly in the inner stance a consultant takes in relationship to the client world, to knowledge, and to himself. By *inner stance,* I mean the feelings, beliefs, viewpoints, and perspectives that drive one's actions. It is the place we "come from" when we act.

I want to make clear that I do not deny the importance of expert knowledge in the consulting process. Quite the contrary, knowledge is enormously valuable. An overreliance on knowledge, however, without significant attention to one's inner self, the process of consulting, and the quality of the relationship, results in limited success. It will be even less effective in years to come.

WHAT IS CONSULTING MASTERY?

By *consulting mastery* I am not referring to mastery in the sense of "control over." Nor am I positing some lofty expert knowledge that only a few can know. The mastery I am talking about arises from the artistry of consulting, driven by effective expression of the inner qualities of the consultant himself. Mastery has little to do with the science of consulting; it is more about the moment where wisdom is deftly applied in a way that moves the client toward deeper and more profound action. Mastery, in this sense, is not a place where one arrives, definitively and permanently. Rather, mastery comes in moments, and is often elusive. Like others, I have moments when I tap into an inner state in which I am at my best. These moments usually come when I am calm, centered, open, fluid, and confident. Naturally, I have moments when I am also at my worst, stuck in some turmoil of my own psyche from which I cannot seem to escape. Mastery happens when we are open to the lessons our experiences have taught us—and honest with the clients we seek to help.

Consultants who explore the inner aspects of the consulting process challenge the key assumptions in the consulting field. Many of these consultants are brilliant in their work yet get little credit. That is because they have guided their clients so successfully that the clients receive—and deserve—the credit themselves.

Masterful consultants seldom shy away from self-reflection when faced with an unsuccessful consulting situation; they know that their inner stance is what matters most in their work. They value a trusting partnership with the client, the deft application of knowledge, and the inner character required to inspire others. Success, for the masterful consultant, is the result of a powerful blending of these three capabilities. Like streams merging into a single river, the confluence of these three components is redefining and giving new shape to the consulting industry. As we will see later, reliance on any one of these streams, to the exclusion of the other, results in limited consulting success.

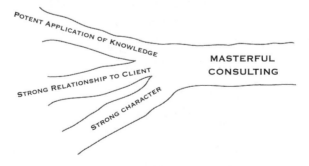

STREAMS OF THE MASTERFUL CONSULTANT

This way of thinking represents a paradigm shift in the consulting process, one in which the wholeness and health of the consultant himself are of crucial importance. A healthy inner stance produces these things, all of which are crucial to consulting mastery:

- The ability to see and think holistically

- A sense of self-certainty, self-esteem, and self-value

- The ability to be honest, genuine, and to inspire trust in others

- Neutrality, deep listening, and a spirit of collaborative inquiry

- An ability to set up an empowering relationship with the client

- Knowledge about the change process

- The ability to be present

These and other features of the inner aspects of consulting will be explored throughout the book. It is my hope that by continuing to read this book you may call into question some of the deeper, possibly even hidden patterns that structure your own consulting behavior. As a result, you may see a path toward greater effectiveness and begin making an even bigger difference in your consulting practice. We begin by understanding the goals and strategies of the typical model of consulting.

PART I

UNDERSTANDING CONSULTING MASTERY

CHAPTER 1

THE DECAY OF
THE CONSULTING
PROFESSION

We have met the enemy and he is us.

—*Pogo (Walt Kelly)*

A FEW YEARS AGO, I was involved in a consulting engagement, part-nering with what was then one of the "Big Five" consulting firms. We were helping a multinational Fortune 100 company implement SAP software as their new company-wide software system. This changeover took well over a year and required a ton of planning, training, and dealing with all the issues one deals with when under-taking such a massive change. Early on in my work with the con-sulting firm, one of the young, extremely bright, talented, and dedi-cated consultants (we'll call her Diane) showed me with great pride a document they had been developing—the consulting firm's plan for leading the changeover to the new SAP system. This plan was over 400 pages long and showed over 1000 different things a man-ager needed to pay attention to in order to successfully lead the implementation of the new system. This document had sections on how to train others, how to listen to others' concerns, how to gath-er information, etc. It was truly a magnum opus of SAP planning, custom tailored (so they said) to meet this client's particular need.

I cannot begin to guess how many consulting hours it took

Diane and others to develop such a document. I'm sure hundreds of hours. What caught my interest, though, was not the huge investment in time and the client's money. It was the pride that Diane felt about the work, believing in her heart that this was truly value added to the client. With some degree of surprise on my part, I asked her how this document was used, and she reported to me with consternation that it seemed to have been given short shrift. The clients were, in her words, "resistant" to using it. In fact, she offered, "few even read it in the first place." Diane seemed to believe that if they were truly motivated they would actively read and use such a document and that their lack of use was a sign of their failing, and not hers or her firm's.

Diane's whole thinking and presumably that of the project leaders of the consulting firm was driven by a belief that good information and good analysis should carry the day. Rarely is this the case when it comes to influencing organizations. Organizations, and people for that matter, respond to a different song. To get organizations to change, they need to be inspired. Not much damps the human spirit more than breaking down an organizational problem to its smallest parts. Dissection rarely produces movement in organizational life. Diane was well on her way to being a good consultant. If she continued down her path, however, being a masterful consultant would elude her, for what she was learning in her firm had little to do with making a big difference.

It Starts with Goals

To understand the difference between good consultants and great ones, we need to go beneath the surface of the rules of typical consulting approaches and examine the goals and strategies that drive those rules.[1] We will start with goals, for the goals of consultants, as for any human being, form and inform the strategies they use.

Take a moment and ask yourself: What do you want as a consultant? Why do you consult in the first place? You could want many things. If you are like most consultants, however, your goals probably fall into one of three areas.

- To add value (fix a problem, plug a hole, introduce a new process or system)

16

- To make a lot of money

- To make a profound difference—to shift the organization to a new level.

The primary goals of many consultants employing the typical rules of consulting are to *add value* and to *make a lot of money.* In the story described in the Introduction, Sam was drawn to consulting because he wanted to achieve these two things as well. To make a profound difference would be icing on the cake, but not essential. He believed that making a big difference does happen from time to time, but since it is so elusive to him, he believes it is best to focus on adding value and making money. Not surprisingly, Diane had the same goals. Both were young consultants eagerly following the footsteps of a generation of consultants before them, wanting to help and to earn a very good living.

To add value and make money, the consultant typically offers help in the form of expert advice or an expert process. In a competitive bidding situation, often the consultant must also convince the client that this expertise cannot be found elsewhere and not only is it well worth it, but the client is at risk of failing without it. In most cases, clients are inclined to believe this is so. In addition, the consultant will often leverage the talents of others to expedite the consulting process for the client.

These goals, to add value and to make money, get translated into strategies, which in turn directly affect the actions and the outcomes of the client engagement. Let's begin with the primary strategy that drives most consultants' actions and behaviors.

THE SAVIOR STRATEGY: THE PRIMARY STRATEGY OF THE CURRENT RULES OF CONSULTING

Every day, throughout the country, clients and consultants are participating in a silent and powerful contract, often unaware of its existence. It is the basis of what I call the *savior strategy.* To understand this strategy, we need to strip away the complexity of consulting and get down to its essential form.

At the core of any consulting activity is the desire by the

client to get help and by the consultant to offer help. Help tends to take the following form:

- Client defines a problem.

- Client hires consultant to either solve the problem or tell the client how to solve it.

- Client pays for this service and sometimes implements the advice.

The desire to be helpful runs deep in the psychological make-up of most consultants. They have spent many years honing their craft, driven by this desire. More specifically, they have a belief in how organizations can be better run, and a genuine desire to show clients the way.

Simultaneously, clients often have a deep desire to be helped. Rarely seeing consulting as an aid for growing or developing the organization, they often seek out consultants when something in the business is not working well or is "broken." Out of consultants' desire to help and clients' desire to have something "fixed" is born the *savior strategy*. To occur, the savior strategy requires two consenting parties—the helpers and the receivers of help. The helpers must be motivated to help and also believe they have a better way. The receivers of help must want to be saved, believe they are capable of changing, and believe that the helpers have a magic elixir obtainable only from the helpers.

Many consulting firms are brilliant at playing the savior game and preying on the fears of clients that, without the firm's help, the company is either doomed or in deep weeds. These consulting firms make impressive presentations, backed up by recent research, demonstrating the trends that are impinging on the company, followed by multiple examples of how clients have been helped enormously by the consulting firm's intervention. That these charts are often pseudoscientific is usually not evident, because the client so wants to believe that the consulting firm will save them. It is a lesson carried over from the snake oil salesman of the 1800s, who made a good living selling exotic elixirs to "cure all that ails you." When you want to be fixed or saved, you are easily prone to being convinced.

IMPRESSING CLIENTS WITH SLEIGHT OF HAND

One very wealthy consulting firm that I have worked with was brilliant in their ability to demonstrate added value through "research." One of their most powerful presentation slides was a graph comparing their clients' stock progress in the past 10 years versus the Dow Industrial Average, showing in dramatic fashion how their clients had significantly outpaced the market. This demonstrated, or so the firm wanted the client to believe, that the consulting firm's intervention made the difference. What more compelling argument could there be? The client seldom considers that there is a self-selection process going on, and that certain companies are predisposed to use the consultant's services. What is also hidden is the selective methodology used in defining a client. In this case, only clients of long standing were cited. Those who dropped the consulting firm were likewise dropped from the research. In effect, the data offered was no test of the consulting firm's ability at all. A "before and after" picture of *all* clients would have been a far better measure of actual results.

Preying on the client's need to be saved is a significant modus operandi for many consultants, particularly those that employ an "expert" model of consulting. What better way to hook the client into believing in the necessity of hiring the consultant than to cleverly participate in the game. To be fair, most consultants don't seek to "hook" the client at all (at least not consciously). They simply want to be of service and to add value in the best way they know how—by solving a problem. Nonetheless, both consultants and clients participate in the same implied contract. You, the client, need help. I have what you need. I'll sell it to you, and then you'll have it.

It sounds so wonderful. But the negative consequences of the implied contract can be severe. Once the consultant leaves, the client organization will *not* have more knowledge than it had before, because knowledge—the consultant's stock in trade—cannot be given away. You can give people information; it's like giving them a bag of groceries. But knowledge transfers less easily. In the realm of human and organizational dynamics, knowledge must be learned and earned through exploration, deep shared thinking, and often struggle. Many consultants do indeed often have useful knowledge, but by the time it is transferred in the form of a presentation, report, or other form, it is rarely more than information.

Since the knowledge behind that information is rarely transferred, it is never truly owned by the client organization. The bookshelves and credenzas of managers around the world are laden with well-crafted consultant presentations—collecting dust.

Yet in spite of this, clients are happy to pay for information and to expect positive results. This willingness to be "done to" and be "given to" is natural. Most organizations are overwhelmed, and they look for the quick fix. Most consultants are happy to oblige.

I used to work in a consulting firm that had a well-developed process for "transforming" organizations. Our primary intervention was a 4-day "team building" event that many people described as life changing. The beauty of our approach was that we started with the executive team, helping them through very difficult issues. The executives came out the other side with a renewed sense of passion for their leadership and for working together, thus, they were ripe to sign on the dotted line to have others throughout the company experience the same thing, for a hefty sum of money. We also did a number of other things to help the client "align" its resources and create a high-performing culture, but the team building was the primary transformation vehicle.

Having led many of these interventions, however, I noticed a pattern. In most cases, the executives were happy to have us "roll out" our process throughout the company. The more we could do for them, the better, thereby freeing the executives to focus on things they were more comfortable with—strategy, dealing with investors, planning, etc. Metaphorically, it was as if they wanted us to wave a magic wand over them. And we did. However, in almost every case, little or no change took place in the client organization. Individual people might be transformed, but the client organization as a whole remained stuck in neutral.

In the few cases where we struck a different relationship and where the client took full responsibility for the transformation process, we had much better results. Naturally we preferred the latter scenario, because we sincerely wanted to see enduring results from our work. However, we were perfectly willing to accept the former scenario. As one of my colleagues, Tom Shenk, puts it—"great payday, no difference."

SECONDARY STRATEGIES OF THE CURRENT RULES OF CONSULTING

The goal to add value and make a lot of money gets enacted and expressed through the primary savior strategy. This strategy, in turn, produces secondary strategies that support the desire to help and to make money. These strategies, in turn, determine the kinds of choices consultants make. The typical strategies of the consulting process fall into one of three categories. They are: the consultant's relationship to his client; the consultant's relationship to knowledge; and the consultant's relationship with himself— his character, in other words.

In the arena of *relationship to client,* most consultants employ a strategy that gives them tacit power over the client, and they use that power to try to get the client to do what they believe is best for the client. In the arena of *relationship to knowledge,* most consultants claim and use specialized knowledge, processes, tools, and techniques as their primary added value. In the arena of *relationship to self,* most consultants seek to develop presentation and sales skills for gaining more business. Let's look at each more deeply and its consequences.

CREATE A "POWER OVER" RELATIONSHIP TO THE CLIENT.   Most consultants say they want a partnership with their clients. They talk about the importance of give and take and in working together to solve a problem. And, indeed, in most cases that is what they desire. However, many consultants are unaware of the multiple ways their behavior implies a different relationship—one best described as having "power over" their clients.

Consultants who consciously or unconsciously employ a "power over" strategy do a number of things that are designed to maintain control over the client and the consulting process. For example, they chop up the business into parts in order to analyze it. On the face of it, this seems sound. However, the more consultants do the work, the more likely they will understand the business better than the client (at least those aspects relevant to the consulting engagement). Consultants then use this understanding as leverage to get clients to do what the consultants think is best for them. Additionally, many consultants control the consulting process as much as possible, convincing clients that these "tried and true" methods guarantee best results. Since consultants know these methods, and the clients do not, a "power over" dynamic is created or maintained. Finally, the very act of promising to deliver success feeds off the client's desire to be fixed or saved and puts them in a childlike position in relationship to the consulting "parent."

CLAIM AND USE SPECIALIZED KNOWLEDGE, PROCESSES, TOOLS, AND TECHNIQUES AS THE PRIMARY ADDED VALUE.   Most often, the added value consultants provide in the form of knowledge, tools, and techniques is really worth something. So is the research they tailored to meet the unique needs of the client. Conducted by bright and eager consultants and led by savvy partners, consultants do provide useful analyses, sound techniques, and thoughtful recommendations, much of which has real value for the client. The only rub is the claim that it is specialized and unavailable elsewhere.

Consultants place a high value on being special, on having something the client cannot get anywhere else. Sometimes they claim that the knowledge may not be special, but the methods for implementing that knowledge are. However, rarely does a consultant have something a client can't get elsewhere. Many times I have seen consultants scramble to put together a presentation from a recent *Harvard Business Review* article, slap their logo on it, and claim to have specialized knowledge. Astonishingly, it works. They dazzle the client with presentations, delivered with panache. In truth, if this knowledge is this available, how "special" can it be? The real added value comes not from the information but from the ability to get clients to actually use this knowledge well. This ability is indeed a rare commodity among expert-based consultants.

DEVELOP "SELF" SKILLS FOR GAINING MORE BUSINESS.   Many firms teach their new consultants the importance of presenting themselves well. Partners "dress for success" and encourage their consultants to do the same. They place a high emphasis on conforming to the kind of social etiquettes that appeal to those in positions of power in their client organization. And they hone their influence

22

and persuasion techniques. To them, developing "self" is about outer image and presentation, not about the "inner self." Indeed, you might argue that the "inner self" has little to do with effective analysis. Masterful consultants take issue with this, however. One masterful consultant I know left her highly successful partnership in a firm finally fed up with the over-attention to image and inattention to issues of character and lack of true commitment to the client. In her words, "the hypocrisy of how the consulting firm ran counter to the very principles it taught clients was too much for me to bear."

Each strategy can generate an endless number of actions. Many actions, however, fall into a typical set, represented in the far right column in Figure 1-1. Since this book focuses on consulting mastery, I will summarize only the actions of the current approach to consulting. In future chapters, we will look into the actions of masterful consultants in far greater detail.

Many of the larger, more "successful" consulting firms use two additional and very questionable strategies as part of their financial wealth plan. They often use less experienced consultants and charge far more to the client to create high profits. And they offer high-margin "bolt-ons" ("how about some fries with your burger") as a critical added resource.

While I think the typical approach in Figure 1-1 is fair and close to reality, it is also a caricature. Few consultants truly operate exactly like this. Many do some of these things as well as some that are more masterful. Certainly, few consultants will ever admit that they are focusing primarily on making money. In subtle ways, however, they make choices that are not in the client's best interest. Sam was a great example. His mentor taught him that the client often can't see what it needs, and that he and other members of the consulting firm knew better than their clients. Had the client known better, it is reasoned, the client would not have needed to hire Sam's consulting firm in the first place. This frees up Sam to recommend things the consulting firm has to offer without hesitation or concerns.

Consultants throughout the land are following the same process. In some cases, the consultant follows these strategies and actions and does indeed help solve the problem and leave the client

---

FIGURE 1-1   THE TYPICAL GAME OF CONSULTING

Goals	Primary Strategy	Secondary Strategies	Actions
Make Money	Be a savior	Create a "power-over" relationship	Chop up the business into parts and analyze the business—use the analysis as the primary source of added value to the client
Add Value			Control the process to the extent possible
			Promise to deliver success, and feed off the client's desire to be saved or fixed
		Claim and use specialized knowledge, processes, tools, and techniques as the primary added value	Offer value in the form of deep analysis and thoughtful recommendations
			Claim to have developed expertise unavailable to clients
			Dazzle the client with presentations and sound technique—deliver with panache
		Develop "self" skills for gaining more business	Attend to and develop one's image
			Hone one's influence and persuasion techniques

---

satisfied. In some cases, it is a waste of effort: Remember those bookshelves of reports collecting dust. Rarely, however, does advice giving or help in the forms most consultants provide make a difference. It rarely adds energy to the system. It does not challenge people to think differently, nor cultivate deeper understanding. It rarely penetrates the underlying patterns that form and shape the client and keep them from achieving a higher level of performance.

**"THE SYSTEM OF CONSULTING AS TYPICALLY
FOLLOWED IS BANKRUPT AND MOST CONSULTANTS
AND CLIENTS DON'T EVEN KNOW IT!"
—A HIGHLY SUCCESSFUL CONSULTANT'S VIEW**

HOW THE RULES OF CONSULTING WERE CREATED

One *can't* just declare the need for "a new model for consulting"—first one must understand how consulting came to be the way it is today. Without this understanding, we are destined to perpetuate some of the very forces that have led to the decay of the consulting field. To understand how the current consulting business has been shaped, let's look at each of the following:

1. The historical roots of the typical consulting model

2. Why large businesses buy into it

3. How our educational system supports it

THE HISTORICAL ROOTS OF THE TYPICAL CONSULTING MODEL

Since the early 20th century, when, for all intents and purposes, the consulting field was born, consultants have made a simple promise to clients:

The Consultant's Promise

I, the consultant, promise to have knowledge that you, the client, value and need. I promise to demonstrate that value and transfer the knowledge and/or its benefits to you. The process I use to transfer this knowledge to you will be structured and understandable. I will charge you a consulting fee for that transfer. I promise that if you use this knowledge, you will be better for it, and it will be worth the price you pay.

Why has this contract been so successful? Two main reasons: expertise packaged in a structured form, and leveraging the gifts of talented people.

WELL-PACKAGED EXPERTISE.   The inception of the expert-based, structured approach to consulting harkens back to the early 1900s, when Frederick Taylor began to apply quasi-scientific principles to the task of management. Taylor, scion of a wealthy Philadelphia family, came into prominence when the industrial age was in full swing, and machinery was taking the place of manpower in the production of goods and services.

The railroad had recently replaced the horse as the primary source of rapid transportation, and with it big businesses began to flourish as the possibility of using railroads as a powerful distribution system came into being. Steel was becoming the backbone of industrial society and oil was just emerging as a powerful source of energy. Cities were the heart and soul of our nation's growth.

These changes did not happen overnight, and when compared to modern times, the business world remained relatively stable and predictable, production processes relatively inefficient, labor inexpensive and its supply seemingly unlimited.

Early in his career, Taylor was fascinated about what motivated human beings. As a result of repeated efforts to study humans in production settings, Taylor developed what he called "scientific management," a rather crude, yet effective application of the methods of science to the increasingly complex problems of managing people in rapidly growing, labor-driven businesses.

Through systematic study and logical reasoning, Taylor broke down the process of production into its smallest parts, and based on the assumption that it is the responsibility of management to "control" labor, developed a method of optimizing the process of production. Taylor's system of analysis required the consultant to study how people used their time, and how the process of production flowed, and then to find ways of making use of time and production flow more efficient. These "time and motion" studies were all the rage in the early 20th century. Many consultants adapted his methods and, with them, helped companies become more efficient and more effective. His methods were popularized and even parodied in books and movies such as *Cheaper by the Dozen* and Charlie Chaplin's wonderful comedy, *Modern Times*.

Taylor's methods were simple yet profound.* He would study a client organization, using a structured methodology that was designed to help clients solve both human and organizational efficiency problems. Enormously lucrative, Taylor's methodology paved the way for countless other consultants who saw the advantages of applying an expert-based, structured methodology to address business problems. To this day, almost all major consulting firms use the same process, although the underlying expertise or knowledge may be quite different.

LEVERAGING OTHERS. While expertise packaged in a structured way is the first ingredient of the typical rules of consulting as currently practiced by many, an important second ingredient produced management consulting's hypersuccess over the past 50 years. Many refer to it as the "leveraged model of consulting." At its most basic form, it looks like this. When a consulting firm's partner sells a large piece of consulting work to clients, most of the legwork is farmed off to the firm's less experienced, often young, consulting talent. The difference between what the consulting firm charges for its time and what they pay the young consultants is huge, and the margin is an incredible wealth-making machine for the firm. While I am not sure who pioneered the leveraged approach to consulting, I am sure that it became famous at McKinsey, historically the most successful and lucrative consulting firm in the world.

Here's an example of how the leveraged model works in more detail. A partner sells a piece of work—let's say a $5 million consulting engagement for a Fortune 500 company. Typical fees for such an engagement might be: $3000/day rate for consultants, $3500/day rate for project leaders, and $4000/day for the account manager's time. When a client signs a contract and work begins, often, unbeknownst to the client, each consultant's total cost to the consulting

---

* In addition to efficiency, Taylor was also very motivated to create fair wages for employees and to reduce the abuse of blue-collar labor that was rampant at the time. His humanitarian aims have often been lost in the more recent popular trend to uniformly question his tactics and impute his motives.

LEVERAGING TALENT THE MCKINSEY WAY

In 1926, James O. McKinsey, an accounting professor at Northwestern University, founded McKinsey and Company. Joined by Tom Tierney soon thereafter, they began auditing clients' books to identify opportunities for cost savings and improved efficiencies. The firm was not really distinct from other firms started around that time, such as Booz Allen, until 1933 when Marvin Bower, a Harvard Business School and Law School graduate, joined McKinsey and Company. Bower was the true visionary behind the firm, committed to creating a high degree of professionalism in what was then not recognized as a true profession. A few years after Bower joined the firm, McKinsey took a temporary position orchestrating a turnaround at Marshall Field & Company, one of the leading retailers in the country. McKinsey died shortly thereafter, in 1937. Bower and Tierney, the two leaders of the firm, disagreed over how to run McKinsey and Company and broke the firm into two halves. Bower continued to run McKinsey while Tierney formed A. T. Kearney.

Shortly after taking over McKinsey, Bower began making profound changes that revolutionized the consulting industry. For example, up until that time, consulting firms typically hired gray hairs with significant industrial management experience. The prevailing belief was that on-the-job experience was crucial for consulting success, if not at least for credibility. But Bower went against the patterns of the times. Feeling that experience often brought baggage, he instead sought intelligence. "I respected intelligence as much as, if not more than, practical experience," he told *The Edge*, a Wharton Business School publication. "We needed intellect in the firm as consulting was becoming an increasingly thought-intensive process."[2] In new hires, he sought character, intellect, personality, and drive.

With youth comes openness to learning, and so Bower and his partners developed and taught "The McKinsey Way" to an eager group of budding consultants. Bower's system of hiring and training produced a highly skilled workforce that could be easily leveraged and replicated in multiple situations. Given that McKinsey and Company and most other large consulting firms based their success on analytic expertise, the research and analysis underpinning most consulting jobs could be done without a lot of experience. Moreover, the use of younger talent exactly fit McKinsey and Company's emerging style, tailoring the diagnosis and work to match the circumstances of each client. Where other firms in the early days of consulting would start with a solution in mind, the McKinsey way was to break client problems down into elemental parts, then seek causes and solutions to these parts. This appetite for detail and analysis was well suited to bright young, consultants.

Over time, Marvin Bower built the most successful and dominating consulting firm in history, and the premises upon which it was built are replicated in almost every successful consulting firm worldwide. These assumptions are rarely questioned, primarily because it has worked so well for over 60 years. In particular, it works for the consulting firm itself, a magnificent money-making machine.

firm is on average about $225,000 per year, including salary, bonus, benefits, overhead, etc. This nets out to about $1000 per day assuming the consultant works in a client engagement on an average of 225 days per year. The difference between what the consultant costs the consulting firm and what is charged is pure margin, thereby leveraging the talent and time of the consultant. Similar margins apply to higher-level consultants. The net effect is a system where the sale occurs at the higher levels of the firm, but the bulk of actual work is done at lower levels. The more the partner can repeat this process the more money he makes for the firm (and for himself). All consultants in every major consulting firm know this process extremely well, and each receives a handsome salary and bonus based on his or her ability to use the system to its fullest.

WHY LARGE COMPANIES BUY INTO THE CURRENT RULES OF THE GAME

The second force shaping the prevailing consulting rules is the expectations of large industry leaders and the relationships they form with large consulting firms. Together, industry leaders and major consulting firms form the power elite of the business world. Interestingly, they show us what was successful in the past, not necessarily what will be successful in the future. For example, *Fortune Magazine*'s list of most admired companies almost always features those companies with the largest number of people or the greatest market share. These companies and their leaders were extremely successful in earlier approaches to business. They typically follow a hierarchical form of organizing and a tightly controlled system of management. While some have evolved to adopt alternative models of organization to help them grow and change, most rely on more structured, systematized approaches to change. To them, this makes sense. By the time a company gets large enough to become an industry leader, it often relies on rules, processes, policies, and systems of management that move people in lockstep fashion.

Ironically, what it takes to *manage* a large system is not the same as what it took to *become* a large system. Most large companies were innovators in their time—IBM, Hewlett-Packard, United Airlines, and Dupont to name a few—but now focus more of their energy on successfully managing their complex system than on creating a new model for success.

Not surprisingly, these large organizations typically hire large consulting firms that match their needs. They expect consultants to come in and offer a systematized approach to change and apply it to their monolithic, rule-bound organization. Together, the large business and the large consulting firm create a self-reinforcing system of exchange: larger organizations seek help from larger consulting firms whose structured approaches are tailored to meet the needs of larger client organizations.

While perhaps successful in the past, these structured methodologies are no longer enough. They reinforce a dynamic in which the client becomes dependent on the consultant for their change process. While change may occur in the short run, the client is no more capable of leading change in the future. Expert knowledge may (or may not) be applied, but the client is no wiser for this knowledge.

Moreover, many employees within these firms frequently resist the changes recommended by the firms employing this structured model because they don't feel it belongs to them. They are being told what to do by another set of bosses (the consultants, this time) often without the feeling that the consultants value their point of view, knowledge, or expertise. Trust is not established between the client's employees and the consultants, and this is fatal because trust is so crucial to change. While the consultants and the leaders of the organization may like the structured change process that is being "rolled out," the workers themselves often feel like they are being "rolled over."

I have worked with many large clients over the years. One was particularly memorable. In this organization, many of the workers were initially highly suspicious of me, even though we had never worked together. When I asked why, many reported that they had just been working with one of the large consulting firms and felt insulted by how they were treated. They felt disrespected and even demeaned by the way the previous consultants acted. One worker put it this way: "I can't believe the firm sends us these snot-nosed consultants—who have never worked in a company—to tell us how to run our business. We started working with one of the senior partners. He seemed to know what he was doing, but then he left us with these young kids, fresh out of the university, who knew very little except their book learning. These kids are now telling us what we're supposedly doing wrong. I resent it."

But let's not blame large businesses too quickly for their emphasis on structure. Let's also recognize that many human beings desire structure. In an ever-changing world, the hunger for quick answers to troubling questions is quite natural. Structured approaches to problem solving provide comfort to people, many of whom are used to feeling like cogs in a large system. Also, on a deep psychological level, being told what to do protects us from consequences should the change process fail. In these ways, the structured system meets our needs.

On an even deeper level, though, big companies' expectations of the consulting process reinforce the very rules that necessitate many consulting practices in the first place (see Figure 1-2). Most large businesses need consultants because their organizations are not good at change. They have difficulty changing because their systems and practices are not adaptable. Their systems and practices are inflexible because the companies are overly structured and rule-bound, and the parent/child, leader/follower pattern their workforces labor under is an inescapable feature of the underlying rules of its own game.

These rules, in turn, cause large businesses to seek consultants or consulting firms who do a good job of structuring the consulting process to fit their own underlying rules, thereby reinforcing the very dynamic that gave rise to the problems in the first place.

While not all client-consultant relationships follow this pattern, most do—particularly those between large consulting firms and large companies whose expectations define the business landscape.

How Our Educational System Supports the Current Rules of the Game

While the most financially successful consulting models fit the knowledge-centric mold, it did not come from out of the blue. The

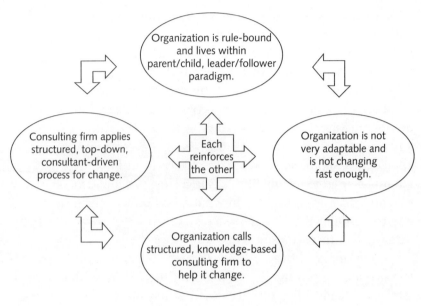

FIGURE 1-2 A SELF-SEALING SYSTEM

primacy of knowledge-based expertise began in our educational system, and is rooted in its bias of *thinking* over *doing*.

This bias is to be expected when the primary purpose of our school system, and of higher education in particular, is to arm students with the knowledge believed necessary for business success. Nearly all of us were trained under this system, and we seldom pause to examine its assumptions about what is important to learn.

Having grown up in this system, consultants pay a great deal of attention to knowledge, and much less to their ability to act upon it effectively. How could it be any different? To earn a higher degree, a student must demonstrate an ability to write papers, pass exams, and—if in a doctoral program—add knowledge to the field through a dissertation. These are primarily "thinking" processes. In short, we are taught about knowledge and thinking, not about effective action.

Our learning institutions reinforce this bias through the system of tenure and promotion and through the structure of their organization itself. For example, most universities obviously value publication over skillful teaching techniques in awarding tenure.

Consider the stereotype of the unkempt, disoriented, nutty professor, as an illustration of the preeminence of brilliance over behavior.*

While good at providing critical knowledge and sometimes developing students' thinking skills, this system is bad at teaching students how to work with others, how to tap into the collective creativity of groups, how to inspire others toward action, or how to create new markets or new products. This kind of competency, this skill in action, requires much more than knowledge or individual thinking skills. It requires interpersonal skills, emotional intelligence, and the ability to create together. This is the stuff of successful organizations in this day and age. Sadly, it is not well taught in our schools at any level.

THE TYPICAL APPROACH TO CONSULTING IS RAPIDLY BECOMING OBSOLETE

Together, these three factors—our history, the expectations of leading companies, and our systems of higher education—conspire to perpetuate the old system of consulting, in which knowledge is king and the structured demonstration and transfer of that knowledge is its queen. This system, which served us well throughout most of the 20th century, has been so successful that some of its fundamental assumptions are rarely examined. It is a system that's remarkably inflexible. Even worse, as the world of business moves to hyper-speed, it is a system that is rapidly becoming obsolete.

While the expert, leveraged model worked well in the past, the winds of change are howling today. The consulting profession must listen to that call. Change is the norm in this day and age, not stability. The Internet, genetic research, quantum technological advances, and global competition have given rise to a whole new world. Now more than ever before we must question the fundamental assumptions and beliefs underlying the consulting field.

---

*Lest I leave the wrong impression, I have met numerous professors who don't fit this stereotype, and who have earned their place in both the consulting and academic worlds for their ability to develop knowledge and effectively apply it through resourceful action. They are, however, the exception to the rule.

The remainder of this book explores an alternative way of approaching the consulting process. Ironically, this alternative way is a system without a system. Built instead on a set of principles, this alternative, when effectively applied, causes profound and enduring positive changes in organizational life. This new system—let's call it a model—redefines what it means to be a good consultant, and what it means to add value to our clients. It does not oppose structure, nor does it discount the value of knowledge. Instead, this new model for consulting takes a more holistic view of consulting in which process matters as much as content, and the relationship between consultant and client is primary.

We begin with an overview of the model underlying masterful consulting. Then Parts II through IV look at this model more deeply—exploring closely the three key relationships in consulting mastery: our relationship to clients, our relationship to knowledge, and our relationship to ourselves. In each chapter, you will hear the words of masterful consultants, as well as my own. You will hear examples of counterproductive inner stances and productive ones.

As you read counterproductive ones, I hope you will avoid asking, "Do I do this, or don't I do this?" If you ask that question when looking at a counterproductive stance, you may decide, "Nope, that doesn't apply to me," and then disregard the message. Similarly, when reading about stances that evince mastery, and you say to yourself, "That *is* me," and then miss seeing ways you might bring that principle more into your consulting life. Instead of the "Do I or don't I" question, I invite you to see yourself as a person unfolding, throwing off armor you don't need, and picking up new possibilities and making them your own. So the question is not, "Do I do this?" The question is, "How do I do this, or how can I do this even better?" None of us is perfect in all of these areas, including the masters that I interviewed for this book; indeed, they would be the first to admit their failings. Perhaps if we gently consider how to learn to embody these principles more fully, we may advance toward mastery.

CHAPTER 2

The Masterful Consultant's Inner Stance

One must not always think so much about what
one must do, but rather what we should be. Our
works do not ennoble us; but we must ennoble our
works.

—Meister Eckhart

JOHN LEFT THE DEBRIEF SESSION of the consulting engagement thinking he had done a decent job. He had helped the client accomplish the task, had met all his commitments, and felt satisfied his deliverable was better than most could have done. The debriefing went as expected, with nothing unusual. John shook hands with the client, leaving her with this message: "Sheryl, if you ever have any other work like this, please don't hesitate to call." Sheryl assured him she would. John was comforted in her response.

Months went by and there was no call. Through his connections John learned there were indeed two other similar projects that required his kind of expertise, yet he was never called. After eight months, he decided to take action. He called Sheryl to ask her why he was not considered. She gave him two reasons related to their internal decision making, both of which seemed compelling but did not persuade him. He asked her again if she was pleased with his work, and she indicated she was.

What John did not know, and would likely never find out from Sheryl, was that his work was adequate, but not great. He had done everything he could, but she felt no connection with him. Moreover, she felt that his work would not take them to the next level. He fulfilled the contract but did not impress. The problem wasn't his method or his reports. The problem was that he lacked the inner magic that inspired others to challenge their assumptions. He was good, but not masterful. Sadly, he yearned to be great, so not getting called back was painful. He didn't believe her answer to his question, yet had no way to probe deeper to learn what the real problem was. He felt rejected and confused.

While much research exists on the practice of consulting, the profession is still far more art than science. John pays attention to the science and comes equipped with the latest techniques and models. But he misses the artistry that is the essence of masterful consulting.

THE ARTISTRY OF A MASTERFUL CONSULTANT

Like a great painter, the masterful consultant relies on more than simple technique. He knows that each client situation is unique—a blank canvas. While there are principles to guide his actions, he must create anew the process and the relationship to produce the greatest effect. Where the painter works with paintbrush and palette, the masterful consultant works with "self."

All good consultants have an inventory of theories, models, tools, and techniques to draw on. Without them, most would be lost. Yet what differentiates master consultants from others has nothing to do with this inventory. It has all to do with the "feel" of the situation, with the ability to act effectively "in the moment"—to sense what is going on in a given situation and then take the action that meets that moment. To do this well requires consultants to divest themselves of the past and the future, of fears, anxieties, and desires, to be present, and then to take action without ego. Theory, models, instruments, and techniques can't teach this, because it arises from the consultant's *inner stance*—that invisible quality elusive to so many.

Robert Bly, in a collection of poems entitled *The Soul Is Here for Its Own Joy,*[1] recalls an ancient African tale illustrating the power of that invisible quality, which I paraphrase here:

> A man had twelve cows, and he loved them very much. But one day he noticed they were giving less milk. He decided to stay up and see why they were giving less milk. At midnight he saw a light come down from the stars. Inside the light was a luminous woman. He said to her, "Are you the one who has been stealing milk from my cows?" "Yes," she said, "my sisters and I like the milk from your cows very much."
>
> Taken by her beauty, and her love of his cows, the man proposed to her on the spot. She agreed, but with one condition: "I have brought this basket with me, and I want you to agree that you will never look into this basket."
>
> The man agreed, and they were married. But his curiosity soon got the worst of him, and one day he broke his promise and peered into the basket. To his surprise, he found it empty.
>
> His beautiful wife returned that day to find the basket open. When she confronted him with the question of whether he opened the basket against her wishes, he confessed. "I did!" he said, laughing frantically. "I opened the basket! There's absolutely *nothing* in it. There is nothing in the basket!!"
>
> The mysterious woman replied, "I must leave now. What I brought with me in the basket was spirit. It's so like human beings to think that spirit is nothing!" And she was gone.

So too with the best kind of consulting. We expect to look into the basket and discover easy explanations for deep transformations. Oh, we might see ordinary things—those tools, techniques, exercises, models, and specialized knowledge that anyone can see. What is also there, but invisible, is the consultant's spirit—his inner stance. I am not talking about spirit in a religious sense but rather about the spirit with which we do our work.

Mastery emerges from a healthy inner stance. A consultant's inner stance can be felt and experienced from his demeanor and mindset, in what he pays attention to and what he cares about. Presence, confidence, openness, and commitment are all vital elements of a healthy and vital inner stance. A consultant's inner stance colors every dimension of the client-consultant relationship, so it deserves considerable attention. Invisible it may be, yet it shows up in everything good that we do. Perhaps Albert Einstein said it best when he said: "All means prove but a blunt instrument, if they have not behind them a living spirit."[2]

A master consultant I interviewed said something important about the consulting process that is relevant here. When I asked what advice he would give to others about becoming a masterful consultant, he said simply:

> Be in a constant learning environment. The research shows
> that eventual success is a hockey stick in which the length of
> the stick is directly correlated with the length you have been in
> an apprenticeship mode. People who don't succeed go for
> money right away and never learn. I say you ought to get paid
> the next 10 years in the form of learning experiences.

What learning experiences did he mean? Those that include the inner stance. Too often, consultants seek the quick fix, particularly early in their careers, and don't commit themselves to the learning that mastery requires. Like their clients, they too want a magic pill they can offer to help companies be successful.

Unfortunately, no magic pill exists. Those who seek it rarely achieve true, enduring success. In contrast, none of the masterful consultants I interviewed adopt a one-size-fits-all solution. Instead, they are armed with a rich array of intervention tools, models, and approaches, which they use flexibly and creatively. Becoming masterful didn't come easily. It came from long, hard work on their inner stance, and much experience. This work results in a set of goals and strategies that stand in sharp contrast to the goals and strategies employed by those who adhere to the prevailing rules of the consulting game.

THE MASTER CONSULTANT'S GOALS AND STRATEGIES

Every organization is driven by a set of *patterns*. The way we hold meetings has a pattern. The way we communicate has a pattern. Our leadership style has a pattern. These patterns form, mold, and harden until they become the very culture of organizations. The *goal* of consulting mastery is simple: *to impact the fundamental patterns of the client organization in order to produce profound and deep change.*

To accomplish this goal, masterful consultants adopt a primary strategy best characterized as an *empowering partnership*—one designed to shift the client organization to a new level of health and performance. An empowering partnership is one where both consultant and client are touched by each other. Together, they create an authentic, vulnerable relationship, where the client, the process, and the relationship itself are all explored, deepened, and enhanced. They see their work together as co-creative and filled with learning that is every bit as imaginative as it is well designed. Scottish philosopher David Hume said it well when he wrote: "The sweetest path of life leads through the avenues of learning, and whoever can open up the way for another, ought, so far, to be esteemed a benefactor to mankind." This avenue of learning traveled by an empowered relationship is the heart of the master consultant's primary strategy.

Following this primary strategy, masterful consultants use three secondary strategies, each fitting the three arenas of consulting: relationship with client, with knowledge, and with self.

1. **THEY DEVELOP A CLIENT-CENTERED PARTNERSHIP.** They see clients as a whole system and encourage their clients to do the same. They are clear that clients have the capacity to grow themselves. Therefore, they position themselves as guides or partners, not experts. Finally, they see their clients as responsible for the outcome while remaining a partner in the process.

2. **THEY SHARE KNOWLEDGE OPENLY AND FREELY.** Masterful consultants know that the key to effectiveness is in

applying knowledge in real time. In addition, they seek wherever possible to transfer knowledge and enhance the wisdom of their clients.

3. **THEY SEE THE QUALITY OF THEIR CHARACTER AS A CATA-LYST FOR TRANSFORMATION AND LEARNING.** Masterful consultants recognize that the most important differentiator between good and great consultants is the quality of their character. As a result, they spend a great deal of time developing their inner self.

To better understand these three strategies, let's examine each one more thoroughly.

HOW MASTERFUL CONSULTANTS RELATE TO THEIR CLIENT ORGANIZATIONS

The empowering relationship masterful consultants form with their client organizations may be obvious to many, but it is also difficult to attain. Almost all consultants believe they form relationships with their client organizations with the intent to empower them. They say they create conditions in which the client *owns* the process or the outcome, and that their intent is to *leave the client more capable* than when the consulting process started. This mindset alone, however, is not what differentiates masterful consultants from others. It is the degree to which they behave congruently with it. While many consultants espouse the importance of the client owning the process, and of creating a true partnership with the client, their behavior, too often, tells another story.

Let's look at one example. Craig is a competent consultant who believes strongly that his client needs to own the process and the outcome of the consultation, and he believes the members of the client organization need to implement his ideas themselves in order to grow. During a planning session to develop a two-year plan to execute a fairly radical Six-Sigma process throughout the company, Craig led the way. He offered a model for executing the ideas, and walked the group of key executives and HR staff through each carefully designed step. They followed Craig's lead, feeling a need for his guidance in an area that seemed overwhelming and highly complex and made decisions consistent with Craig's framework. When members of the planning team offered ideas that Craig believed were unwise, he deftly and compassionately explained why and offered an alternative suggestion. The team felt persuaded by his viewpoint, never controlled. Based on initial positive feelings about Craig, all appeared to be going according to plan.

Had you looked at Craig's behavior more closely, however, you might have noticed signs of a less-than-ideal outcome. Throughout the meeting he made suggestions far more often than he asked questions or invited comments. When he did ask questions, it was almost always with an answer already in mind. Subtly, Craig steered the group toward the pre-existing answer. Neither did he solicit feedback about how they were feeling about the process or decisions made. Additionally, numerous nonverbal signs were ignored, such as crossed arms and restive expressions suggesting that team members were disconnecting from the process. Regardless of these signs, Craig left feeling successful, having imparted his hard-earned wisdom to the members of the team. The CEO felt as if he got his money's worth. After all, wasn't he paying Craig for knowledge?

The missing ingredient here was that the team, while following Craig's lead, did not psychologically *own* the change process or the outcome, because they never had to think it through for themselves. As a result, they did a poorer job in the implementation phase than they did in the diagnosis. Midway through the process, the implementation stalled as other business concerns came to the fore. To this day, Craig blames the team members for their lack of commitment and ability to act with conviction, not himself for the subtle and mounting ways he precluded their own learning process.

In contrast to Craig's experience, masterful consultants keep their clients in the driver seat, committed to their ownership of the outcome. It's a conscious process, one that calls for rigorous self-observation and attention to the potential to want to act in a heroic fashion and "fix" the client's problems. Masterful consultants seek feedback to minimize their own unconscious patterns that might result in taking power away from their client organizations. In other words, they walk their empowering talk. Unlike Craig, masterful consultants will more often ask questions than give answers. They act as a facilitator, committed to having the planning team members think the process through for themselves. They might offer a model, but at the same time readily accept one of their client's if it achieves the outcomes of ownership and committed action necessary to implement change. Masterful consultants know that the magic is not in the models, but rather in the intangibles: the learning process, the consultant's relationship to the client, and the consultant's character.

Masterful consultants behave more congruently with their beliefs because they examine their own behavior deeply and fully. They are also deeply committed to the client having freedom of choice, ownership of the process, and valid information upon which to make decisions.[3] They are far more *consciously facilitative* than someone like Craig. While Craig says he is committed to those same principles, his greater, unconscious commitment is to being "brilliant" in the eyes of the client—and to being "right."

Owning the outcome is one of three features of the client relationship that masterful consultants form. In addition, masterful consultants treat the whole system as the client, and wisely negotiate the dilemmas posed when the person paying them acts inconsistently with the needs of the whole system.

Underlying masterful consultants' success is their abiding commitment to a partnering relationship, one where power is shared equally between client and consultant during the change process. One thing that differentiates masterful consultants from others is the depth to which they hold true to this principle, not merely paying it lip service. In the act of defining a consultant-client relationship, for example, most masterful consultants have a very candid conversation with the client about mutual boundaries, expectations, and desires. While other consultants tend to wait to discuss their relationship until problems arise, masterful consultants deal with it up front. In the contracting phase of the consulting engagement, they will place as much if not more emphasis on defining the desired qualities of the interpersonal relationship as on the financial relationship. They discuss and agree upon who is in charge of which meetings, when and how to give feedback to each other, under what conditions either party can exit the relationship, expectations about honesty and vulnerability, and much more.[4]

THE WHOLE SYSTEM IS THE CLIENT

One master consultant I interviewed was engaged by a highly conservative organization to coach an executive on how to become a more effective leader. The targeted executive (let's call her Nancy), was known to be mercurial in her behavior, and often rubbed people the wrong way. After conducting many interviews, the consultant concluded that Nancy's behavior was only part of the problem. The other, more fundamental element was the organization's hidebound intolerance of creative ideas that ran counter to its traditional ways of doing things. This straitjacketing resistance to change frustrated Nancy, who wanted to give people a jolt. In her frustration she often acted ineffectively, barked orders, and blamed others for their unwillingness to take risks. These were coping behaviors that only served to exacerbate the perceived problem.

While most consultants would be happy to spend most of their time coaching Nancy, keeping her as the focus of the problem, this consultant chose to help the organization as a whole, particularly the executive team, to reevaluate some of the more creative behaviors Nancy exhibited. Simultaneously, he coached Nancy on how to offer her ideas in ways that were more palatable. As a result, Nancy and the rest of the team were able to move beyond the previous, polarized dynamic, and find mutually accommodating approaches. The consultant's attention to the whole system, coupled with his deftness in straddling the needs of all concerned, was an example of consulting mastery.

HOW MASTERFUL CONSULTANTS RELATE TO KNOWLEDGE

While I have argued strongly against the *overemphasis* on knowledge in the hierarchy of consulting abilities, I am not dismissing it altogether. Indeed, a threshold of knowledge is necessary to be even a half decent consultant. The importance of knowledge was reinforced through the client interviews I conducted to understand their views of consulting mastery. When describing the most effective consultant they had ever worked with, many described how bright and knowledgeable the consultant was. Clients often spoke about not only the consultant's conceptual capability but also of his or her ability to see clearly through the fog of the client's difficulties. Similarly, the intellectual horsepower of each of the consultants I interviewed was quite evident. At the same time, none of them wore their intelligence on their sleeve. Quite the opposite; almost all were astoundingly humble.

Knowledge, then, is crucial to consulting mastery, as is the ability to think clearly. Without some threshold level of knowledge and a keen intellect, the consultant will not fulfill the client's tacit need to be given something (knowledge) the client believes it lacks.

However, brilliant thinking does not make a great consultant. Brilliant thinking may impress, but it doesn't empower the client to make changes. Instead, all of the masterful consultants interviewed displayed an impressive amount of emotional intelligence. Their ability to understand their clients from a human standpoint, to see client problems more clearly, to help them make sense of their own organization, and work with them to the point where true change occurs is what separates them from the pack. Most consultants have the requisite knowledge and analytic capability. Few have the emotional intelligence to produce lasting change in their client organizations.

In this day and age, both good and masterful consultants are more than adequately equipped with expert knowledge in their field, and are able to communicate their knowledge effectively. In the knowledge arena, what distinguishes masterful consultants is the way they hold and use knowledge. They hold their knowledge with certainty and confidence, not arrogance. When they communicate, they often describe the complex set of unfolding dynamics in ways that create clarity out of confusion. Most importantly, masterful consultants are guided by a set of theories about change, which provide a map for how to navigate the complex and choppy waters of change. One master consultant I interviewed said it well:

> Too often consultants are walking around and they don't have
> a solid ground to stand on in terms of either a theory of change
> that they can use across multiple levels of system or a theory of
> phases of development. Without those two things, they are
> almost certainly going to end up basically leaning on tools and
> techniques.

In addition to offering concepts cleanly and simply, masterful consultants will pick and choose their spots when intervening into the client organization. Ever aware that the client must own the change and take action based on the knowledge offered, masterful consultants seek not to dazzle the client with knowledge. Instead,

44

they guide and support the client toward the discoveries necessary for action. Even more important, they seek to create conditions in which these discoveries are so strongly experienced that the outcome is a profound commitment to change. While I have no hard data on the subject, anecdotal data combined with what I have observed from countless examples of consultants following the principles embedded in this book show that the ratio of implementation success to failure is quite high and leaves those that employ the typical model of consulting in the dust.

HOW MASTERFUL CONSULTANTS CARRY THEMSELVES AS PEOPLE

The quality of character of masterful consultants is evident in how they talk, how they relate to others, and how they act. Behind these behaviors must be integrity, confidence, and humility. Behind this, deeper still, must be strong self-esteem, often borne of years of self-reflection and intense inner work.

In my experience, masterful consultants strive to live by a set of principles. We all have principles that guide our actions, sometimes tacit, and sometimes explicit. What distinguishes masterful consultants from others is their adherence to those principles, their commitment to examine themselves in relation to these principles, and their willingness and ability to self-correct. Ralph Waldo Emerson, the famous 19th century transcendentalist philosopher, put it well: "Self-command is the main discipline."

Not surprisingly, the principles of self-command are not typically taught in most consulting training courses. Nor are they discussed in great detail in daily conversation among consultants. But they are held deeply by each of the consultants I spoke to, and by other great consultants I have had the pleasure to observe in action. Here, then, are the principles shared by masterful consultants.

THE MASTERFUL CONSULTANT'S PRINCIPLES OF CONDUCT

1. ALWAYS TELL THE TRUTH, AT THE DEEPEST LEVELS

2. COMMIT TO LEARNING—FOR SELF AND FOR THE CLIENT

3. BRING MY WHOLE SELF IN FULL PARTNERSHIP

4. PLAY A BIG GAME

Always tell the truth means being honest with one's self and with others at all times. Great consultants are typically courageous and value honesty before caution. At the same time, they find ways of speaking honestly in ways that others can hear. They do not bludgeon others with honesty. Instead, their honesty goes down easily because it is coupled with respect.

Commit to learning has to do with a stance in life. Great consultants are inquisitive. They spend far more time and energy exploring issues than they do offering answers. They respect and abide by the process of discovering, and encourage answers to unfold, rather than delivering them in machine-gun succession.

Bring my whole self has to do with being vulnerable and with being whole—mind, body, and spirit. Great consultants are acutely aware of their shadow self, and rather than deny or hide some areas of their self, they seek to bring them out. They see the process of consulting as a very human process, and know that the more we know and respect our own self, the more we can understand, respect, and guide others.

Play a big game means working with others to make a larger difference. Great consultants don't get embroiled in either/or thinking. They focus on ways of working that expand possibilities to produce win-win outcomes, and that open up vistas clients were not even aware of.

Simple as they may seem, these principles are profound in their implications. As I look back on the moments when I was less than successful, I can almost always trace them back to either avoiding or not embodying one of these principles. Masterful consultants know deep in their bones that failure in consulting is almost always attributable to violating one of those principles; therefore they strive to live by them impeccably—to be in command of self. Deviating from them creates an inner disturbance. Once they notice the deviation, they immediately course-correct.

By saying that masterful consultants live by the principles I have described, I am not suggesting they are perfect. To the contrary, any principle or value is a beacon of light to strive for; not a rule to be gripped by. What differentiates masterful consultants from others is their commitment to the principles, their never-wavering intention to look themselves in the mirror, and their ability to self-correct without self-blame.

These qualities do not come easily. They are the result of years of self-exploration, self-examination, and the support of many others—therapists, counselors, coaches, mentors, friends, and family—all of whom challenge the consultant to live up to his full potential as a vehicle for positive change. It takes a strong sense of self—an unusually high level of self-esteem—to attain mastery, and it is driven by a continual commitment to self-awareness.

MASTERY IS NOT SOMETHING YOU CAN GO OUT AND GET. THERE IS NO MAGIC PILL. IT IS SOMETHING ONE EARNS.

Underlying the four principles of conduct is a deeper awareness held by all masterful consultants. Masterful consultants do not see these principles as static. Nor do they see themselves as perfect. They see themselves on a journey toward fully realizing these principles, a destination that is never fully achieved. This is a journey toward being a more conscious and self-aware human being, and not just a good consultant. It is a journey of self-discovery.

In short, these principles are a guide for how masterful consultants conduct themselves, always. The principles determine the consultants' actions, decisions, and choices. It is their powerful inner guide, and in living by this guide, consultants become effective, trusted, and positively influential.

Together, these arenas of consulting, relationship to client, knowledge and self, come together in the thoughts and actions of masterful consultants (Figure 2-1). They are in stark contrast to the past and present model that underlies most consulting practices and while perhaps more difficult to enact, represent the potential future of the consulting industry.

THE THREE STRATEGIES ARE AN INTEGRATED WHOLE

As a system, the goals and strategies of masterful consultants do not exist in isolation from one another. Trying to enact one strategy

FIGURE 2-1 THE MASTER CONSULTANT'S MODEL			
Goals	Primary Strategy	Secondary Strategies	Actions
Make a difference	Empowering Partnership	Develop a client-centered partnership	See the client as a whole system, and encourage the client to do the same
			Be clear that the client has the capacity to grow them-selves, and position yourself as a guide and a partner, not an expert
			Keep the client responsible for the outcome, while you partner in the process
		Share knowledge openly and freely	Recognize that the key to effectiveness is how to apply knowledge real-time
			Seek to transfer knowledge and enhance the wisdom to the client
			Respect the client and build genuine trust
		See the quality of your inner stance as a catalyst for transformation and learning	Recognize that the most important differentiator between good and great consultants is the quality of their inner stance
			Develop your inner stance and act with integrity

without the others is like a three-legged stool missing a leg. Inevitably, it will fall.

To illustrate, let's look at three examples. I know one consultant (let's call him Paul) who is quite brilliant, and who has conceptualized a way of working with clients and helping them transform that is as well thought out as any I've ever seen. Paul also acts with the utmost of integrity. However, when he works with clients, they often feel that he is aloof, professorial, and sometimes self-absorbed. Paul has generated many new clients, but few stay with him over time. Fewer still call him back for more work. They rarely tell him the real reason for not continuing to work, masking it with excuses such as, "we aren't ready to go forward yet," or "we want to slow the process down for now." As a result, Paul has no clue why his client work comes up short. His relationship to knowledge is strong and his character impeccable. But his ability to connect to people in a heartfelt way just isn't there.

In contrast, I know another consultant (call her Sandy) who demonstrates enormous integrity in her dealings with others. Sandy has a wonderful way of engaging with clients, and they experience her as warm, caring, and appropriately empowering. Nonetheless, her Achilles heel appears to be her ability to communicate her ideas clearly. While she is bright, having earned a doctoral degree, she often speaks in a way that meanders or is verbose, and often obfuscates her key points. As hard as Sandy tries, clients are often left confused. This is particularly problematic in that one reason an organization hires consultants is to help them better deal with their own uncertainty and confusion. Sandy's ability to relate effectively is clearly without question, and her integrity beyond reproach. But her relationship to knowledge is flawed. Consequently, she has difficulty obtaining work, and when working, sometimes has difficulty helping clients move in a clear, coordinated way.

Finally, I know a third consultant (Greg) who is clear thinking, holds knowledge in a way that supports clients and their learning, and establishes a strong partnership with them, yet his integrity is suspect. Frequently, Greg unconsciously acts in a self-serving manner. His need for work sometimes causes him to be too aggressive with clients, so that he comes across like a used car salesman. Greg sometimes "shapes the truth" to get what he wants. In other words, his character is compromised. As a result, clients often end up not trusting him, to the point of severing their work with him.

There are endless examples of consultants whose imbalance or inadequate capability in one of these fundamental arenas compromises their consulting effectiveness. In contrast, while all the masterful consultants I interviewed appear to have a particular strength, none of them are weak in any one of the arenas. They have worked hard to develop all three, and recognize them all as crucial to their consulting success.

Having summarized the key features of consulting mastery, the bulk of the book is devoted to deepening the reader's understanding of the details of what it means to be a masterful consultant. The last two chapters then explore mastery more fully and provide guidance on how to move toward it.

PART II

MASTERY IN ACTION

THE MASTER CONSULTANT'S RELATIONSHIP TO THE CLIENT

CHAPTER 3

CLIENT-CENTERED CONSULTING

The more we look out for others,
the more we look out for ourselves.

—Terry C. Warner

I WAS WORKING FOR THREE DAYS with a CFO and his direct reports at a mid-sized health care organization. The organization had been a client of mine for a couple of years, one with whom I had experienced some success. In this particular case, I had been asked by the CEO to help the CFO and his team to strengthen their leadership and teamwork, a challenge I felt well qualified to meet. The CEO felt strongly that the offsite would be valuable for the CFO and his team—a gift to them, of sorts—and he believed I could lead it well. However, there were also warning signs that I should not have taken the work.

I ignored them all.

The strongest indication was the CFO's ambivalence about the offsite. He expressed reservations from the onset and again several times during the planning stage. I assured him each time that I could add value and that it would be well worth it.

The team, for its part, seemed disinterested, as I quickly discovered during my assessment interviews. They were overloaded and felt no need for team development at that time.

Rather than listen to this, I told myself, "Well, all leadership teams can improve at every stage of development. Why not this one?" And so I pressed on. As part of the offsite plan, I suggested we use a number of different data feedback instruments each of which required a lot of work on everyone's part. In spite of their reservations, I continued to assure them the offsite would be worthwhile.

It was not.

The whole process felt flat, and getting them engaged was difficult throughout. At the end, they reported that the offsite was not worth the time spent. Moreover, some people indicated that they did not feel comfortable with my style. A couple of the team members even described me as disconnected and condescending. They felt that I was guided less by their needs than by my own agenda to "teach them something."

I deserved the feedback. It had been many years since I had facilitated a process with such mediocre results. Upon reflection, it had to do with "where I was coming from" with this client. I had pushed past clear warnings and my own significant reservations about the project, and then, during the offsite itself, tried to confront issues the client was plainly not eager to explore. In pushing my own agenda, I really was acting in a condescending manner, ignoring the reality in front of me. My work with them was centered on me, not them.

In this chapter, I explore the hidden tendency on the part of most consultants to focus on themselves. I then point out the features of a more powerful focus for the consultant—the client-centered view. This focus is most often employed by the consultants who consistently demonstrate mastery.

Some Fundamental Questions

Heard in too many organizations throughout the world are comments like these about consultants:

"They have their own agenda."
"They just don't get us."
"If only they had asked us, we could have told them that."
"I just don't trust what they are about."

The biggest complaint of all is that "we spent a lot of money but the work made little difference."

When many consultants hear these things, they tell themselves that the client is to blame. "If only they had [fill in the blank]." But what if the problem had little to do with the client? Perhaps the problem had something to do with the consultant's definition of consulting success.

What does it really mean to be successful in consulting? It's a question we often fail to ask ourselves. Is success measured by how much we earn? No. Some great consultants earn less because they choose to work only part time. Is success measured by how much we charge? No. Too many successful consultants choose to charge little because they want to work with a set of clients that cannot afford large fees. Is it measured by the size of the consulting contract? Hardly. I have seen too many huge consulting efforts fall short of their targeted outcomes. These financially driven goals do not define success well. Another definition is called for, one focused on meeting client goals.[1]

MEETING THE CLIENT'S GOALS. To meet the client's goals, we must first ask: Who is the client? For most consultants, the answer is simple: the person paying your bill. This person's needs must be understood and met. Hence, his or her goals dictate the consulting mission.

An alternative school of thought is that the whole organization is the client. This view defines consulting success as meeting the goals of the total system and leaving the whole organization healthier as a result of the consulting process. The consultant seeks to understand the whole organization's needs, aims, and goals, and be in service to that. More specifically, system health might include:

- Achieving the goals set out in the initial contracting process with the client

- Helping the organization maintain fluidity so it can adapt to a changing environment (in other words, *learn*)

- Meeting the needs of its members

This view requires that the consultant bring to light potentially competing goals embedded in the client organization and seek to resolve them. It requires that the consultant be willing to put the consulting engagement at risk in the service of the greater needs of the organization. It requires that the consultant be willing to confront the person paying her if that person's behavior is hurting the client organization as a whole. This is the view that masterful consultants most often adopt. This outlook has significant implications for how a consultant joins the client in planning the consulting process and how together they make decisions along the way.

If the client is the whole system and the goal of masterful consulting is to meet the system's goals and leave the organization stronger, then the natural question becomes: What inner stance must the consultant adopt, relative to the client organization, to produce such outcomes? I believe, as do the masterful consultants I interviewed, that the answer has to do with a *client-centered approach* to consulting.

MASTERFUL CONSULTANTS SEEK TO LEAVE THE WHOLE ORGANIZATION MORE HEALTHY, STRONG, AND VIABLE.

CONSULTING APPROACHES THAT MISS THE MARK

To understand the client-centered approach, let's first contrast it with some alternative approaches to consulting. The more common are: consultant-centered, task-centered, payer-centered, and technique-centered.

CONSULTANT-CENTERED CONSULTING. In this often-used approach, the consultant spends a great deal of time and energy thinking about her own needs, sometimes to the exclusion of the client's. The phrase "full wax job" derives from this approach.[2] Consultants who adopt this approach spend time trying to convince the client to use specific services, not because it is in the client's best interest, but because they are high-paying, high-margin activities for the consultant. Sorry to say, I have witnessed many conversations within consulting firms in which the topic was on making more money, sometimes to the detriment of the client's well-being.

In her book *Final Accounting,* Barbara Ley Toffler provides an insider's view of the consultant-centered view in action at Andersen Consulting. She reveals, among other things, the pressure she felt as a consultant to "bill our brains out." As one of many examples, she describes a consulting opportunity that she believed should have cost about $50,000 or $75,000, extremely small by Andersen's standards. Here is how Andersen Consulting beefed up the billings.

> We took advantage of our neophyte (new and unsuspecting client(and steadily built a dependency on our team by such things as giving her weekly "homework" assignments to help her learn about her new position, and devising a monthly step-by-step plan that basically said to her that she wouldn't be able to sustain her responsibilities without us being present. Before she knew what hit her, she had an action plan priced at around $250,000 a month. We had seen a key vulnerability . . . and pounced.[3]

When the primary goal is to make a lot of money and client needs are less important, consultants perpetrate such dubious tactics. Consulting firms, driven by profit goals, find clever ways of doing it, including leveraging young consulting talent as described earlier, hiding costs, preying on the client's fears, and pushing unnecessary services on them. Too often, customer needs are secondary.

The consultant-centered approach is not an official approach per se. No consulting firm would articulate it as a modus operandi. It does not appear on a brochure or website. Although invisible, it reflects an inner stance, driven by an attitude of scarcity or self-serving interest. It is particularly natural for young consultants to adopt this way of relating to a client. Early in my career I sometimes took work that I should not have. I did it either because I felt I needed work, or because I felt I would grow from the experience. My clients often paid the price.

Similarly, many of the consultants I interviewed said that the biggest mistake they made as a consultant was to take work that they should not have, motivated by their own, self-serving desires. They freely admitted that this was hardly something to be proud of. This consultant's comments echoed the sentiments of many:

> When you have a practice and you're having a hard time mak-
> ing payroll, you do stupid things. When you are making deci-
> sions based on money and you don't have enough of it, you're
> going to make mistakes. My biggest mistake as a consultant
> was in taking work I should not have in order to pay the rent. I
> stayed in the client organization too long and tried to oversell
> them stuff. It all starts with issues inside myself. It starts with
> greed and fear. These were mistakes I have learned not to make
> any more.

TASK-CENTERED CONSULTING. The task-centered approach focuses all energy on the task at hand, often to the exclusion of the client's true needs. This type of consulting often occurs when a client already has a solution in mind, and then seeks the right consultant to provide that solution. Many times consultants will be happy to take the work and seek to deliver the solution asked for. "I'm only doing what the client has asked" is the justification. Too often, however, when con-sultants learn that the solution asked for does not truly meet the needs of the client, rather than surface this issue, as would happen in the client-centered approach, the consultant continues to deliver the work. You know the refrain: "great payday, but no difference."

The task-centered approach is too myopic. Tasks can be suc-cessfully accomplished even as the client suffers severe damage. Let's say the client is setting up a project designed to introduce a new product line, one that will eventually replace the old one. In the task-centered approach, the consultant will do everything in her power to facilitate the desired outcome, regardless of the effect on the entire organization. Moreover, she may collude with the client in keeping the project "hush-hush" so as not to disturb the rest of the organization or slow down the results. She may sense a political problem but ignore it since it isn't a part of the task definition. In the short run, the task may be accomplished, but the organization loses more than it gains. Going behind the organization's back fosters mistrust and resentment among the very people the new project will depend on for success.

PAYER-CENTERED CONSULTING. The payer-centered consultant views the person paying the bill as the client. On the surface, this approach makes perfect sense. Why not focus on that person's needs? After all, if he or she is not pleased, there will be no more consulting income. Note the focus on getting paid versus meeting the needs of the client.

The main problem with this approach is that the payer is almost always part of a larger system. And sometimes what the payer wants is not what the system needs, which would rarely be surfaced, discussed, or addressed in this approach. The consultant would simply carry out the needs of the payer. Very often, the payer's attitude might be part of the problem. Unless his or her role in that dynamic is addressed, no true difference can be made in the health and well-being of the client organization as a whole.

An example might be instructive here. Let's say the CEO hires an organizational development consultant to help make the people in the organization more responsible and proactive. On the surface, this seems like a worthy goal. However, more often than not the reason people have not been acting responsibly or proactively has to do with the relationship between the CEO and others, or between the senior executive team and the rest of the organization. Leadership behaviors that inhibit others from taking responsibility might include:

- Withholding of information
- Confusing direction
- Coercive leadership style
- Lack of integrity.

A leader who wants more responsibility and initiative from others can easily exhibit many of these behaviors. The payer-centered approach does not produce a conversation about leadership behaviors. Instead, the effort is to "fix" others. My prediction: "great payday, little difference."

TECHNIQUE-CENTERED CONSULTING. Responding to the client's need for structure and certainty, and preying on their need to be saved, many consultants come to a job with a predetermined solution. They then try to convince the client that this solution is what will treat their ailment. This approach reminds me of medieval doctors who believed that almost all medical problems were caused by bad blood. The natural solution was to suck blood from the patient, often using leeches.

A limited toolkit, coupled with excessive faith in its utility, can be a dangerous elixir and is the modus operandi of the technique-centered consultant. I have seen this approach quite often used by inexperienced consultants or those who prefer a formula. They tend to mirror the client's preferences for the comfort of structure or simplistic approaches. Consultant and client together tread a path that, more often than not, is destined to fail.

Many faddish trends in consulting are variations on this theme. Potential examples include Management by Objectives, TQM, Process Reengineering, GE's "Workout," Myers-Briggs–based Team Building, The Balanced Scorecard, and Portfolio Management. In and of themselves, they can be wonderful tools in the right situation. When they become the sole approach or model, however, in the hands of a consultant inexperienced in other ways of working with clients, they can be dangerous.

THE CLIENT-CENTERED APPROACH

The client-centered approach stands in shining contrast to these approaches. The goal of the client-centered approach is to consult in such a way that the client as a system is left more whole, healthy, and more capable. It requires that the payer and the consultant both be focused on this outcome. More specifically, the client-centered consultant practices with the following tenets:

1. The client is ultimately responsible for the consulting outcomes—ownership is key to success.

2. The client's needs are paramount in the mind of the con-

sultant—all efforts are designed to be in service to the goal.

3. The client is a unique client and all services need to be customized to meet that client's unique needs.

4. Client learning is at the core of all consulting activity.

5. The client is capable of solving its own problems and transforming itself.

THE CLIENT IS RESPONSIBLE FOR THE OUTCOMES. In almost all consulting situations, both client and consultant want to see the client achieve its goals. They both also want to avoid failure. Consultants, who come in like a knight on a white horse, taking advantage of the client's desire to be saved, end up encouraging their clients to avoid responsibility for achieving those goals. The clients just want the consultant to make their problems go away, so they can go on with business as usual.

Playing the consultant-as-savior game works well for both client and the consultant if the goal is avoidance. It frees the client from taking full responsibility and doing a lot of the hard work necessary to reach a new level of effectiveness, while meeting the consultant's need to appear heroic.

Clients and typical consultants unwittingly collude in multiple ways to make the outcome the responsibility of the consultant, including:

- Putting the consultant in the driver's seat of the consulting process

- Emphasizing what the consultant will do in the consulting situation rather than what the client will do

- Contracting for consulting outcomes and deliverables rather than client deliverables

Each of these—and many more—create conditions where the client divorces itself from responsibility.

The alternative is to be very clear at the outset that the client has the responsibility to achieve its own outcomes. Many of the masterful consultants I talked to held this as a guiding principle. Said one:

> When you start owning the outcome you are in trouble as a
> consultant. The client owns the outcome, not me. If I ever
> allow the client to try and foist that one on me, I have a sense
> of failure. I don't let that happen. I make it very clear in the
> contracting up front that the outcome is theirs. I'll do every-
> thing to help them have a positive outcome but I absolutely do
> not and will not own the outcome. At the same time, we co-
> own the process to get to the outcome.

Another saw clearly the ownership dynamic in terms of a metaphor of electrical power.

> I think of myself as an electrician. I have the ability to hook
> into this tremendous power that I don't own. I didn't bring it
> or create it. There is a huge grid out there where power runs
> between people and that power is the human potential within
> the client organization. All I do is hook up to it. It is their
> power, not mine. I just help them harness it and channel it.

In the client-centered approach, the consultant is not divorced from taking responsibility for outcomes. The consultant is responsible for partnering well, for providing important expertise, and for acting as an effective facilitator or a guide to the process. In all cases, however, the client remains in the driver's seat.

THE CLIENT'S NEEDS ARE PARAMOUNT. How often have you been asked to do something as a consultant that you knew would have little effect, but did it anyway because it paid well? I think this happens quite a lot. We are human, after all, with a natural tendency to act in ways that are self-serving. If not managed, however, this need to take care of ourselves can make us ineffective in the long run. Masterful consultants rarely, if ever, take on work they believe is destined to fail. They take a long-term view of their work and recognize that losing work or turning it down in the service of clients' needs pays off in the long run.

Let me emphasize that I am not saying the *payer's* needs are paramount. I am referring to the needs of the whole system—which are sometimes in direct contrast to the needs of the payer. In placing the needs of the system first, the masterful consultant may choose to do a number of things that can cause her to lose the consulting opportunity, such as:

- Confront the payer

- Help the payer see how he or she perhaps unknowingly participates in the very dynamics he wants to change

- Focus on interventions designed for learning—learning that can be quite painful

- Surface issues the client is unwilling to discuss

- Turn away from the work knowing it is destined to fail.

In sum, the masterful consultant will sometimes put herself in harm's way in order to be successful. Let's look at an example

Unbeknownst to Mark, the CEO of one of Brenda's most important clients, there appeared to be strong signs that many people in senior positions were about to leave the company. Mark knew some were dissatisfied, but did not know it was this bad. Moreover, he certainly did not see himself as the cause of this dissatisfaction. During Brenda's conversation about the issue, Mark was very defensive, due to both his surprise and his tendency to believe that problems start with others and not him. Brenda pointed out that she experienced him as defensive, at which point Mark defended his defensiveness. Gently, yet assertively, Brenda pointed out that she was having difficulty getting through to him. She pointed to his behavior of "defending his defensiveness" as an example of defensiveness and that it was preventing him from hearing her. Mark got quiet for a moment and then started to consider the validity of what she was saying. He asked what could be done to learn more and how he could address the issues she was raising.

Before and during the conversation, Brenda felt she was taking a risk, possibly pushing the issue too far, too fast, and that as a result Mark might decide she was not a good consultant for him. Yet she pressed on. Her deft handling of the issue, combined with the courage to persist in spite of his pushback, impressed Mark. It made him feel confident she could help him learn.

Clients, much like the consultants I interviewed, valued working with consultants whose focus was purely on client needs. They saw being client-centered as an important factor that distinguished masterful consultants from others. One client spoke clearly on the difference:

> The difference between most consultants and great ones is that most are self-serving, while the best are customer-serving. You can tell those that were interested in improving their own reputation or extending their contract, versus those who were there to get the job done in the best possible way. The best I've worked with wanted to know they were leaving us having done what we needed and done it well.

THE CLIENT IS A UNIQUE ORGANIZATION. Many consultants and consulting firms tend to take a cookie-cutter approach to consulting, whether or not they admit it. They operate like Procrustes' bed in Greek mythology. Procrustes, a bandit in the Greek myth of the hero Theseus, had an iron bed that didn't fit anyone short or tall. He ambushed travelers and, after robbing them, made them lie in the bed. If they were too tall, he cut them down to size. If they were too short, he stretched them to fit, in the manner of a medieval torture rack. In either case, they fit, but they died.

The procrustean efforts of many consultants to make clients fit their system of consulting do not take into account the unique characteristics of each client. Instead, they mercilessly try to make each client the same. For example, a few years back, a *Wall Street Journal* article chronicled the efforts of one of the top employee benefits consulting firms whose advice to each of its seven clients was virtually identical. The recommendations were the same and replicated almost all of the firm's 54 basic strategies and tactics.[4] This kind of practice exists in consulting firms throughout the world under the guise of caring advice. Rarely does it help. Instead, it fills

the firm's pocketbook and is driven by the desire to maximize efficiency and produce high margins. Indeed, the whole leveraged
model of consulting firms described in Chapter 1 is based on this
aim. And who can blame them? After all, they are businesses, interested in profitability. The answer is: Clients blame them, silently.
One client I know had this to say:

> I'm constantly surprised how infrequently consultants ask me
> what I need. They seem perfectly content telling me what they
> could do and having said that, leave satisfied with what they
> said, feeling they had a successful meeting with me.

In contrast to so many others, masterful consultants put
client outcomes as their most important aim and subordinate everything else to it. They respond flexibly to the needs of clients. They
make the bed fit the client—not the other way around.

In viewing the organization as unique, it is crucial for the
consultant (and the client as well) to first learn about the client
organization and then tailor the consulting solution set to meet its
unique needs. Questions that might be asked include:

- What is the organization's history and how has this affected its current state?

- What factors underlie the organization's current dynamics?

- What are the aspirations of the key members of the organization?

- What opportunities exist for this organization?

Answers to these questions invite a unique set of solutions.

Recently a client said something that was music to my ears.
We had worked together in the past, and I had helped his executive
team form a strong company culture during the company's inception. Now, three years later, he wanted my help in continuing to
strengthen the company's leadership. He asked me how I might
approach the work, and I replied that there were many options. I
wasn't sure which of these would best suit his organization at this

point in time. He then replied (and this is the music), "Tell you what. Let's meet for a few hours. I want to show you our financials, some of my plans for the next year, and share with you what has been happening recently. Maybe then we can discuss what makes most sense from your perspective." Crafting the consulting process together flows naturally from this kind of understanding.

You may be asking yourself: What does understanding clients have to do with mastery? Every decent consultant wants to know about his or her client. This is Consulting 101. My answer is this: The difference is not in the activity. The difference is the *inner stance* that drives the activity. The ordinary consultant wants to know about the client in order to better fit her solution to the needs of the client. The masterful consultant does not come with a predetermined solution at all. Instead, she comes with a lens through which solutions will be discovered or created anew.

The ordinary consultant only has a hammer in his tool kit and wonders what kind of nail he's dealing with so he can apply his hammer better. The masterful consultant won't consider a tool or technique—a solution—until a deep understanding of the client organization starts to emerge.

The consultants I interviewed understand this well, and spoke passionately on the importance of treating each client as a unique entity. Clients did the same. In reflecting on the best consultants, one client said:

> The best consultants I have worked with were not trying to sell me a package that they prepackaged, but were openly trying to understand our organization's issues. They were sincerely interested in our organization as opposed to trying to sell a piece of business for them.

Another client put it differently, but conveyed a similar message:

> I know a lot of consultants who listen but don't hear. They listen in order to fit their canned solution to the problem. The best consultants I have worked with hear the problem and assimilate the information based not on a canned solution but out of experience. As a result, they come up with creative solutions.

66

CLIENT LEARNING IS AT THE CORE OF ALL CONSULTING ACTIVITIES. Most consultants seek answers. Masterful consultants seek learning. Answers to problems come easy. They rarely produce learning. A colleague once told me that Ralph Waldo Emerson used to greet friends with the question: "So what is clearer to you now?" Such a question invokes the spirit of learning. Learning, individual or organizational, produces clearer understanding than what one had before. When learning is the central activity and aim, organizational growth is more likely to occur.

Recently, in checking in with individual clients I have not seen for a while, I have gotten into the practice of asking them: "What is your learning edge?" I don't remember how this question came to me, but I have been finding it enormously valuable to ask. Often, they take a while to think about their answer, and what they tell me points to where I might support them in some meaningful way.

Masterful consultants understand this well, and create contracts with clients in which learning is the goal. They emphasize its importance at the outset of the client contract, and more importantly, they model learning at each step along the way. In this modeling of learning lies an essential difference between average consultants and masterful consultants.

Many consultants prefer to act invulnerably. They want to know, and they seek solace in their knowledge. Not knowing disturbs them, particularly those who lean on knowledge as the source of their power. They feel that not knowing reveals a chink in their armor. After all, if I am offering expertise in the form of knowledge, then missing some piece of knowledge represents a weakness. In contrast, not knowing does not disturb the masterful consultant. *More often than not, it is an opportunity*—to probe, to discover, to explore, and to learn. And it is an opportunity to model what it means to learn well.

Masterful consultants use questions remarkably well, all in the service of learning or discovery. These questions come in many forms. Sometimes they are questions to seek knowledge. Sometimes they are questions to seek answers, or to seek clearer understanding. Often their questions are designed to reframe a problem, so that a new perspective on the problem emerges. Masterful consultants understand the differences between these types of questions, and use them appropriately in different situations. I will explore this concept in greater depth in Chapter 11.

THE CLIENT HAS THE CAPABILITY TO SOLVE ITS OWN PROBLEMS. Carl Rogers, the great humanistic psychologist, authored the concept of client-centered therapy. In direct contrast to other forms of psychotherapy, in which it is believed that the therapist has knowledge that the client lacks, Rogers believed strongly in clients' ability to heal themselves. The therapist's role is not to pour something into a client, but to draw something out. Interestingly, the derivation of the word *education* has the same meaning. Educate comes from the Latin infinitive *educare* which literally means "to foster" or "to draw out."

Similar to Rogerian therapists, client-centered consultants are more educators in the original Latin meaning of the word, drawing out their client's natural capability. This approach is predicated on the belief that *people and organizations naturally move toward growth and healing* and that much is already known within the system about what its own health might look like. To the client-centered consultant, the trouble with most organizations isn't the lack of knowledge, but the lack of ability to let this knowledge surface and drive organizational choices.

So much of what is unhealthy about organizations could be viewed as the unexpressed or unmet desire for health. For example, when employees are angry, it is often because of their inability to meet their needs through the current organizational policies, procedures, and practices. Leaders of organizations can either try to make people stuff their anger, or try to get underneath it and learn the deeper motivation behind the anger's expression. I believe that more often than not, anger in organization is a "cry for health."

From this belief in the organization's capacity for its own learning, growth, and healing, client-centered consultants do a number of things. They will:

1. Listen generously (nonjudgmentally) with a deep desire to learn about the organization.

2. Communicate what they learn with others in the service of shared learning.

3. Invite healthy and real communication and expression of feelings throughout the system, driven by a belief that the knowledge for effective change is already there and is aching to come out.

4. Help the client explore its aspirations and discover for itself the factors that both facilitate and inhibit living those aspirations.

5. Treat the whole system and everyone in it with the utmost respect and care.

6. Act congruently—be a model for healthy and conscious expression of thoughts, feelings, and compassion.

This list represents not a set of actions, but an inner stance. When consultants come from this way of being, their actions naturally cultivate exploration, honesty, tough decisions, and acts of enormous integrity.

Michael Lindfield, in a lovely article that draws a corollary between masterful consulting and cultivating a garden, points to an example of the inner stance that emanates from a client-centered view.

> Patience is rewarding. So in working with my client groups, I do not worry when we encounter a period when nothing seems to be happening, because I know that something is building on some level. It is only a matter of time and right conditions that will cause the invisible to become visible. Whenever I sit with my clients and the room suddenly goes silent, I let the silence build and resist the temptation to jump in and "make something happen." The silence is the pregnant pause before the birth, and my role is to "hold the space"— the psychological atmosphere in which the group operates and from which the answers will be generated if given the opportunity.[5]

A wonderful example of the power of trusting the client came recently to me in a way that was somewhat unexpected. For about a year, I had worked with a client organization helping it get clear about the fundamental assumptions needed to build its business, as well as the key tasks needed to grow to the next level. The inquiry was extremely successful and spawned a number of activities. I was privy to many of these and, in fact, facilitated some. I recently learned that since my initial work, the client had conducted a number of highly successful continuous improvement efforts, all facilitated by its own internal continuous improvement experts, many of whom had felt way too uninvolved in the core aspects of the company. The resources had always been there, begging to be used prior to my initial work, but were hamstrung in some way. After the organizational visioning work, people naturally started to seek out these expert resources. Moreover, the vision and focus that came from the work with the client helped shape the direction of these improvement efforts. In other words, I did not have to do anything further to make the organization focus on continuous improvement. It was already there, naturally. It just needed to be located and unleashed.

If we want to understand truly what it means to cultivate the client's capability, one need look no further than Lao-Tzu, author of the *Tao Te Ching:*

> A leader is best
> When people barely know that he exists,
> Not so good when people obey and acclaim him,
> Worst when they despise him . . .
> But of a good leader, who talks little,
> When his work is done, his aim fulfilled,
> They will all say, "We did this ourselves." [6]

If you replace the word "leader" with the word "consultant," this simple statement speaks volumes about client-centered consulting.

A CLIENT-CENTERED VIEW OF LIFE

The features of this client-centered view of consulting cannot be used in a piecemeal fashion to produce mastery. Instead, they represent a holistic view of consulting. For example, being committed to learning makes no sense if one continues to treat every client the same. One can't hold the client responsible for outcomes while feeding them all the answers. No consultant who believes in the client's inner wisdom would then follow a prefabricated structure or process.

Those consultants who adopt a client-centered view tend to take this same approach to life in general. They often ask questions, no matter where they are. They listen generously to others. They seek to understand the bigger picture—the system as a whole—and attend to its needs. Families, communities, countries, and the planet can all be viewed from this perspective, and people who do so tend to seek richer, deeper, and perhaps more enduring solutions to human problems. Those who don't may solve some problems, only to create others.

CHAPTER 4

Seeing the Client
as a System

Everything flows.

—Heraclitus

MOST ORGANIZATIONS ARE STUCK and can't see beyond their "stuckness" because they don't see how their parts are all interconnected—how they are part of a whole system. Too many consulting efforts start and finish with a narrow view of the organization. They focus on such forces as leadership, strategy, the technical system, the marketing approach, the culture, the structure, etc. What causes their consulting to be ineffective is not any single action but the isolation of that effort from the other key forces shaping the organization. Clients and consultants collude in this willful blindness, rarely recognizing the counterproductive consequences of their choices.

Instead, they live in an illusion of independence, autonomy, and separateness. We in Western culture, with our mechanized view of systems, are particularly susceptible to this illusion. With this view we justify much of the pollution that goes on in the planet under the name of progress. With this view we justify war, believing we can eventually kill off those we despise, with little consequence. We focus on our differences and fail to see the deep penetrating sameness that courses through us all. We believe we humans are better than animals and justify killing them in the preservation of our own species, and in so doing fail to realize we are killing our planet,

73

the vessel we all share. So many of us in Western society miss the simple wisdom taught in the Disney movie, *The Lion King*, about how we are all connected in the great "circle of life."

In one of the memorable scenes of that movie, Mufasa, the Lion King, talks to his son, the future king, about how we never die completely. Instead our bodies become part of the soil, which in turn nourishes the plants. Animals eat these plants, completing one of the many ways in which we are all part of the same natural cycle.

Native American cultures, along with many others, are very clear on this point, as they pay homage to all animals, and give them thanks for the food they provide. Killing isn't done for sport in such cultures, only by participating in the great circle of life. Witness excerpts from "The Valley of Peace," a Native American poem by Monterey Hulsey:

> . . . Of Father Sun . . .
> who lights our world
> Of Mother Earth . . .
> her flesh, the path we trod
> Always with . . . never upon
>
> From the four directions
> come the winds
> to unite as one
> and circle the valley again
> The circle of life
> The circle of time
> The circle of the red way
> in my mind . . .
>
> . . . Red men, yellow men, black men, white
> Make them all welcome here tonight
> For red are the hearts beating inside
> White are the last teardrops
> Sister Moon cried
> Black is Mother Earth,
> from which we all grow
> Yellow is the shining light inside every soul.[1]

In the Valley of Peace the circle of life is revealed. All beings participate in this great circle. The Valley is seen as a whole, the parts can't be separated. Similarly, all organizations, and the people within them, participate in circles of life. To see this requires that we see less sharply and more fully—that we step back and squint our eyes and see how things blend—how they interrelate.

Perhaps the greatest gift we consultants can provide our clients is the gift of seeing more expansively and more holistically. To do this, we must see more expansively ourselves. We must learn to see organizations as we see mountains and rivers and trees—as part of a more meaningful whole.

So many of the masterful consultants I interviewed spoke about the importance of this expansive view. One of them said this:

> I think masterful consulting is about responsible consulting. It is about looking at the impact of my choices on the larger whole or the next larger frame than where I'm looking. An example of a leverage point is being able to create strategy that has far-reaching impact as opposed to coming up with a project plan for one intact initiative.

Another said:

> Most successful consultants are very nimble intellectually and are very good synthesizers and integrators. They are not narrow. They help their clients see from a whole systems approach where many components have to come together. Often each of those components in the organization are comprised of people who have either vested interests or separated projects with consultants working with them in a separated way. The ability to integrate and synthesize and show how it's all part of the whole is incredibly important. Conversely, where I've seen consultants fail is where they are so rigid in their language and philosophy that they can't see how it fits in with the whole.

Many of the clients I interviewed also spoke about the importance of a more holistic understanding of the client organization as a system. Said one, for example, in commenting about what the masterful consultant had to offer:

> She's a holistic thinker. She wouldn't see the issue in narrow
> marketing terms, which was the way it was presented to her.
> She saw the issue as a corporate issue. She was always coming
> to a higher level of understanding of the situation. She would
> understand how IT, Development, HR and Marketing were all
> linked together. She looked systemically at problems, holistical-
> ly and analytically at the same time.

Many models out there are designed to help us see systemical-
ly. We are not lacking in cognitive understanding. Moreover, many
people, too numerous to mention, have offered wonderful ways of
understanding organizations as systems, including Daniel Katz and
Robert Kahn, Peter Senge, and Meg Wheatley, to name a few.[1] The
fascinating question remains, in spite of the plethora of knowledge:
Why do so few consultants truly understand organizations holistically? Why, in the face of potential deep understanding, do we still
create separation in our minds and in our choices?

Perhaps the answer lies in our hunger for a singular answer. I
remember a meeting a few years ago with colleagues where we sat
around dissecting a case study of a faltering organization. We were
tasked with analyzing the problems of the organization and offering
solutions. While each consultant was competent in his own right,
what intrigued me was how the solutions each offered seemed to
match point for point with his or her own area of expertise. The
strategy consultant viewed the problems as a strategic failing; the
culture change expert saw them as the failing of a weak culture; the
marketing consultant focused on lost marketing opportunities and
failed positioning. It became evident to me that consultants could
see no further than the paradigm upon which they were schooled.
Could it be that the organization and its leaders suffered from the
same narrow understanding?

So many volumes have been written about understanding
organizations as systems that it would be folly for me to do the idea
justice in this space. There is no magic wand I can wave that will forever change the way you see things. But I can describe a few ways a
consultant can start seeing differently—and how that change develops mastery.

I am struck by how little consultants (and leaders, for that matter) understand organizations as systems. We seem to gravitate to the easiest, simplest approach—a perspective we all agree on. We pick apart the organization and see its parts. In so doing, much is lost, and unwittingly, much damage is done. Witness the number of mergers that occur with so little attention to the culture clash that the mergers create. So many mergers are forced through without acknowledging the tremendous power of each company's culture. Most estimates and research I have seen suggest that over 75% of mergers fail, often due to poor culture fit between the two companies. This separation of strategy from culture reflects a willful blindness to the holistic nature of organizations, to the "big picture," and the foolishness of seeing them as interchangeable parts that can be snapped together or pulled apart.

Many consultants have their own pet intervention, their own pet solution. Myers-Briggs enthusiasts have their personality styles. Branding consultants have their market positioning. Strategic planners have their models—their cash cows, their scenario building. Organizational assessment consultants have their survey-feedback processes. Process reengineering consultants have their workflow charts. Outdoor team builders have their ropes courses. All are useful. None, by themselves, are powerful, or make a big difference.

Many consulting efforts fail due to the inability to see the organization as a system. I remember the time I participated in a huge consulting effort designed to change a large consulting firm's culture, from highly competitive to a more collaborative nature. We spent three years putting just about every employee through a four-day culture building experience, coupled with efforts to help the organization change internal practices to become more collaborative. All to little effect. After about three years, the consulting effort died out, with little change to show for our efforts. This occurred despite the fact that the culture building activities were perceived almost universally as successful, and for many they were a life-changing event.

I believe the failure had several causes, the most important of which was trying to alter a single aspect of the organization (its competitive culture) that the rest of the organization flatly contradicted. Organizations are made up of a number of elements that weave together to create the fabric of organizational life. These elements include the organization's vision, the quality of its leadership, its strategy, its structure, its culture, its systems, the skills of its staff, and its policies and practices.

We assessed one aspect of the organization's culture without considering other elements—its strategy, its leadership, its practices, and the skills or tendencies of the people it hired. It was like mixing a little oil with a lot of water. The company's strategy was based on a highly aggressive approach to consulting. Its leadership was extremely "command and control" oriented. Its compensation system was based on an "eat what you kill" approach. And the people it hired were not only among the best and the brightest, but also among the most arrogant.

These factors determined the company's culture far more than our team building activities. As long as these factors remained, the bulldog culture was not about to metamorphose into a friendly St. Bernard.

Culture change consultants are not the only ones who fail to see the organization as a system. Any consultant or consulting firm whose focus is on one of the key elements of organizational life to the exclusion of others is guilty of the same narrow perspective that limits and even kills consulting efforts. Strategy consultants, IT consultants, marketing consultants, culture change consultants, HR consultants, process efficiency consultants, and a host of others hang out their shingle as experts in one area, usually yielding less than masterful results.

Thankfully, a movement today is beginning to meld consulting capabilities together. For example, many branding firms are beginning to recognize that branding can be seen as a fundamental rethinking of an organization and its direction. As a result, they are partnering with culture change consultants to help their clients' new brands come alive in the organization itself. I see some strategy consulting firms starting to reconsider the process by which they do strategic planning so that more of the organization's culture is kept in mind. I also see many culture change consultants learning more about how to facilitate strategic understanding within organizations.

Nevertheless, the movement to integrate is too slow in the making. Consultants and consulting firms that follow the expert-consulting model have particular difficulty seeing the larger system, due either to their inability to understand the totality of an organization's dynamic, or to their own hubris that assures them they have "the answer." Such a belief serves them well in the marketing of their services, but poorly in their execution.

To see what I mean, let's look at two distinctly different approaches. These fictional accounts are drawn from direct experience. Susan is a strategy consultant, who tells clients she is much more than that. She believes strongly in the importance of strategy and that an organization's strategy must fit its vision and its culture. Yet her behavior belies her true belief. Susan has been schooled in her consulting firm's approach to strategy, and it is, for the most part, all she knows about how to help an organization grow. However, she knows it well.

After a competitive bidding process against a number of other consulting firms, Susan and her firm won a contract to help a medium-sized hospital system rethink its strategy over the next 10 years. The hospital system was concerned that its market share was going to be eaten away by competitors and wanted to do something proactive to anticipate this and respond swiftly. Susan had done a bang-up job of demonstrating her knowledge of industry forces and pointed to a number of successes her firm had in the past doing similar kinds of work. The graphics on the presentation slides were particularly impressive, as were the highlighted financial outcomes proving the firm's record.

The process for consulting Susan and her team described was straightforward and classic. She and her team would work with a few members of the management of the hospital system to analyze the market, understand the system's strengths and weaknesses, and produce a report with specific recommendations for strategic changes. If needed, the consulting firm would then be available for helping in the implementation. After all, pointed out Susan in the proposal, "a strategy is only as good as its execution." These pithy phrases spoke to some of the issues and concerns the hospital system had, and the numbers of supposedly successful results from their consulting efforts were impressive.

After three months of heavy data collection and analysis, Susan and her team submitted the report and a presentation to the whole senior staff. The presentation urged the system to shift from a highly community-based approach to hospital care and delivery to one that had produced high efficiencies, streamlining operations, and cutting unnecessary costs. In addition, it suggested beefing up its marketing to become more visible.

During the meeting, there was much discussion and debate over the wisdom of such a shift. Many of the old-timers felt that the community-based approach was their strength, and was consistent with the deeply held faith-based values of the hospital system. Many of the new-timers felt the same, while acknowledging that something must be done to deal with some of the cost-cutting expectations of the HMOs. In the end, they decided to implement a modified version of Susan's recommendations, to be implemented starting in six months. By the time six months rolled around, the project was scrapped for more immediate concerns. The total cost to the hospital system was well over a million dollars. Good payday for Susan and her firm. No difference for the hospital system.

Perhaps, given the title of this chapter and the principles laid out here, the problem is obvious. It was not obvious to Susan, however. Susan did everything she had been taught. She included key people along the way (to gain buy-in), she was up front with her assumptions and her approach, and she worked diligently in the service of an effective strategy for the client. And her analysis of the strategic opportunities was beyond reproach. Her biggest error was that she underestimated the power of culture in affecting or limiting change. She severed culture from strategic change, and in so doing, focused on only one part of the company and its needs. Moreover, her perspective blinded her. Her training in strategic planning in health care was deep, but not wide. She did what 95% or more consultants do as they work with clients. She saw the problem in a narrow framework, the resulting solutions were inadequate for the task, and presto, another brilliant report collects dust on the bookshelf.

Now let's compare that with Joe, a masterful consultant with a talent in the same arena of strategy as Susan. Joe was asked to work with an insurance company experiencing stagnation in its markets. The company wanted to seek alternative markets and/or shift its current market offerings so that the company could move beyond its current plateau.

When asked how he approaches such situations, Joe pointed

out that there is no such thing as a typical situation. This alarmed the client at first, who was seeking simple solutions to a knotty problem. Nonetheless, the executives regarded his reticence to offer pat answers as clearly different than other consultants, and refreshing. What sealed the consulting engagement was his unwillingness to take the project without significant commitment on their part. While other bidding consultants focused on the work that they would do, and its potential payoff to the client, he focused on the work the client needed to do, and his role as a guide in the process. The client found this approach sound, and at the same time troubling, because it implied much more involvement than they were initially ready to provide. He recognized the dilemma they were feeling when faced with more work, and was patient in explaining how anything less than full involvement on their part was likely to produce poor execution downstream.

They were also impressed with his sensitivity to their desire for simpler solutions coupled with his ability to help them recognize that no simple solutions existed. If they existed, he believed they would have found them already. This acknowledged what they had been feeling, namely their difficulty in getting past their current plateau. He seemed savvy about business and about many aspects to it, including strategy, structure, culture, technology, and many of the challenges in their particular industry. It was the totality of what he understood that impressed them the most, coupled with his humility in admitting that there was much he did not know. He believed his greatest added value was in asking good questions.

He began his work by forming a team of people, mostly from the client organization, who were going to get their arms wrapped around the problem together. He offered a model for understanding organizations that included leadership, strategy, structure, culture, systems, and environmental factors such as industry trends, government regulations, and societal trends and asked the team to conduct an assessment to understand the relationship among these factors. The team, in turn, found ways to include many key people in the analysis, including the Board of Directors. This was a particularly smart move because in the end, the Board backed what they had in mind and helped fund the next stage of development of the company with a secondary offering in the stock market.

Their analysis came as no surprise to most key players in the company. In fact, after about six months of effort, the conclusion was almost ho-hum. It was a natural outcome of the data many were involved in collecting along the way. It did not require a major entrance into new markets. Instead it involved an amplification of the work they were doing, coupled with paring down some efforts that were too far from their "knitting." In addition, it was clear that they had become sedate in their approach as a company, too comfortable with past success. As a result, they had become bureaucratic. Changing this proved more difficult than the 45-degree turn in their strategy, yet it was essential in making the new focus work. The assessment team came up with a multi-layered approach that included changes in personnel, more rigorous hiring strategies, and clearer performance expectations. They called this "raising the bar." What's more, they staged these changes over a three-year period, recognizing that if they went too far too fast, they could cripple their current clientele, and maybe the company as a whole.

At the end of the consulting process, Joe looked back with pride at how much the client had achieved over a three-year effort. Equally as important, he had done little compared with the client's own efforts. This was typical of his experience, yet the results of his efforts were consistently gratifying.

Joe was far more successful than Susan because he saw the work from a holistic perspective, he took a client centered approach to his work, and he was extremely sensitive to the issue of buy-in. What eluded Susan, and what Joe understood so well, was the importance of treating the client as unique, and of seeing the organization as a complex set of interweaving forces that cannot be separated and "fixed." His choices moved the system, while fixing nothing in particular. Put simply, Susan, like most consultants, saw organizations as problems to be solved. Joe saw them as patterns to be guided and shifted.

Too often leaders and consultants miss the patterns. Their interventions fix problems yet don't make a difference. This doesn't have to be the case. The wise leader helps her organization not only see it as a system, but share in the responsibility for it as a totality. The wise consultant partners with the leader to help accomplish the same.

CHAPTER 5

SHARED OWNERSHIP OF THE PROCESS

We talk about the quality of a product or service.
What about the quality of our relationships and the
quality of our communications and the quality of
our promises to each other?

—*Max Dupree*

THOM WENT TO MEET with a potential new client, a division of a large software development company. The head of the division, Christine, and two of her direct reports were seeking a consultant to help them become a high-performing team and better leaders of their division. In the previous four years, they had worked with three different consultants. They had been disappointed in the results: In each case, the consultant didn't deliver what they expected. The first consultant was fairly knowledgeable, but the mountain of information she unloaded on them did not help them become more effective as a team. The second had a lot of nifty exercises, and everyone enjoyed doing them—but in the end, that made no difference either. The third confronted them repeatedly and was rather abrasive, so they deemed him ineffectual and discarded him.

After hearing of their consulting frustrations, Thom saw that the problem was not the consultants per se. Nor was it the team, for

Thom could see they were eager to be helped. The problem was in the relationship between the two. The executive team's description of what they wanted strongly suggested they were looking for a magic pill to address their needs—as if they were expecting something to be done *to* them, not *with* them.

And so, unwittingly, each consultant took turns playing the savior game. Each appreciated the client's enthusiasm and welcomed the opportunity to ply its trade. While trying to act like facilitators, they wound up acting like experts, in the sense of providing something vital the client needed, for a price. Each colluded with the executive's desire to be saved. The familiar result: great payday, no difference.

After hearing their story about failed efforts, Thom offered his diagnosis of why the consulting efforts did not work well. Thom challenged their expectations and proposed a different kind of relationship—one based on shared responsibility and shared ownership. He helped them see what was missing in the other relationships, as well as the role they played in their own disappointed results. This appealed to Christine, in particular, and Thom was hired.

If we question the assumptions upon which most consulting processes are built, the reason why the first three consultants did not work starts to reveal itself. The model they all followed is simple—and misses the mark. Consultant offers knowledge for a fee. Client pays for that knowledge, and the knowledge is (supposedly) transferred. In the case above, the knowledge came in the form of content, team-building exercises, and confrontation—information, tools, and technique. All of these approaches put the responsibility for change squarely in the hands of the consultants. No matter how effective the consultants may be, no matter how clever, they would not be able to turn the client into a high-performing team. Nor could they ever. Their knowledge was fine, but their inner stance (and the client's) was way off-target.

THE POWER RELATIONSHIP BETWEEN CLIENT AND CONSULTANT

The typical client/consultant contract—pay in exchange for consulting knowledge—seems self-evident when the transaction is put so simply. And because it seems so obvious, some of the fundamental assumptions underlying this contract go unexamined. One major assumption embedded in the exchange, for example, is a relationship of power: The consultant or consulting firm is "one-up" in power in relationship to the client. I/we know something you don't, and therefore have power over you.

This relationship of power is often played out in much the same way as a parent might guide a child. The consultant (parent) claims to have knowledge the client (child) seeks. The client, hungry for the knowledge says, in effect, "give it to me" (put me through your process). Typically the client (child) does not take responsibility for the process, which makes sense since the consultant (parent) has promised that if the client follows the consultant's lead, the client will reap benefits.

In this exchange, the client/child has surrendered its power to the consultant/parent. In surrendering, the client takes little ownership of the process and is therefore less likely to implement the consultant's solutions. When that implementation does not occur—or goes sour—the client can easily blame the consultant and wash its hands of responsibility. "If only the consultant had delivered the goods, we would be fine." Yet the consultant can wash her hands of responsibility as well by claiming, "If only the client had listened to me, the consulting process would have succeeded." Both feel justified in their blame and, at the same time, are often unaware that they engaged in a power relationship fraught with pitfalls. This relationship is rarely examined, yet it typifies almost every consultant-client situation in which the expert/structured approach to consulting is offered in exchange for money.

One reason this relationship goes unexamined is that it worked quite well in a world where change was slow, and efficiency was the primary driver of business success. That was Frederick Taylor's world and his methods suited it well. But the world has changed, so much so that in most cases, structured, knowledge-based approaches no longer fit the business world these approaches are tailored for.

The other extreme, a client relationship in which the consultant gives away all his power, is also beset with problems. Too often consultants, particularly those who fall purely in the process-consulting camp, withhold their own point of view, or manipulate the client to their own ends under the guise of facilitation. For example, some use Socratic questioning strategies when in fact they know the answers in advance.

Consulting mastery avoids both of these extremes: "power over" or abdication of power. Instead it has to do with sharing power between the client and the consultant, and co-ownership of the consulting process.

The tendencies toward the "power over" or "power under" extremes of the client-consultant relationship are expressions of the consultant's inner stance—they arise from the consultant's unconscious and unexamined power drive, reinforced by the client's attitudes about power. All too often, consultants fail to look deeply at the tacit relationship they form with clients, partly because they have disowned a remote corner of their own psyches. Let's examine this phenomenon more closely.

Many consultants enter the field with a desire to make a difference. This is an influence desire. It is a desire for power. While aimed at adding value for the sake of the organization, it is a power desire nonetheless—one that draws many consultants not only toward consulting in general, but to expert consulting in particular. In the expert consulting model, the consultant can wield power directly by claiming to have knowledge the client lacks. In too many cases, power in the form of knowledge is wielded with flamboyance or even arrogance, to the detriment of the client's ability to produce lasting change. Many of these very same consultants claim to be committed to empowering their clients, yet try to control the change management agenda, overstructure the change process, or use data to prove their point rather than to create conditions for shared learning.

At the other extreme, many consultants, particularly those who take a process consulting approach, are uncomfortable with admitting they like power. They see how unbridled or unconscious power creates damage and are on a constant crusade to avoid that damage. Too often the result, however, is that the power motive simply goes underground and is expressed in manipulation or avoidance. Many consultants who operate in an extremely facilitative manner are often blind to this power motive, as they psychologically disown their own power needs. By "disown" I mean that they do not recognize the desire for power as a part of themselves. They may see it clearly in others, but due to their negative judgment of power, they fail to see it in themselves.

But the power motive is there in every consultant, lurking somewhere in the psyche. When the desire for power is disowned, that motive gets expressed in counterproductive ways. One masterful consultant I interviewed spoke volumes on the subject of disowned power in a self-revealing manner:

> Dad had a lot of overt ways of demonstrating his power, so my Mom had to find indirect ways of establishing her power while at the same time always denying it. Right to her death, she denied that power. I think in many ways consultants, particularly OD consultants, are often kind of sneaky about how they establish their power. Not always, but there is a potential for it, and we do it in ways much like my mother did—flirtatious, friendly, self-deprecating, bowing, scraping. Often we don't come to terms with what we are really seeking. We place a lot of blame on people who have a lot of power because we've disowned so much of our own.

CONTRASTING EXAMPLES OF CONSULTING

To understand the effect of the power relationship between consultant and client, let's compare two consulting situations with similar goals, but very different outcomes. The first cost a great deal but resulted in little to no change. The second resulted in a great deal of change for a lot less money.

A FAILED ATTEMPT AT CHANGE. Steve was an extremely articulate consultant with a formidable presence. He stood 6'4", had a deep, resonant voice, and held a long and impressive record of successful leadership. He had once been a CEO, orchestrating a difficult turnaround for a failing retail company and was now a relatively successful senior consultant, with many marquee clients. After a number of key meetings with a large company in the energy industry, he had successfully negotiated a $2 million contract to help change the company's culture. His persuasiveness in the face of hesitation on the part of the CEO and other members of the senior management team was a testimony to both his skill and his genuine belief in the value of culture transformation. While the fee was hefty, even to this company, the potential benefits far outweighed the costs.

The process, similar to most culture change efforts, would start with an effort to reinvigorate the company with a new vision and strategy, followed by a series of learning experiences for everyone in the company.

During the sales process, and many times during the initial stages of the consulting effort, Steve explained to the clients that the consultant's role in the process was that of a guide. He said he would facilitate key meetings and help them come to decisions. The decisions ultimately were theirs.

On many occasions, however—throughout key meetings, preceding the vision process, and throughout the two years of working with the company—there were signs that all was not well. People would raise concerns about the change process, about its necessity, and about the company's readiness. With each reservation, Steve had a quick rebuttal, adept at asking questions designed to get the client to see the wisdom of the change. But one growing almost invisible phenomenon was not addressed—the locus of control over the process, which was rapidly moving to Steve's hands.

Over a series of interchanges that lasted many months, Steve became more than the symbol for change; he became its leader. The CEO deferred to Steve on key decisions, having doubts about his own leadership, and feeling that Steve knew more about changing a culture. Steve filled the void happily, oblivious to his inner desire to be in charge. Simultaneously, Steve managed the dynamics of the senior team well, deftly facilitating key discussions or using the magnetism of his own personality to assuage concerns and build confidence in what he was doing. None of this was intentionally manipulative. Steve believed deeply in what he was doing, and saw their collective hesitation as the natural resistance that comes with the territory of change.

The culture change initiative went along as planned, with

each series of events accomplished by the culture change consulting team. The team felt they had created a set of learning experiences that positively impacted the organization as a whole. While at the same time, there were increasing indications among the leadership of the company that the initiative was losing ground.

About two years into the project, the CEO was asked to step aside and was replaced by one of the senior executives. The new CEO had great respect for Steve as an individual and as a professional. At the same time he had reservations about the culture change effort. Slowly but surely, the change effort lost steam, becoming just another of a series of "flavor of the month" changes that were notorious among the rank and file of the company. At about this time, Steve focused on other consulting projects, losing interest in the senior team's own inability to "get their act together," as Steve put it.

Sadly, this is a familiar story.

A SUCCESS STORY. Contrast this with a similar situation, with dissimilar results. The client was a medium-sized insurance company, which, like the company Steve tried to fix, had stagnated in a highly conservative industry. Alex, the company's CEO, brought in Sally and a team of consultants to help shift the organization's culture and make it a much stronger player in their industry.

Much like Steve, Sally spent a lot of time helping the client understand that the client had to "own" the culture change process for it to work. Like Steve, she explained that she and the other members of the consulting team were simply agents and guides. It was the client's responsibility to make it happen. The difference between how Steve and Sally played this out, however, was palpable.

Sally was actually less experienced than Steve, both as a consultant and as a businessperson. What she lacked in experience, however, she made up in her genuine belief that the client was responsible for the results. She embodied this belief in a number of ways. For example, whenever she sensed a member of the client organization was hesitant, she asked that person why, and then respected it as a natural reservation rather than confronting the person in a sales-like manner. She also helped Alex listen to his own intuition, and adjusted the change process accordingly. In addition, rather than push differing views of change onto the senior management team, she helped them come to solutions that often respected their own dissent. She didn't see people as "resisting change" or "dragging their feet." She saw them as having legitimate concerns that needed to be addressed.

Over time, it became clear to management that the change effort was indeed theirs, for better or worse. Sally was a trusted advisor, but the client remained in the driver seat. A significant event occurred about eight months into the project, one that would have sounded a death knell for almost any other significant change. The Board removed Alex, the CEO who had brought Sally and her consulting team in. The prevailing sentiment was that he lacked the horsepower to lead the company through the growth process and was not the leader of the future. This decision came in spite of the positive momentum that seemed to be taking shape.

The new CEO, Mark, had never led a company before but had a track record of success at a much larger competitor. He showed no interest in the culture change effort at first, viewing such efforts as "touchy-feely fluff." A hard-nosed businessman with a powerful, analytical mind and a nose for numbers, he was also very achievement driven, wanting to succeed in his new effort as CEO.

In spite of his own inclination to put the brakes on the culture change effort and replace it with a more disciplined "manage by the numbers" approach, he was impressed by the enthusiasm among the leadership team and rank and file for the culture change. So rather than make blocking a perceived positive effort his first statement as new CEO, he decided to let it ride, at least for the time being.

After witnessing Sally facilitate key meetings, he began to appreciate her as an ally. In short order, he instituted regular meetings with his senior team designed to continue to build their teamwork, and began having Sally coach him to become a better CEO. Mark impressed Sally with his genuine openness, his integrity, and his interest in improving his leadership skills. Rather than "selling" Mark on the change effort, she asked him to consider two things: (1) the change effort could go on without him, but it would be far stronger with Mark in the lead; (2) if Mark were to lead it, he would have to to do so genuinely, and put his own "stamp" on it.

After thinking it over, Mark elected to lead the change effort, and he made a commitment to become an effective CEO and the leader of the change process, with Sally's guidance. Sally's work with Mark and the team lasted almost two years, during which the company moved from being an also-ran to being one of the leaders in the industry. Many changes took place including breakthrough profitability, a shift in culture from a rather complacent employee population to one of high initiative, and improved teamwork throughout the system. Eventually, an industry leader bought out the company, but not before it earned strong revenues—and strong profits—in a wilting insurance market.

IT'S ALL ABOUT THE RELATIONSHIP

These contrasting examples illustrate what masterful consultants know well. While the client must own the outcome, both client and consultant must own the process—together. For the client to own the process exclusively takes all responsibility away from the consultant and denies an important part of his added value—to guide the process. For the consultant to own the process exclusively, on the other hand, divorces the client from its responsibility for the outcome, and denies the fact that each client is unique, and its knowledge of itself is critical to the process.

Given the importance of shared ownership, the most crucial factor for success is clearly the relationship between consultant and client. And the essence of the relationship for masterful consulting is one of *partnership*. The spirit of partnership is not in what one does; it is who one is. It is perhaps the most fundamental feature of a masterful consultant's inner stance—the characteristic from which all else emanates. And it's not complicated. You either come from a stance of partnership or you don't. One master consultant I interviewed put it directly:

> I don't think this relationship thing is such a big puzzle. It's not hard to figure out. I'm amazed when people ask me how I develop a trusting relationship. We've made this complex because we want to avoid the behavior that's required. You're really stating something that for me is very obvious but I do understand how difficult it is for people to realize. *Who I am is*

91

not a technique or a process. My partnership comes from who I
am—and it comes freely and easily.

Partnership means that *the consultant is committed to her clients
and they to her.* They are engaged in a mutually satisfying, mutually
beneficial relationship in which a particular exchange must take
place and in the process, the client must be improved. And at the
core of partnership is the sense of compassion the consultant feels
for the client. Said one consultant I know: "What makes my partnering easy is the genuine love that develops between me and my
clients. They get that I care deeply about them." Note how far
removed this is from the typical, clinically analytic view of consulting and of business. Note also the tension between this and the rev-
erence many consultants place on objectivity and emotional distance.

Partnership means that the consultant operates from the following set of principles or commitments relative to the client organization and the individuals within it:

- I am committed to your well-being and effectiveness.

- I tell the truth and expect you to do the same.

- I act with integrity and expect you to do the same.

- We recognize that to be successful in the process, each of
  us has to be successful.

- We encourage each other to be our best and give and get
  feedback to support this.

- Nothing is held back. I put my heart into this relationship
  and to an effective outcome and so do you.

These principles are, not surprisingly, reminiscent of the
Christian concept of Agape and Martin Buber's view of an I/Thou
relationship and stance in life.[1]

Almost all of the consultants I interviewed spoke with great
passion about this issue of partnership:

> One of the other things I feel strongly about is that the rela-
> tionship with the client is a partnership. I don't assume I have

the answer or solution, but will continuously try options and give the client a good deal. I feel in partnership with them and share the responsibility for what occurs.

If you were talking to a friend, you would never use language like "own the process." I actually believe for the complexity and the anxiety that are now growing in all our lives together, it isn't about taking ownership. It's about being together, trying to figure it out. A young Danish woman gave an image to me. She said, "I feel like we're holding hands, walking into a dark forest." That describes the kind of relationship with the client I seek.

As a consultant I try to establish a relationship of some equality where our power in the relationship is about equal. When functioning well you wouldn't say the client or I were more powerful. You'd comment on the synergy of the relationship.

In addition to partnering with clients, partnership is an inner stance that masterful consultants come from in life. It is not a switch they turn on and off but an eternal state. Many masterful consultants I interviewed spoke about this eloquently, and it was evident in the way they related to me in the interviews, eager to hear my perspective as much as to tell theirs. Reverberating throughout the interviews were thoughts like these:

I view all change as collaborative. I'm collaborating with colleagues as a member of a team. I'm often an external change agent paired with an internal one. I look at my clients as collaborators, co-inventors, co-researchers. At the bottom of it is the ability to develop a relationship that essentially maximizes empowerment.

Many clients I interviewed, as well, attached the same importance to partnership. One client put it this way when reflecting on the best consultant he had ever worked with:

She was stronger than other consultants; had more hands-on experience, a deeper character, was willing to stand firm when necessary and call me on my own issues. But the thing that stood out for me was that I felt like I had a friend. She brings a whole bag of tricks and skills, but more than that it's the relationship she built with me that made this other stuff so useful.

**FOR THE GREATEST EFFECT,
THE CLIENT MUST "OWN" THE OUTCOME
WHILE TOGETHER CLIENT AND CONSULTANT
JOINTLY OWN THE PROCESS.**

To help understand the principle of partnership more graphically, let's look at how partnership might work during one aspect of the consulting process: the proposal phase. We can explore the principle of partnership anywhere in the consulting process, but I choose to illustrate partnership during the proposal phase, for the beginning of the consulting process sets into motion the rest of the consulting engagement. Like the opening sequence to a movie or play, the initial proposal phase sets the tone.

PARTNERING AT THE PROPOSAL PHASE

In the typical consulting engagement, after some conversation between client and consultant, the client asks the consultant to put together and submit a proposal. The act of offering a typical proposal forms a relationship in which consultant is seller and client is buyer—one who offers and one who receives or to put it more graphically, the consultant is the "doer" and the client is the "done-to." By not participating in the process as a partner, the client already begins to form a passive relationship to the consulting process. If the client's key players are not actively involved in the development of the process of change, they are less likely to take action. Net result for the consultant: great payday, no difference. Net result for the client: flavor of the month.

Because of the tacit assumptions and counterproductive features in the typical proposal process, many masterful consultants

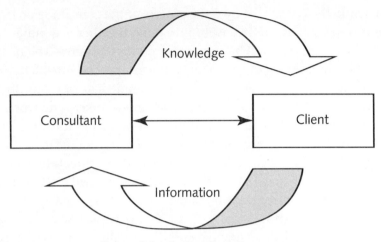

FIGURE 5-1   SHARED RESPONSIBILITY

have been exploring a different process, one that appears to have a much more positive and powerful outcome for the client—a shared proposal. When a client suggests to a masterful consultant that she develop a proposal and submit it, the masterful consultant will explain some of the problematic qualities of such a process, and offer to develop the proposal together instead. Doing so requires that the client become actively engaged at the outset in thinking about the whole change process, and what it will take from both parties—consultant and client—to produce effective results. The process of discussing a shared proposal becomes the beginning of a contract spelling out involvement of both parties at each step along the way, and also shapes the quality of relationship that needs to be formed for a successful outcome.

Part of the explicit agreement that gets formed during this approach is that knowledge and information will be shared fully and readily so that, working together, consultant and client can form the change strategy that will best produce enduring results. A second agreement that gets formed is that the goal is not merely the targeted change but also strengthening the ability of the client to create similar changes in the future. In other words, learning is also a goal. In this scenario, consultant and client work together over time to find the best way of accomplishing the desired change. The client and the consultant own the process of the consulting engagement, and see it as a relationship they build together over time.

A shared proposal has two other positive features. The first is that the development of the shared proposal itself becomes a testing ground for the relationship, providing an immediate opportunity to see what it will be like to work together and to determine whether the relationship will help support optimal outcomes for the client. The second is that it becomes a way for the consultant to demonstrate her ability to consult with the client on a real-time basis. Instead of relying on what the consultant says she will do, the client can make an informed decision based on actual experience working with the consultant. Naturally, this puts the consultant in a more vulnerable position—having to demonstrate value—but it is precisely this requirement that promotes the greatest likelihood of success down the road for both partners. Working together at the proposal phase also requires that the client be more vulnerable as well. I contend that greater vulnerability is a necessary condition for both client and consultant to create the kind of relationship where true insight and change can occur.

Once the agreement to co-own the process of the consulting engagement is in place, many positive elements naturally follow. The client and consultant meet regularly to plan each activity; they meet often to discuss progress and make adjustments to the plan; and they ensure that the client remains ultimately in the driver seat of the change itself.

An example: Seth began to work with a new client—a medium-sized company just sold by the founder and CEO, with a new president brought in. She and the Chief Administrative Officer currently act as co-leaders of the company. They both feel strongly that while the company is in good shape financially, its culture is stuck in the 1950s. The former CEO was quite paternalistic and created and cultivated a culture where everything flowed through him. People liked him a lot, and appreciated his care for the company and its people. At the same time, they grew extremely dependent on him —the outgrowth of a typical benevolent autocracy. The company's two new leaders, by contrast, seek to change the culture to one where employees exhibit much greater initiative and self-responsibility. They also want to learn what that really means in terms of their individual leadership as well as their shared leadership of the whole company.

They asked Seth to help them change the culture over time. Having agreed on the goals of the client engagement and their mutual expectations in working together, they decided to begin with an organizational assessment. As part of the assessment process, Seth suggested that instead of having his consulting firm tell them how to do an assessment, he would educate them in what goes into an assessment, and point out a number of key decisions they need to make in the process. Decisions included whom to survey, whom to interview, what questions to ask, how to administer the survey for best rate of return, whether and how to group people in the interviews themselves, etc. With Seth's guidance, the client convened an assessment planning team made up of the two co-leaders of the company, the HR director, one of the sales directors, and the head of marketing. Over a series of meetings Seth helped them learn about the importance of a high rate of return on an organizational survey they chose, and different ways to get one. The team explored the different outcomes that come from individual interviews and group interviews. They discussed different ways to think about the data they will get from the process and what to do with it. They talked about who owns the process, who owns the data, and what to do if the data looks bleak. Over time, Seth guided them in making key decisions at each step along the way.

Two results naturally came from these meetings: First, the assessment team felt high ownership of the process to the point that they were "on it" when it came to executing the plan. Second, much shared learning occurred so that the plan itself had a higher likelihood of working well within this unique organization. All this occurred without Seth making one decision on their behalf, and only one recommendation. Naturally, if they made a decision that seemed unwise from his point of view, Seth would tell them so. But he didn't need to. He believed that when good, capable, caring people learn and are committed to making a decision in the best interests of the whole organization, they would.

A year and a half later, Seth continues to work with the company, and changes are starting to pay off. The senior team as a whole acts with a high degree of responsibility for the company in contrast to the prior regime, and they feel clearly in the driver's seat of the organizational change. In that space of time, the company's market value has grown five times its size and has spawned three new areas of new business.

Too often, the reason consulting efforts do not achieve significant outcomes is that the consultant and the client view it as an exchange. I give you money and you provide me a service. I give you a recommendation and you implement it. Such an exchange works when the service is easily "wrapped in a package." A massage, a shoeshine, or weeding your garden are all services for which little mutuality and collaboration are required. Too often, the consulting process is treated in the same manner. Hence, little synergy occurs.

By contrast, a successful consulting engagement is characterized by a true partnership with significant amounts of interchange. It is often messy and fraught with pitfalls. Rarely is the answer truly obvious. If it were, the client would likely not require help. If the problems faced in consulting situations are knotty, complex, and challenging, then the quality of the relationship needs to be characterized by shared learning. Partnership and shared ownership are the only goals worth attaining if the consultant aims for mastery.

PART III

MASTERY IN ACTION

THE MASTER CONSULTANT'S
RELATIONSHIP TO KNOWLEDGE

CHAPTER 6

APPLYING
KNOWLEDGE

A little knowledge that acts is worth infinitely more
than much knowledge that is idle.

—Kahlil Gibran

ACQUIRING THE INNER STANCE necessary for consulting mastery is
not like putting on a hat. Most consultants develop their craft by
attaining vast amounts of knowledge, altogether missing the more
elusive qualities that define consulting mastery. Most of us have
spent many years as consultants acquiring the skills, techniques,
and craft-specific knowledge to enable our clients to become more
effective. We believe strongly that the more we hone these skills,
and learn how to share the benefits of our knowledge effectively
with clients, the more impact we'll have. And to some extent this is
true. Much of this knowledge is indeed valuable. Clients seek knowledge and expertise from consultants to solve problems they can't
solve themselves. Most consultants develop specific knowledge and
then sell some of that knowledge, or the information derived from
it, to clients for a fee. This exchange is natural, fair, often mutually
valuable, and worthy of respect. What kind of information are we
talking about? A specific and critical business system; a report
explaining competitive forces within a particular industry; information about what kinds of organizational structures work well in
what kinds of specific situations, to name a few.

**TO SIMPLIFY THE WORDING THROUGHOUT
THE REMAINDER OF THE BOOK,
I WILL OFTEN USE THE TERM "KNOWLEDGE"
GENERICALLY TO ENCOMPASS THEORIES,
IDEAS, MODELS, TOOLS, AND TECHNIQUES
OF THE CONSULTING TRADE.**

Knowledge is useful not only to clients but to the consultants as well. Without it, we are lost. A consultant's ability to communicate to and influence clients through his knowledge—a kind of knowledge in itself—is a necessary condition for success. The synthesis of knowledge, intellect, and analytic skills helps a consultant make sense of the client organization and its challenges.

Yet there is more to the consulting process than knowledge offered and bought. For many clients, the problem isn't lack of knowledge. It is often readily available somewhere in the client organization. Their problem is their inability to act on this knowledge effectively.

Despite this, the thirst for ever more knowledge remains the norm. To understand why so much importance is placed on knowledge, let's look at a typical consulting situation. A client calls the consultant in with a specific problem or need. Presumably, the client feels it cannot solve this problem by itself, or it wouldn't ask for help. Notice the implicit assumption here, that the consultant offers the client something the client doesn't have. What do most consultants have to offer? Knowledge, or so they believe.

At the beginning of a potential consulting opportunity, most consultants demonstrate the extent and power of their knowledge in order to gain the work. The more brilliant the consultant is, and the better his presentation, the more the client is dazzled, and the deal is sealed. The silent and often unconscious collusion between consultant and client begins to form. The client is saying, in effect, "Please save me." The consultant, in response, replies, "I will save you." And the means of that rescue, expected by both parties, is knowledge.

From this stance, knowledge appears to be crucial. It also appears that the more knowledge, the better, because knowledge dazzles the client in the sales process and offers the promise of valuable help. But here's the rub. Knowledge will go only so far. How often have we seen clients receiving knowledge, or information derived from that knowledge, in the form of a report, a redesign, or a set of recommendations that go nowhere? What is crucial to consulting mastery is how this knowledge is applied—how well the consultant paces the client, how the knowledge is offered, and how the knowledge is received and put to use.

To clarify, let's make a simple distinction between the two phases of a consulting process—Phase 1: diagnosis, and Phase 2: implementation. In the span of a change effort, Phase 1 (which includes assessment, analysis, feedback and planning) represents about 10–30% of the change process, while Phase 2 represents 70–90%. In Phase 1, thinking and analyzing skills are clearly important. In this phase, assumptions are made and thoughts and plans are organized so that everyone is operating on the same conceptual playing field. Galvanizing a client organization toward action—and getting people to think the kinds of thoughts that will produce change—is a big part of the Phase 1 process. In Phase 2, however, analysis fades in importance and the focus shifts to the skills of human interaction.

Many consultants simply drop off at the end of Phase 1, leaving the client to deal with the challenge of implementation. Others continue to work with the client, but end up withdrawing at some point as they see their efforts falling short of the desired change. Few make it through to the end. Fewer still do so successfully. I contend that it is during Phase 2, when influencing clients to mobilize resources effectively, that the masterful consultant's inner stance shines through.

SIMPLY PUT, HELPING AN ORGANIZATION MAKE SIGNIFICANT CHANGES IS NOT A CONCEPTUAL PROBLEM. IT IS A HUMAN PROBLEM.

KNOWLEDGE WAS NOT ENOUGH AT DEC

In a brilliant analysis of the rise and fall of Digital Equipment Corporation (DEC), one of the most remarkable companies of our time, Edgar Schein makes this point all too clear. In explaining why DEC was unable to pull itself out of a monumental tailspin, he points out that the information about why troubles existed at DEC was readily available and apparent to all. And yet that knowledge was not enough. He said, "I observed repeatedly (in meetings) that critical information was surfaced, discussed, analyzed, and then rationalized away. . . . Too often we assume in our management literature that if we could just show people what is going on, they would act to fix things. . . . One of the deep lessons of cultural dynamics is that if the remedy would require an organization to violate some of its deeply held cultural assumptions, that remedy will not be applied. Instead, the organization will rationalize that what it is doing will work out in the end, or it will apply quick fixes and organizational Band-Aids that provide an illusion of problem solving."[1]

This proposition is lost on many consultants who feed at the trough of knowledge. Strategy consultants, for example, clearly must know a fair bit about strategic planning and thinking, about the industries they work in, about how to study and analyze the competitive landscape, and about what questions will prompt the client to understand and/or rethink their business. But this considerable array of knowledge is not enough to be masterful. How often have you seen a brilliant strategy consultant deftly communicate his expertise without truly helping the client actually make the change? In many cases, this is exactly what happens.

More often than not the cause of the problem is not that the ideas are wrong but that the client firm has little except money invested in the solution. The cost of implementing most consulting solutions is far greater than the consulting fee. When it comes to implementing the actual solution for a problem, the client hasn't amassed enough internal psychological commitment (buy-in) to warrant the effort. As a result, most consulting reports collect dust— all that expertise, wasted!

When implementation is poor or recommendations miss the mark, a mutual blame process often follows. Consultants blame clients for lacking the ability or guts to implement what is clearly the right thing to do. Or consultants blame clients for poor execution. Clients, in turn, blame consultants for not handling the process well, giving bad advice, or performing poorly. In either case, both clients and consultants often absolve themselves from responsibility for either the process or for the lack of follow-through.

Since the consulting firm can cite an ample number of success stories, its failure to make a difference can be easily justified, particularly if the consultant believes it was the client's fault for not implementing. "We did our part. They didn't do theirs." All paradigms tend to be self-sealing in the sense that, in the face of contrary data, we hold onto our beliefs about how the world works. I don't know the success rate of consulting engagements, but I will tell you it's much less than consulting firms will lead you to believe.

To be masterful, consultants must know much more about how to manage or guide this process of change. They must be able to influence others through a complex set of challenges and help them deal effectively with all of the forces that arise naturally to prevent change. Resentment, anger, hope, cynicism, excitement, confusion, despair, enthusiasm and ennui are all by-products of the change process. These feelings directly affect the process as well. Without the knowledge of how to navigate the muddy and often choppy waters of change, the implementation of a new business strategy, product branding, or ERP effort (for examples) is much less likely to succeed. Sadly, knowledge about the process of change, and the skills needed to execute it, are rarely taught well in prestigious consulting firms.

Masterful consultants typically know no more than you—in fact, they sometimes know less. They are rarely any more skillful than you in explaining a model or designing a process. As one master consultant said when I interviewed her:

> I'm not very good with staying current with the new models. I guess I should be more up to date. There is some good stuff out there, and I probably ought to keep abreast of it. It just isn't crucial to my work.

Relative to knowledge, what distinguishes masterful consultants from others is how they hold and communicate that knowledge. They hold it gracefully and confidently, they communicate it with care, and they apply it with wisdom. These attitudes comprise the difference between good consulting and great. They don't lead with knowledge; they lead with their inner stance and then use knowledge judiciously.

Most of us lead too often with knowledge. We have all been in many situations where we have presented our models, ideas, theories and beliefs to clients and not had an impact. Even worse, clients sometimes respond with a yawn: "Been there, done that, ho hum." But even after experiencing this outcome many times, we lead with our knowledge anyway. Perhaps we don't know any better; perhaps our knowledge is familiar, comfortable, and safe. Perhaps it's the way we wield power. Yet by leaning on knowledge so much, we become imbalanced. There is much more to effective consulting—and to life—than one's intellect. The heart and spirit matter just as much, if not more.

When I was nineteen, I had an epiphany that has guided my life ever since. I was a university student, taking a walk in the woods near the university, reflecting on my life. I thought about how unfulfilling my life had been up to that point, and how deeply disconnected I was from my feelings. My train of thoughts led me to the troubling realization that I had never had the experience of truly having loved anyone. I may have uttered the words "I love you" to my mother and father—and the occasional girlfriend. And each time I said those words I *thought* I meant them. But on this day, I realized those words had been hollow. I had never actually *felt* love.

At the time, this was all deeply disturbing. And yet this reflection ushered in a whole new life for me. I suddenly realized that I had spent far more energy developing my intellect and far too little energy developing my heart. Right then, I made a commitment to myself. Starting now, and for the rest of my life, I would learn how to feel the care and love I had for others.

This revelation may seem strange for the reader, particularly if love and care are familiar feelings. At the time they were distant concepts to me, devoid of authentic experience. Up to that fateful moment in the forest, my life had been a testimony to the primacy of the intellect. Fortunately, I made an early course correction.

I am not alone in having bowed to the altar of the intellect. By focusing on intellect so strongly as a young man, I was prey to the same intellectual bias that underlies business life: that knowledge is king, that science, models, theories, structured methods, and ideas are what define successful people and successful organizations.

This bias has and continues to be perpetuated in the field of consulting as well as most other professions. It calls us to read, research, and write about tools, skills, and techniques, all the while losing sight of a deeper phenomenon, one not easily available to scientific scrutiny—that our inner stance matters and it matters a great deal. Without understanding the centrality of our inner stance in the actions we take, we create a skewed, imbalanced approach to consulting for ourselves, one that has, I believe, brought a sense of imbalance to the whole consulting profession.

So the question that makes a big difference is not: What knowledge is best? Rather, it is: how does one hold knowledge? Recently, one of my colleagues, a masterful consultant in her own right, impressed me greatly with the way she communicated her knowledge to a client. "When you get right down to it," she said to a group of participants in a leadership workshop, "being an effective leader is not necessarily a complex proposition. It boils down to just a few key points. When you live these few key points, you are a great leader." The participants were immediately eager to hear, their pens ready to take notes, their eyes alert, their hearts pounding for they knew they were about to hear something significant. She then drew on a flip chart the five points and their meaning. "I get it," said one participant eagerly, "but how does play win-win differ from seeing the system as a whole?" The consultant answered assertively, yet without arrogance. "Great question. I actually think there is some overlap. Like any distinction, the world never falls neatly into our own models. Here is how I see them as different." The consultant went on to explain in simple, graphic terms and then offered an illustration of each so the difference could be understood clearly.

No big deal, you might think. I can do that. I can display five points on a flip chart. I'll do that and I, too, will be masterful. Not so. What led this consultant's presentation to work was a combination of factors, which together created the conditions for effective knowledge transfer:

- Her solid understanding of the points she was offering

- Her ability to portray them simply and clearly

- Her modesty in conceding that her points were not exclusive

- The fact that she had been a living example of these principles throughout the beginning of the workshop and so had earned the respect of the participants

- She offered them in a way that went down easy—with confidence and, at the same time, openness.

To the uninitiated eye, one might think the points themselves were the magical part of the equation. And sure, what she said was important. It was how she said it, however, and how she lived it that made the biggest difference. The following sections focus on this point, and are intended to clarify the proper relationship to knowledge that masterful consulting is all about.

SOME KNOWLEDGE IS CRUCIAL

To begin, let's acknowledge that some knowledge is critical for consulting mastery. While this level may not be as high as we might think, it does exist. One of my surprises in talking with master consultants was how important they felt knowledge was. I was expecting them to tell me it was almost insignificant. They didn't. Instead, they acknowledged its role in consulting mastery. To understand what that role was. I asked each masterful consultant to weigh the following in terms of its importance to consulting mastery:

- Knowledge (what one knows)

- Experience (one's ability to apply what one knows and one's ability to deal with unique and challenging situations from experience)

- One's self (one's inner stance)

While there was some variation, *Knowledge* was seen as somewhat important, on average, receiving 25%. *Experience* got 28%. But *One's self* got 47%. Interestingly, client interviews revealed a stronger emphasis on knowledge. Many of the clients interviewed spoke of their respect for the best consultant they ever worked with in terms of knowledge. But as I spoke to people, I learned they valued one kind of knowledge above others: insight. Clients felt that high knowledge in one's area of expertise, coupled with wise application of that knowledge, was crucial. When wisdom and knowledge combine, the result is insightful knowledge. Without insight, knowledge is an also-ran.

At the same time, clients felt that how you hold that intelligence, how you use it, is far more crucial than raw intelligence or knowledge itself. I will discuss more of this in later chapters.

GUIDED BY A THEORY OF CHANGE

Geoff Bellman, one of the master consultants I interviewed, in his wonderful book, *The Consultant's Calling,* said, "The world does not make sense. *We* make sense."[2] This quote speaks volumes to the importance of having a theory or set of theories to guide yourself. I believe he meant that there is no meaning in the world apart from what we humans make of it. It is up to us to make sense of it. And how we make sense, through the lenses we use, makes all the difference in the world. Many master consultants said that while specific knowledge is not so important, being grounded in a set of theories about change is very important to their work. Part of their job is to help their clients make sense. They indicated in many different ways that one of the reasons they are so successful is that they enter a client situation feeling grounded in their own capability. An important part of that grounding is a result of holding a small set of theories about change or about organizational effectiveness that guides them. One consultant I interviewed had this to say:

> Many consultants are walking around without a solid ground to stand on in terms of theory of change or a theory of development they can use across multiple levels of a system. Without those two things, they are almost certainly going to end up leaning on tools and techniques to be effective.

While not every consultant I interviewed echoed these sentiments, clearly all were grounded in a set of theories that guided them, while at the same time they were not imprisoned by them.

These theories, and their way of seeing the organization, produce the kinds of insight that make a difference between good consulting and great. Each consultant was a living example of what Kurt Lewin said a half a century ago, scoffing at those who dismissed the importance of theory: "There is nothing more practical than a good theory."[3] One model, for example, emphasized the importance of client ownership of the change process. Another emphasized the power of dissonance, or incongruity between vision and current state, as a major impetus for change. There were many others.

Regardless of the particular theory, two things are instructive here. One, how each consultant felt the models for change helped him. Two, how grounded he became in the models. Without these models, I believe many consultants easily get lost in the client's own confusion about itself. They wander through the consulting process and justify such wandering as being client-focused. Amid the tangle of complicated challenges that afflict most organizations, consultants without workable models are not helping their clients at all.

I am not talking about rigid structure here or a simplistic connect-the-dots approach. A good model is often highly fluid in its expression and application. Indeed, any model to be effective needs to recognize that living systems are, in a very real sense, ordered chaos. In such an environment, we need cognitive maps that help us wend our way toward a change that is sustainable, knowing all the while that our maps are fallible—they are not the territory.

THE COGNITIVE MAPS FOR MASTERY

An effective cognitive map for consulting mastery has three important features: (1) Masterful consultants are guided by a set of theories, not just one. (2) They use their knowledge to reveal patterns that others may not see. (3) The theories are in the background of their awareness and not worn on their sleeve. The magic is really their ability to see "in the moment." Let's look at each, in turn.

A SMALL SET OF THEORIES. No one theory can effectively account for all of the phenomena occurring in a complex organization. One reason is that so many dynamics exist in organizational life that no one theory can explain or predict them. Consultants wedded to one theory to the exclusion of others will likely try to forcefit the client situation into the theory, as opposed to using multiple theories to understand the reality of the situation.

Let me give you an example. I am currently working with an organization in the performing arts, one of the second-tier organizations in its field, that is seeking to become both stronger as a whole and among the top tier. In many ways, the organization has felt stuck as an institution, working hard to give birth to the next evolution. A host of factors influence its current organizational dynamics (both strengths and weaknesses), including the long tenure of the institution's leadership, the relationship of the board to the institution (a volunteer board made up of members of the community), the current economy, the personalities of all the leaders, the history of the institution, the relationship between the performers and the institution, the industry itself and its expectations.

The situation is complex. To work with all these people effectively, I can't rely on any one theory to guide me. Clearly there are relevant theories of how the personalities of the leaders affect the institution as a whole. There are relevant theories about the power of environmental factors on any given organization. There are relevant theories about the process of change and which levels to push, and pull, and when. There are relevant theories about labor-management relations that clearly affect some of the institution's sense of feeling stuck. Any one of these many useful theories will tell me something about the dynamics. But to act on any one without considering the others would be folly.

In addition to having a set of theories to guide you, these theories must be not only comprehensive but also integrated. One masterful consultant said it like this:

> The key is to give clients a way of making sense out of a very confusing set of dynamics . . . the most successful consultants are very nimble intellectually and are very good synthesizers and integrators. They take a whole system approach so many components have to come together. Often people either have vested interests or projects that result in them only seeing the parts. The ability to integrate and synthesize and show how the parts impact the whole is what distinguishes great consultants from others.

His statement illustrates the masterful consultant's stance as it relates to theory or knowledge. He reported to me in the interview that he feels confident as a consultant, in part, because he knows he can understand just about any client situation he faces. He has his theories to guide him, and together they explain and/or predict what he is facing. He will share whichever theory is relevant with the client, only when it makes sense, and he will not confuse his client with too many theories or with competing theories. In other words, his theories for change come together to produce a whole system of understanding.

THE IMPORTANCE OF PATTERN ANALYSIS. A good theory needs to help the clients see more lucidly into its own dynamics. Great consultants are great, in part, because of their ability to see patterns. At the dawn of Western science, Pythagoreans distinguished pattern from substance, viewing the former as deeply impacting the latter. As Gregory Bateson put it:

> The argument took the shape of "Do you ask what it's made of—earth, fire, water, etc.?" Or do you ask, "What is its pattern?" Pythagoreans stood for inquiring into pattern."[4]

Seeing patterns is at the essence of viewing organizations as systems, and shifting those patterns over time, as required, is the goal of consulting mastery. I believe almost all great consultants shift patterns rather than fix problems. Witness the following comments by some of the consultants I interviewed, whose fascination with patterns has taken them far from the commonplace understanding of organizations:

> As a consultant, you can bring industry or content expertise. You can bring analytic horsepower. You can bring particular methodologies. Pretty generic stuff. When I think about what I bring myself, I think it has a lot to do with pattern recognition—the ability to help the client make sense out of what can be a chaotic situation very quickly.

> Part of my skill is to pay attention to the way I diagnose some-

thing as I try to change it. You don't diagnose things statically. Instead, you look at what happens when you try to influence the organization in some way. Then the issue is, do I respect the thing I'm trying to influence—do I respect the resistance itself as a very important part of the change situation. I have found myself being much more leery of strategic plans and much more interested in pattern analysis and a lot of things that go with chaos and complexity theory.

I feel like I'm an African tracker, noticing very small incidents, details, and discerning what they mean. Minute things are not obvious, yet they are crucial. I spend time developing the pattern making ability and the seeing. I'm amazed when I'm with trackers. They just glance at the earth and are able to tell a whole history of what went on there, what animal showed up, their state of health. That's how I regard myself as a consultant.

Pattern analysis does not happen overnight. Like the tracker in Africa, it comes from years of practice and time and experience looking for patterns. One of the consultants I interviewed spoke luminously to this phenomenon:

I now have enough experience to dig deeper—to find a pattern about the human dynamic. Many years ago I read a piece that talked about how really superb chess masters, when they look at a board, they see hundreds of patterns on the board whereas a mediocre player would see 20. I'm clear that in all of my dealings with the subtleties of human dynamics, it takes time to learn these patterns. You have to be in the work long enough to develop that kind of mastery.

The goal of pattern analysis is to penetrate the deeper patterns that together combine to keep the organization stuck in its current model. It is to see what others do not readily see. I'm reminded of a quote by the philosopher Albert Szent-Györgyi who once said: "Discovery consists of seeing what everybody has seen and thinking what nobody has thought."[5] Organizations remain stuck because of the deeply embedded mindsets and beliefs that prevent shifts in understanding, as well as the structures and systems that calcify over time. These mindsets prevent others from seeing the deeper patterns. If the goal of masterful consulting is to shift the organization to a new level, then attention to these patterns becomes ever more crucial.

THEORY IS BACKGROUND; BEING "IN THE MOMENT" IS FOREGROUND. All of these comments point to the same conclusion. Far more important than the knowledge itself is how the knowledge is applied. The Greek word *praxis* is instructive here. *Praxis* means to put theory into practice. Implied in the notion of praxis is the coming together of knowledge and action. Too many consultants are running around with good theories for change, development, transformation, etc. without the ability to put those theories to work in real time. Let me go one step further. While the ability to apply theory is essential to great consulting, it is not enough. What differentiates masterful consultants from others is the ability to intervene effectively in the moment—it is praxis. Indeed, *when the intervention meets the moment, that's when consulting begins to make a difference.*

**MAGIC OCCURS WHEN THE INTERVENTION
MEETS THE MOMENT.**

Ron Tilden, one of the best consultants I know, typifies the spirit of praxis. He has this to say about the magic of "being in the moment":

> Fundamentally, I am an improvisational jazz musician in terms
> of DNA, while active in this more traditional consulting profes-
> sion. I am so grateful for my training, yet those training wheels
> have fallen off over time. What is left is the improvisational
> artist in me that really trusts the moment. The key to my suc-
> cess is to be prepared and then let go, to just jam with people.

Many of the clients I interviewed similarly spoke in different ways about the best consultant they had worked with and how present, fluid, and "in the moment" they were. One client summarized how important this was to her. In reflecting on the necessary qualities of masterful consultants, she said:

> They have the ability to be in the moment and to make the right call in that moment. You've only got a finite amount of time to make a difference as a consultant. . . . Sizing up things correctly in the moment, using your intelligence, making the right decisions is what is most crucial.

Rick, a masterful consultant, was in an initial meeting with a new client recently, where this concept of the "intervention meets the moment" shined brightly. It was the first meeting in which the whole senior team discussed the results of his organizational assessment. While the CEO and a couple of senior executives were very eager to have him work with the senior team and the company as a whole, others were reticent. They were not sure whether his work with them would bring the value necessary to warrant their collective time and money. In other words, while Rick had an agreement to work with the client, at that instant, the agreement was fragile.

The meeting went rather smoothly for a while. He shared with them the results of the data he was collecting, and then invited open dialogue about its meaning for them, and implications for the future. The only hiccups occurred a couple of times when the CEO offered a point of view in a very harsh, extremely authoritative manner. In each instance, he spoke so firmly that he shut off any dialogue. Rick could sense that others had differing views—their eyes darted among the group each time to see if others would speak. In both cases, no one responded to the CEO's comments. Not surprising, one of Rick's findings in the assessment had been how difficult it was to challenge the CEO, and that people often described him as impenetrable. Rick followed these executive outbursts with silence, electing not to intervene. Somewhere in the middle of the meeting, Rick began to feel as if the process was going too smoothly—almost flat. It changed rapidly. After a bit of heated and what appeared to be healthy dialogue, the CEO stepped in with another strong assertion—something to the effect of "Thanks for all your input, now let me tell you how it really is." Silence followed.

Here is what I mean by applied knowledge. In this story, Rick is sitting on a boatload of knowledge about the CEO and how others feel about him. Rick is aware that the CEO can easily be defensive, and he has witnessed this defensiveness many times. Rick is also sitting on a great deal of research and experience about groups and the effect of the CEO or leader on them. Finally, he is armed with more theories about group dynamics and intervention than he cares to count. All of this knowledge matters little. It is how Rick uses it that matters most.

In this case, ever aware of the potential for angering the CEO by challenging him publicly, Rick seized the moment nonetheless. He recalls saying something like this:

> I'd like to pause for a moment and explore what I think just
> happened here. I'm feeling hesitant about saying something
> about what I see because I am not yet sure about your expecta-
> tions of me as a consultant, nor am I certain that you all value
> talking about your own team process. So I'd like to share my
> view as a way of not only learning about your expectations, but
> also in sharing one of the ways I believe I can be valuable to
> the team.

Rick hesitated a bit, noticing that they were attentive, and at the same time seemed curious. He continued:

> I observed Jack make a strong assertion about his view, which
> was followed by silence and many people squirming in their
> chairs. This suggested to me that people had some thoughts
> and feelings about what Jack said, yet chose not to respond. I
> observed this kind of active silence in a mild way a couple of
> times earlier in the meeting, and am now wondering if this is a
> pattern in this team. Before we talk about it, I'm wondering if
> others saw or sensed what I saw.

Immediately, one of the members spoke up and indicated he saw it too. Others chimed in, while the CEO remained silent. Rick then turned to the CEO and asked him if he saw it. He said he did as well, and that it often happened. He then got defensive and said that he felt very open to feedback and differing views, and often felt like others were not stepping up to the plate to disagree with him. "I don't want 'yes men' and it frustrates me that people don't speak their minds in these meetings or disagree with me."

Rick then asked if they would find it fruitful to explore this dynamic more fully. The CEO and many others said "yes," and so they did. Rick framed the conversation by suggesting that the goal of the discussion was to learn together, and that it was important that no one assign blame to anyone. They had all participated in creating this dynamic, and blaming the CEO or anyone else would not be productive. They agreed, and proceeded. They discussed how the CEO's own behavior may contribute to the very thing he wants to avoid, and that others were fearful of directly disagreeing with him in team meetings. They discussed how others were shying away from confronting the CEO. And they talked about how CEO-centric the team was.

This discussion went on for about ten minutes, when Rick's role changed to helping them surface their own sense of how this dynamic got created and to ensure learning occurred.

At the end of the meeting, they reported that Rick had not only handled the situation deftly, but that they were feeling a strong need to continue to explore how they can strengthen their own team functioning. And they wanted Rick's help as a guide.

Knowledge is helpful, but what made this dicey intervention succeed was Rick's ability to apply that knowledge effectively and in a timely manner. It was also his ability to describe rather than judge the dynamics he saw. His intervention was risky, to be sure. Yet this is precisely his added value as a consultant—to skillfully do that which the client cannot do well for itself. Skillfulness has everything to do with timing, grace under pressure, integrity, care, genuine openness, and commitment to the client's learning. When all of these are present, then the intervention meets the moment and magic occurs.

Masterful consultants know this well and spend much more time tuning their own capability in these areas than in learning the latest and greatest theory or model. I have witnessed too many consultants armed with knowledge and a brilliant intellect who make little difference to their clients, and I have seen many masterful consultants who may not be up to date on the latest theory or model yet wind up making a profound difference anyway.

CHAPTER 7

CONVEYING

KNOWLEDGE

Make everything as simple as possible,
but not simpler.

—Albert Einstein

MAXINE IS A CONFIDENT MARKETING CONSULTANT who has a theory about buying patterns. She was taught about such patterns in a marketing class in her MBA program, and it has been a guide for years. She has used it in dozens of situations and has learned when and how the model is most useful. The model, in this case, blends understandings of economic factors, market forces, industry trends, and psychological factors. Together, these factors predict buying choices.

Maxine was brought in by a company seeking to take its product line, typically aimed for adults, into the adolescent market. She was confident in herself and trusted her model or theory. Being grounded in the model, she understood the principles upon which the model is based, and could therefore find unique expressions of that model. So because this particular client is dealing with the adolescent population whose buying patterns are notoriously fickle, and influenced by the media, she focused on two features of the model—industry trends and psychological factors—bringing them into sharp relief. Within industry trends, she focused on how the media affects those trends. She then helped her client see how psychological forces inside the adolescent mind affect choices and how understanding the adolescent mind more deeply, in turn, can shape those choices. She did this by facilitating a dialogue that helped the client apply these principles to its target customer base. Economic factors and market forces within the model were touched upon lightly (not ignored) since they were less relevant in this situation. She did not feel she had to fit the situation to the model. For her, it was the other way around. And she did this without calling attention to the model. Instead her whole focus was on the client and its practical use of the model. The net effect was that the client left the meeting with a deeper understanding, making cognitive and practical connections along the way. All of this was done in a smooth, easy fashion that focused on learning and application, not on theory or knowledge. And the client's experience of Maxine was that she was very wise and helpful.

Maxine is not much different than most consultants in her understanding of models, theories, and ideas and their application in organizations. It was the way she carried herself and held her knowledge that made the difference. In contrast to most consultants, she offered her knowledge simply. She sought to reduce the plethora of information to a small set of principles, concepts, or models to guide the client's understanding. It's no secret that the most enduring models or theories are usually succinct. They are memorable, and they clarify. Overwhelming amounts of data only serve to obfuscate.

Maxine also cared more about the dialogue that resulted from her presentation than the presentation itself. She knew that the ability to digest information and discuss its meaning within the group is what helped produce movement in the client organization. People need to explore the meaning of information for themselves. The more they do this, and the more they are allowed to form their own conclusions, the more likely they are to take forceful action. So, like all masterful consultants, she facilitated meaningful dialogue and viewed the integrity of the process as more important than the brilliance of the analysis.

One of the partners in my consulting firm has a way of putting it that I think says a lot about this issue. She says, and I believe this to be so, that mostly what clients want is for us to "help them make sense of the mess." They are calling for help, guidance, or support in some way, usually because they can't make sense of it themselves. For consultants to spend countless hours producing a report, rich in detail, as if richness of detail were the most important value, misses the point. Volumes of data and analysis may give clients comfort, but they don't clarify.

The need to produce large, detailed reports is often driven by one of two things: (1) consultants' need to prove their worth (let me show you how well I understand you and the mess you have and how bright I am); (2) clients' need to protect themselves from some regulatory or legal action (let me prove that I did my homework). Neither rationale has anything to do with solving the client's problem, nor leads, by itself, to positive action.

Rather than wade through an ocean of details, masterful consultants typically highlight key points. They seek to identify the essential features needing attention. They help their clients "make sense of their mess" by focusing on a few key issues. Then they offer models or concepts that lead to action.

And, of course, they use 2×2 matrices to display their knowledge. I say this with a bit of tongue in cheek, knowing how rampant 2×2 matrices are in the industry. For a reason: simple models are memorable. And memorable models are more often put to use.

GROUNDED IN SELF-CONFIDENCE

With great athletes, confidence is crucial. So too with master consultants. Besides communicating knowledge through skillful means, and facilitating meaningful dialogue, masterful consultants hold their knowledge with confidence. During my interviews, I was taken by the paradoxical combination of certainty and humility embodied in almost every masterful consultant I spoke with. I have seen this combination only rarely among individuals, to the point that I would suggest that it happens as a result of deep and consistent work in developing one's "self."

**"I'LL ALWAYS BE NUMBER ONE TO MYSELF."
—MOSES MALONE, HALL OF FAME NBA CENTER**

Abraham Maslow pointed this out decades ago when he observed that one of the characteristics of self-actualized people is this dual sense of inner strength coupled with great curiosity, openness, and humility. I will focus here on the confidence half of the equation. In a later chapter, I will focus on the role in the learning process of its counterpart, humility.

Many of the clients I interviewed felt similarly about the importance of self-confidence. Said one, in reflecting on his experience of the best consultants he had worked with:

> They've got a lot of self-confidence, which comes from being smart, successful, and right most of the time. So there's a certain element of decisiveness. But it's not arrogance . . . it's a sense of "I know what I know."

In masterful consultants, this sense of certainty does not show up as arrogance. Nor does it show up in bloated, ungrounded claims of success that often appear in consultants who are pushy or self-promoting. It shows up as the quiet confidence of a person who knows deep down what she is doing.

A BALANCED STANCE

One of the people who most influenced me in my career, Mike McKeon, had this quality. When he spoke, he had the quiet assurance that he could back up what he said. He often did not speak, but when he did, you knew it came from a deep confidence in his being. One day I asked him why he said so little in meetings yet had such influence. He remarked almost offhandedly that it was simple. He learned long ago to pick and choose his spots. He only spoke when he believed wholeheartedly in what he was saying and the added value he was providing. His comment caused me to reflect on how and when I spoke, and I immediately realized that my speaking was often motivated by other factors and was often not wholehearted. I spoke sometimes to break silence. I spoke sometimes out of my own discomfort. I spoke sometimes to try to impress others. I spoke sometimes to protect people from interpersonal damage. I spoke to appease people's concerns. I spoke to protect myself. I spoke because I liked speaking.

FINDING ONE'S OWN CONFIDENCE

Phillip was facing a challenge in his career. He wanted to make a living as a mediator in public policy disputes and had had difficulty getting into the business. There are many expert mediators in his area, and not enough business to go around. He shared with me during one of our coaching calls that he had just finished mediating a very tough dispute between two agencies that had been fighting each other for some time, and that he was exhausted from this struggle. In exploring his exhaustion, I noticed that there were many moments throughout the day that he seemed uncertain. In reflecting on my experience of him, I began to get in touch with how uncertain he seemed energetically. His comments would often be followed by some communication that caused him to backtrack. For example, he might say things like, "I feel X . . . well, maybe that's not right," or "I would like Y to happen . . . but perhaps it won't be okay." It was as if he often took away his own personal power.

I shared my observations with him and he confirmed that he often interacted with others with some degree of self-uncertainty. This had been true for a long time. We explored this and learned that the sources of this pattern were many, not the least of which was his training as a mediator, which focused on the importance of helping people dislodge themselves from initial positions so that they could negotiate openly. I suggested that there was a relationship between his uncertainty during this recent mediation and his challenges in getting in solid in his chosen profession. In exploring this, he agreed and we began to look at the multiple ways his uncertainty affected his business life. Then we began to look at how his life might change if he came from an inner stance of self-certainty. Over our exploration, he developed an image of himself of greater self-certainty, and his image began to shape his own behavior.

In our next call, he reported to me that he had just done three complex mediations in a row, and that in contrast to the past exhaustion, he felt relaxed and energized. He said the principal shift was operating from an inner stance of self-certainty or trust in his abilities, rather than from self-criticism, which was his usual bent.

Six months later, the country's leading mediation firm in his chosen area of focus hired him.

In reflecting about the numerous non-value added ways in which I spoke, I imagined a bank account where, instead of money, "influence coins" were kept. The more coins in the bank account, the more I was able to positively influence others. I realized that every time I spoke, I either added coins to my influence bank account or spent them. When I speak, for any reason, I am spending influence coins. When I speak from my heart, in a wholehearted way, and when I pick and choose my spots, more often than not, I am adding coins to my influence bank account. Mike had earned a huge amount of coins because of where he came from when he spoke, and because he was careful (full of care) in when and how he used his coins. He spent his coins well, and in so doing, whenever he spent them, he gained more back.

Recently I did something that shows what happens when one is not feeling solid in one's self. I met for breakfast with a colleague and friend, someone I was eager to work with. I was excited about his company and what he was doing, and wanted to participate in some way. Our meeting was designed to explore whether and how I might add value. It went smoothly for a while, but somewhere along the way I sensed that there were no legitimate places for me to do what I do best in his company. Rather than accept this and trust our relationship and my own capability, I began to get pushy. It was not overt, just a subtle shift in the way I participated in the conversation. At one point, I started to tell my colleague of the ways in which I felt I was extremely capable. It was not my finest moment. Suddenly he looked up at me and said, "You know, Keith, you don't have to prove how good you are to me. I already know. I wouldn't be exploring the possibility of working together if I didn't feel you were up to it. So please stop trying to sell me on you."

His feedback stung, but he hit the nail on the head. I was so eager to work with him that, when I sensed the opportunity was slipping away, I became a bit pushy, rather than accepting.

No harm done, he assured me, and we moved on. But I think some harm was done. I suspect he now has questions about my effectiveness as a consultant, where once he had none. His posture was more reserved for the rest of our breakfast; our conversation less fluid. My pushiness resulted in him being less confident in me, rather than the opposite.

There is an image I often use to check whether I am coming from this inner stance of self-confidence. It is an image of my body leaning. When I am not feeling confident, either I lean too far forward (pushy), or lean too far back (apologetic or avoiding). It is not so much that I am leaning physically. I am leaning *energetically*. The same check may work for you. When we lean too much in either direction, we are not coming from a solid stance within ourselves.

Our message suffers when we force people to react to our aggressive-ness (leaning forward) or our passivity (leaning backward). The proper angle of self-esteem and self-confidence is to be upright, cen-tered, grounded, and true.

I just met a young woman, Estelle, who has been consulting and training in her organization for a few years. Estelle sees herself as a highly effective trainer, growing in her ability to consult to her organization. She told me she was frustrated about how seldom her organization uses her advice. "I can't tell you the number of times

FIGURE 7-1   DIFFERENT STANCES

Thoughts	I am worried. I am needy. I am concerned.	I am fine as I am. I am capable. I trust me and the situation.	I don't deserve this. I am not capable.
Feelings	Anxious Unsettled Insecure	Safe Confident Secure	Self-defeated Unworthy Fearful Insecure
Behaviors	Attacking Blaming Overconfronting	Assertive Inquisitive Direct and compassionate	Pulling back Avoiding Apologetic Overly yielding
Outcomes	Others reacting Push back Resistance	Change Positive movement Clear communication	Little movement Tentativeness Disappointment

we have left workshops or meetings with action plans that go nowhere," she said, exasperation in her voice. Here was this skillful, engaging, vibrant woman, committed to helping her organization grow, who felt her work had little impact.

"Could it be," I surmised, "that part of the issue is how much energy for change is coming from you and how little from others? Sometimes the more you push for what you want, the less things change." Estelle's eyes lit up. She got it. She rattled off the many subtle and not-so-subtle ways she had tried to push her agenda for change on to her client, rather than drawing the agenda for change out from the client. The more she thought about it, with a little guidance from me, the more she could see that the problem wasn't in the client. The problem was the way she approached change—kind of like a bully. Bad ideas require arm-twisting. By being pushy with a good idea, you are doing it an injustice.

Self-confidence comes from living, from experience, not from books. It is an essential quality to mastery. One of the masterful consultants I interviewed spoke eloquently on the subject:

> You need to live life to the fullest, like Carlos Castaneda says: "as though death is right there on your shoulder." That doesn't mean being risky and taking wild chances. It means experiencing different cultures, going to different countries, going to the orchestra, going to plays, appreciating different music including rap. It means having as broad a base of experience and phenomenology, in terms of who you are as a human being, as you possibly can, so that you can draw from that incredible rich ground that you bring with you.

Self-confidence comes from self-esteem and from knowledge that is grounded in experience, not thought. When knowledge is grounded, the consultant uses that knowledge appropriately and flexibly. The consultant knows its contours, its areas of application, and its limitations. She wears that knowledge comfortably, like a well-worn shoe. Grounded knowledge, like an old shoe, is not flashy, polished or stylish. It is certainly not perfect. But it fits.

When consultants are armed with grounded theory or knowledge, they are connected to its principles, while molding its expression to fit the client situation. When they are not connected, no matter how brilliant they are, problems occur, and too often they are unaware of it. Let me illustrate.

Jenny blew a tuft of her bangs in relief that the presentation was finished. For the first time she had led a team of consultants as a partner of her consulting firm, and she had just shared with her client's senior team the results of their research. It was impressive. Her presentation was likewise brilliant, measured by the sheer numbers of graphs, figures, data sorts, and well-crafted solutions. She and the team had worked so hard to get to this point that she was not going to leave anything out. After all, the client had paid a lot of money, and she wanted them to see they were getting their money's worth.

The presentation went smoothly enough. A few times she was interrupted by clarifying questions, and now and then she asked questions to be sure the participants were tracking. They must have been, for there were few questions. This made her a bit nervous, wondering what their quietness meant. But her desire to offer a complete and comprehensive package of analysis and recommendations caused here to press on in spite of this discomfort.

Little did she know that their silence was due to two things: First, they were embarrassed that she seemed to know more about their business and industry than they did. Her presentation was so impressive that they were intimidated by it and by her. Second, they were often confused throughout the presentation, struggling with some of her more erudite ideas and complex concepts, but were afraid to show their confusion in front of one another. In spite of having many questions, they preferred to sit quietly and feign understanding.

In the end, after being initially inspired to make the changes she and her team recommended, they were discouraged by the task before them. Moreover, her analysis did not fit their intuitive way of understanding the organization. The complete and detailed analysis was as daunting as the recommendations that followed. So they politely withdrew after pretending to be wowed.

After she left the room, they discussed what to do and agreed to put off her recommendations until they were more ready to "genuinely put them into effect." They never did. Jenny left puzzled by their reticence to take action in spite of the overwhelming evidence that her conclusions were on target.

This story gets played out time and time again, with bright, talented consultants all over the world. Armed with a boatload of data, analysis, and brilliant recommendations, the client's implementation nevertheless falls short of the target. What many of these consultants don't realize is that breaking down an organizational problem to its smallest parts can be dispiriting. Dissection rarely produces movement in organizational life. Brilliant analysis is rarely enough. How the information gets presented and how well it gets digested is more important than the analysis itself.

Not only does analysis seldom move people to act, complex analysis is downright daunting to most people. Most human beings tend to act based on what they can contain in their brain and hearts. There is a principle (and I believe research to support it) that the average person can retain in short-term memory 7 things, plus or minus 2. This principle is the primary reason why phone numbers are divided by dashes. It helps you remember. We remember our area code as one number, not three. We remember the prefix of our phone number as one number, not three. In this way we are remembering 3 sets as opposed to 10 digits.

Jenny would be far more influential with the client by offering a small set of principles to guide her client's thinking and action, rather than a magnum opus. Huge reports don't inspire. Instead, they often deflate.

Simple understanding and the ability to relate information with ease only come with time and a deep commitment to relevance. Many masterful consultants know this maxim: "You cannot take a client further than you have taken yourself." What this means is that the more you are grounded in your own experience in the arena that you consult, the more likely you will experience mastery. Mastery is not given. It is earned. One of the consultants I interviewed explained a piece of the process well:

> There are times I get myself into a snit about something, and I
> ask myself, "What part of your own technology would be most
> helpful to you now?" and then I use it. I say to myself, "You

know this, you teach it, and so now you must live it. You must live it in order to teach it."

This consultant earns her mastery every day, not by being brilliant, but by being committed to living that which she teaches others. This commitment leads her to be deeply grounded in her understanding, and through grounding, can teach others more powerfully. Being grounded in your self and in your theory cannot be taught. It must be hard won. And when hard won, then and only then can your knowledge be held with true confidence and conveyed simply and masterfully.

CHAPTER 8

HELPING CLIENTS
HELP THEMSELVES

If you have come to help me because you feel called
to help me, please go away. . . . But if you have
come because your liberation is bound up with
mine, please stay and let's work together.

—*Unidentified Aboriginal woman*

FOR YEARS I HAVE BEEN STRUGGLING with my tendency to try to control my son. I do it in subtle and not-so-subtle ways, most of which are driven by my own fears of failure. I got it drilled into me early on by my own parents that a "successful" person had to be self-disciplined, focused, and goal-driven. My son, typical of many children, doesn't display these characteristics. He is 13 years old and is generally unfocused around work (go figure!), often procrastinates, and mostly just wants to have fun. He does not like school, although he does get excellent grades. When he exhibits these characteristics, I often get upset and do any of a number of things, from glaring at him, to lecturing him, to setting up consequences for poor behavior, etc. I am aware that none of these behaviors seem to help. Most especially, it has strained my relationship with my son. He knows I love him deeply. But he also wishes I would get off his back and lighten up. To be honest, I wish the same about myself sometimes.

To help me get some perspective on my relationship with my son, I have sought guidance from a therapist. The therapist, Seymour Radin, focuses not on my behavior, but on the "model" that must be guiding my thinking. He says things like, "I wonder where you got the belief that it is your job to teach your son." Or he might ask, "How is that a reflection of the relationship you had with your father . . . what effect did that have on you?" Through questions, I have begun to see my fathering model unfold ever so clearly. And I see the sources of it, the needs that are driving it, and the potential counterproductive consequences of it. I can also see that if I continue following this deeply ingrained unconscious model, I am likely to hurt my son far more than help, and end up with a distant relationship with him.

A couple of months ago I said to Seymour: "Okay. I get it. I want a different model. What do you suggest?" He refused to answer. In typical fashion, his response was: "I can't tell you what the right model is. I'm wondering, though, have you seen examples of parenting that seem to work differently?" I offered a couple and then asked for his recommendation, to which he replied: "I'm not sure, but I am guided often by the principle of wholeness. I wonder how that principle might apply here."

I thought deeply about these questions, and sure enough, slowly but surely a model started to form in my mind that might have a different effect on my son and our relationship. And the model is one that I discovered inside myself. Seymour encouraged me to experiment, to stay awake, and to play with alternatives. The net effect of this process has been profound. After about three months, my relationship with my son began to take a noticeable turn. A different model guides me now; yet at the same time I continue to be pulled by my old model. There is an ongoing argument between two parts of myself: One part trusts the new model and the other part is fear-driven and attached to the old familiar model. Sometimes I fall back to my old ways. But more often than not, I behave consistent with the new model. I have confidence I will continue to learn how to adopt the new model, because it was not placed in me from without. It was one that I discovered inside myself. All it took was some guidance to find it. It's not Seymour's model; it's mine.

Lately I have also been experimenting with a more "guiding"

approach with my clients. More and more, I am giving my clients not advice, but guidance. The difference between the two is both subtle and significant. When we give people advice, we tacitly hold two assumptions: (1) I know better than you; and (2) you cannot think it through for yourself. Guidance is different. Guidance provides clarity—a framework within which clients can think the problem through on their own.

A significant cause of the failure of consulting to affect deeper change is that so many consultants seek a "power-over" relationship to the client. Unconsciously, we want to be king or, at the very least, "the power behind the throne." But for us to have maximum impact, the client must remain in charge. To do this, we need to become guides who serve the king and allow him to make wise choices in his kingdom. This is the way of the magician.

In their book about mature masculine archetypes, Robert Moore and Douglas Gillette tell a story that illustrates this aproach. The prophet Nathan was King David's guide. King David, like many kings, got very full of himself and decided to have his way with Bathsheba, whom he glimpsed rapturously on a rooftop, naked. So he ordered her husband Uriah, a soldier in his army, off to a dangerous assignment, so he would be killed in battle, and he (David) would be free to enjoy Bathsheba's delights. Nathan, who could see clearly the negative consequences of such a decision, came quietly into David's throne room and stood before him. Instead of giving advice he told King David the following story:

> Once upon a time there were two men, a rich man and a poor man. The rich man had many sheep. The poor man had only one little lamb. One day a traveler came to visit the rich man, and the rich man was obliged to give him a sumptuous feast. Instead of slaughtering one of his own sheep, he went to the poor man and took his one little lamb, killed it, and made the feast with it.

Bursting with anger, King David proclaimed that whoever did this deserved to die, to which Nathan calmly replied, "You, sire, are that man." King David immediately saw the wickedness of his actions and repented. [1]

What's good for King David is good for your clients. In the end, the client must make the call. The consultant's job is to offer guidance, to lead the client, but not to bang him over the head with it.

FOR ANY LESSON TO TAKE HOLD, IT MUST BLOSSOM IN THE CLIENT'S MIND AND BELONG TO THE CLIENT.

We see the power of "suggested wisdom" in the great teachers of history. Socrates taught not by telling, but by asking, which compels listeners to come to their own conclusions. Jesus taught by parables, which required listeners to make their own interpretation. The wisdom of science is not to insist on unchallengeable laws, but to invite people to challenge them, one experiment at a time. In each case, a "learning" model replaces a "teaching" model.

It may seem like a small difference, but in fact it's quite radical. The most valuable knowledge isn't "poured in the ear," as many university coats of arms suggest. The most valuable knowledge is the kind the thinker comes to on his own, with a little guidance.

GUIDANCE NOT ADVICE

This concept of guidance suggests that the consultant mustn't control the client or the situation. To do so would not add value. Instead, the consultant enables, teaches, guides, or facilitates. This approach adds energy to the system and helps the system grow. Said one masterful consultant I interviewed:

> One of the ways I see my work as different from that of the Big 5 consulting firms is that I don't see us as producers of power. We are much more like electricians than we are producers of power. What I got from working with some of the Big 5 is that because of the way they work, they don't tap into any of the human energy of their client organizations. They have to bring it with them. They bring this big generator full of a whole

bunch of people and they run around like crazy creating all this power. When they leave, it is gone. The thing I like most is going back to the organization after we've been gone for a while and find it still has a lot of the energy we helped cultivate.

Advice, the preferred tool of the expert consultant, rarely adds energy to the client system. It doesn't cultivate understanding. Yet the desire to give advice runs deep within most consultants, and they spend many years honing their ability to give it. More specifically, most consultants operate from a belief in how organizations can be run more effectively, and want to help by guiding them toward that goal. Isn't the most expedient way to get to this goal to advise the clients—just tell them flat-out where and how they can be better? After all, isn't that what they are paying the consultant to do?

At some level, by giving advice, the consultant is colluding with the client's perceived needs. The client is struggling as a company or has a vision for change and wants to manifest that vision in the most expedient manner possible. The client doesn't know how to do it, or believes it doesn't, and so seeks guidance and help. What better way to help than to tell the client what it needs to do?

A far more powerful approach to cultivating change is to help the client build its own theory of change. Alternatively, you could educate the client about the change process and then help them explore and make decisions from that framework. Masterful consultants "get this," and are committed to client ownership all the way. One consultant I interviewed spoke eloquently on the subject:

> Part of my work is to help the client reflect on how they change and how organizations change. One of the things I'm there to do is to help them understand how change comes about in humans and human organizations and to build their own theory of change. I'll share mine with them either directly or by questions as well, but I want to educate them. A really important element in this education process is reflection— helping them reflect about what they do. I help them stand back from what they've done and comment about it as if they were an outsider. It is a *plan, do, reflect* cycle—something where you are moving on this spiral through time as you move

upward towards the future. In this cycle, both client and I
know that we will regularly reflect on what we are doing
together. It is through this process that the client learns to
make effective decisions relative to their own change process.

All of the above is not lost on clients. Indeed, my interviews
with clients clearly revealed that they valued deeply the ability of
consultants to help clients get to the root of the problems they face.
Instead of dropping information in, after the medieval model, those
consultants drew clients out. As a result of their focus on empowering the client, the clients I interviewed reported that the consultants' work endured far longer than the average consulting engagement.

To illustrate the importance of helping the client think it
through, let's look at two different efforts at Sears, the great retail
company, to orchestrate a business turnaround.[2] The first began in
the late 1980s when Sears was hemorrhaging as a result of a major
strategic decision to enter into the financial services market. Ed
Brennan, then president of Sears, brought in the Monitor Company
to fix the problem. Monitor was renowned as the consulting firm
co-founded by Michael E. Porter, the famous strategy expert and
Harvard Business School professor.

A product of Monitor's work with Sears was "everyday low
pricing," which turned out to be a disaster. This policy caused many
customers to be upset with Sears because they were already condi-
tioned to expect deep discount sales. The company was also not well
set up for such a policy since it was a high-cost operation, in contrast to Wal-Mart, which, being younger and less encumbered by
antiquated systems, was able to organize its business around opera-
tional efficiency. In other words, Sears did not have the business
infrastructure and practice to sustain such a policy.

In spite of the promises on the part of Monitor to change
Sears for the better, the opposite occurred, with plenty of finger-
pointing to go around. At one point, Monitor had over 40 consultants charging $2000–2500 per day per person at Sears. By today's
standards, that is more like $3000–3500. Brennan claimed everyday
low pricing was the brainchild of Monitor, which was therefore to
blame, while Monitor claimed the timing and the implementation

by Sears was at fault, not their policy. Such blaming is the direct result of the consultant making promises to deliver something that by definition is the responsibility of the client organization. When consultants sell their services by claiming their work makes positive change happen, they are, in effect, claiming their work does the job. Clients welcome the promise, and the Savior Strategy is enacted. This enables the client organization to abdicate responsibility, a tactic that rarely ends up well. As 1990 approached, Monitor began to disappear from the scene, and Arthur Martinez, a former vice chairman of Saks Fifth Avenue, soon replaced Brennan.

In contrast to Brennan, Martinez took a very different tack with consultants. He expected his senior managers and himself to be actively engaged on the project. "I want the people who come to present their plans to me to be the people who actually do the work. I don't want the new business pitch from the new business guy and then some other team comes in and takes over."[3] He hired A. T. Kearney, a highly reputable consulting firm with a "roll up your sleeves" approach to business. Through a number of efforts, they were instrumental in helping Sears through a cost-cutting campaign that put the company on the road to recovery. While Kearney provided expertise much like Monitor, Martinez psychologically owned the process. In his own words:

> The process for making this decision was put in the hands of
> Sears people. Kearney was there to provide the support, the
> knowledge, the skill base . . . but it wasn't Kearney negotiating
> with the battery supplier for Sears. It was our battery-buying
> team negotiating on behalf of Sears with the support of the
> Kearney organization and its resources.[4]

But cutting costs was not enough to transform the company. Martinez wanted more. He wanted nothing less than a cultural transformation of Sears. In contrast to many companies who hire large firms to orchestrate such a massive effort, Martinez saw culture change as his responsibility. To provide guidance to him, Martinez hired David Ulrich, a University of Michigan business school professor. At the same time, Martinez kept himself in the driver seat. "We didn't need a consulting organization to provide some sort of a blanket solution," Martinez said. "We needed someone who has seen lots of practical applications and who has seen some of the academic work on motivation. With a consultant, I am asking him to propose a solution. With an advisor, I am testing solutions that we are inventing."[5]

The jury is out on the results. And Sears certainly has not turned itself around consistent with Martinez's desires. Nonetheless, among major companies who have struggled to transform themselves, Sears remains one of the most impressive efforts. I believe it is in no small part due to the fact that Martinez kept himself in the driver's seat.

The simple principle is that when a client psychologically owns the knowledge developed through the consulting process, the client is more likely to take action. When the client and consultant enter into a tacit agreement for the consultant to "save" the client, however, or to give knowledge over, ownership rarely occurs, and the change both sides sincerely want to happen, doesn't.

Guidance, not advice, helps clients to own their actions and their outcomes. At the same time, it is itself something of real value. Guidance can come in many forms. Nonetheless, in observing masterful consultants over time, and through the interviews, I have come to believe there is a small set of guidance behaviors that best influence clients to think through solutions for themselves. They are:

- Framing or reframing

- Feedback

- Asking penetrating questions

Framing or Reframing

Embedded in every decision you and I make, every choice, every action is a *frame*. A frame is the way a person sees a situation or event. It is that person's mental model from which he experiences or understands the situation or event. For example, this book is offering a frame on consulting. Its premise is that your inner stance is an important factor in successful consulting. We could view the consulting process in any of a number of ways: as a set of discrete actions, as a process flow, as a contract between parties, as a symbol of the larger society in which we live, etc. The frame I offer is not the only frame. It is a way of seeing, nonetheless, and it has implications for action.

How a person frames or sees an event or situation determines the choices for his action. If, for example, you walk up to a person and point out that they have mustard on their shirt, and the person says: "So what? Who the hell are you to tell me about how to dress?" and then walks away, you could frame their response in a number of ways, each suggesting a different response from you. You could frame his response as a direct confrontation to you, and then you will likely say something back in retaliation. You could frame it as *He is overwhelmed,* and feel compassion toward him. You could frame it as *He doesn't care about his appearance,* remembering that everyone is different, thereby invoking no particular reaction whatsoever. Frames by themselves are neither right nor wrong. They are merely the lenses through which we view the world.

One of the most powerful things we can do as consultants is offer a frame—a way of seeing—that increases the client's capacity to make effective choices. Masterful consultants get this in their bones, and do it naturally. Here are a few of many examples of consultants I interviewed speaking to the importance of framing:

> I frequently ask questions that help clients become clearer about why they are choosing a certain way. If I feel that it is not an appropriate way as a complete outcome, I may try to find a way to help them see the situation differently.

> It's not that I have the answer and I'm leading the person to that answer. It is that I learn how to formulate questions that actually expand the other person's and my own thinking— learning to ask questions that enlighten.

> I don't use humor to diffuse conflict. I often use it to enhance understanding. It is as if my humor enables clients to get a cosmic chuckle by going high enough in the atmosphere so they can look down on a situation and see what it looks like from there instead of from the middle of it.

I affirm them in their present state of imperfection. I offer
them unique perspectives on the world, I bring a spontaneity
that is often irreverent and breaks them loose from the boxes
they put themselves in.

By definition, a more effective frame is one where the actions
that are implied lead to greater effectiveness, greater outcomes,
greater flexibility, or greater opportunity. For example, I was working with an executive team recently that was constantly in conflict.
Each one saw the other as not effective, and in some ways, out to
undermine the other's authority. After months of bickering, they
decided they needed help in dealing with their interpersonal conflicts. They believed that their interpersonal styles clashed, and if
they could learn to understand each other better, they would reduce
their conflicts significantly. In other words, they viewed the problem from an interpersonal frame. After interviewing each member
for about an hour, I began to form an alternative frame. While interpersonal issues were certainly present, underlying these issues were
a pair of fundamental problems: (1) their model for the business was
not working; and (2) there was confusion about who was responsible for what, fueled by a CEO who was uncomfortable with setting
clear expectations. When we met, I offered this alternative frame on
the situation and invited them to discuss both the vulnerabilities of
their business model and their lack of role clarity. The alternative
frame made sense to them, and they spent two days exploring each
of these issues together. With some guidance from me, they were
able to detect the underlying deficiencies of their business model,
explore alternatives, and clarify each other's expectations in a way
that reduced the structural conflict that was dragging them down.
Interestingly, hardly any interpersonal problems surfaced during the
meeting, and in the months that followed, their relationships were
much more effective.

FEEDBACK

There are a number of premises about how healthy systems operate.
One is that feedback is necessary for a healthy system to function.
Without feedback, the system has no way of knowing if it is pro-

gressing toward its aims, nor can it effectively self-correct. An airline pilot once told me that airplanes seldom travel exactly on course. He estimated that a plane was typically on course about 5% of the time. Built into the airplane's navigational system, however, is a feedback mechanism that tells the computer that the plane is off course, and then the computer corrects the plane. It does this hundreds of times during the course of a normal trip. In this sense, feedback is both neutral and necessary.

Would that human feedback was always so neutral! We often give feedback with a judgmental tone. And even when we give it in a neutral and caring manner, the self-judgment of the receiver causes him to feel stung by the feedback. This is especially true when the feedback is corrective in nature, and even sometimes true when the feedback is affirming. Witness the numerous times you have given someone confirming feedback ("You look lovely today" "What a great job!" "It was one of the kindest things you could have done") and the person receiving the feedback discounts it ("It was nothing." "Anyone would have done the same thing.") This discounting is a reflection of our own negative self-judgment that prevents us from receiving the feedback fully.

Because we often have built in judgments, people and organizational systems often shy away from delivering and receiving feedback—much to the loss of the person or system. One of the most powerful things we consultants can do for an organization is help the system—the people, its teams, the organization—see itself clearly. By providing feedback to the system, or creating conditions where the system can provide feedback to itself, we perform an enormous service for the health and well being of the system. Like the airplane, the information derived from the feedback helps the system make choices that enable it to self-correct.

ASKING QUESTIONS

Many masterful consultants believe that much of the art of consulting has to with asking good questions. Questions often have greater power than answers. Knowing this well, Socrates taught entirely by asking questions. The German poet Rainer Maria Rilke in *Letters to a Young Poet* offers this advice:

> Don't search for the answers which could not be given to you now, because you would not be able to live them. And the point is, to live everything. Live the questions now. Perhaps then, someday far in the future, you will gradually, without even noticing it, live your way in the answer.[6]

Echoing these same sentiments, one masterful consultant had this to say about questions:

> Good consultants have a way of being more in the question, have a sense of asking the right question in the right moment. That rules the process, sometimes profoundly, as opposed to teaching or asserting. The spirit of the work we do, for me, is in the question.

If one of the key criteria for successful consulting is that the client owns the outcome of the consulting to such a powerful degree that the client takes positive and enduring action, and if the key to ownership is thinking it through for themselves, then it would make sense that one of the best ways to create conditions of ownership is by asking the right questions. Witness the following interaction between Bob, a CEO, and Robin (a masterful consultant):

Bob: I am not sure whether I should let go of Andrea, our head of marketing. She is not performing up to what I need, yet I am concerned about letting her go.

Robin: Hmm. What are your concerns?

Bob: Well, we are about to launch a whole new product line and how we position it and market it is crucial for our success. I don't have confidence in Andrea's ability to lead the charge, yet have no one better. She has been a disappointment.

Robin: In what ways?

Bob: (Bob enumerates many concerns as well as the steps he has taken to talk with her, none of which seemed to have made a difference. Robin had been coaching him on this and believes he has done all he could to address the performance issue)

Robin: So what have you been considering?

Bob: I've been considering letting her go, but I'm not sure this is the best time.

Robin: What do you sense as the downside of letting her go?

Bob: For one, Andrea knows the product well, and it will be easier
         for her than to have someone else step in. Also, we have
         made a lot of changes of late in the senior team, and I am
         concerned about the potential disruption on the company
         from yet another change. Finally, she is very well liked, and I
         am afraid that losing Andrea will hurt morale.

Robin: I can appreciate the dilemma.

Bob: So what do you suggest?

Robin: Well, I don't think the answer is altogether obvious. But let
         me ask you: You said that there could be a disruption. Any
         way of testing out the validity of that possibility?

Bob: I guess I am making an assumption that may or may not be
         true. I could talk with a few other members of the senior team
         and get their sense of it.

Robin: How might you do that?

Bob: I'd have to be discreet. I guess I could talk with Terry (head of
         HR) first, and then feel out a couple of others, particularly the
         ones who know I'm disappointed with Andrea. Jim (Sales VP)
         comes to mind.

Robin: I'm wondering what other assumptions might not be true.

Bob: Well, that there is no one to replace her might not be true.
         Come to think of it, I could seek an outside resource for this.
         I know someone in Denver who I used to work with. She
         might be free to fill in, at least temporarily.

Notice that, with the exception of offering an observation or
two, Robin's comments were all questions. And they were real, not
leading questions Robin already knew the answer to. Instead, she
held in her arsenal as a consultant a set of questions that, when
effectively offered, help the client achieve clarity. The goal of mastery is not to prove one's intelligence. It is to enhance the clarity and
capability of the client.

Almost all of the masterful consultants I interviewed valued
their question-asking over their answer-giving. One told the following story depicting the sentiment of many:

> I have a friend running around South America interviewing
> country managers in a pharmaceutical corporation. His ques-

tion was: "What does this work have to do with the reasons you are on earth?" His message was, you are here for a few short years, how does this work contribute? This question has profoundly reformed the purpose and direction of that division of that company. That's what great consultants do. They ask questions that when answered produce a "wow."

Another consultant described the relationship between question-asking and her own intuition.

The first key to my work is making contact. I see my consulting process as forming a relationship. I use my human skills to connect with the person so I can understand who they are, where they are coming from, and what style works best for them. . . . Then I go deeper . . . I ask questions to help establish their current clarity and, using my intuition, I find questions that bring me to understand future possibilities of what they are needing, what they know they need and what they don't know they need but might be of future value to them. One of the key ways I work around defining the future is to listen for what's missing from what they say. I frequently will ask a number of questions and continue to refine my understanding until I get a gestalt of where they are and where I might add value.

So much of the above can be encapsulated in one fundamental principle: *to be drawn toward the mystery of organizations and of life*. Masterful consultants operate from an inner stance that suggests the world is a fascinating place, full of wonder and mystery. Answers are not coins that consultants cleverly pluck from the client's ear, like nightclub magicians. When we finally come upon them, they often seem to have been hiding in plain sight all along. They may even seem obvious in retrospect. The best consultants know their business is not about product (answers) so much as process (questions). And it is in this process of discovery, which is ultimately mysterious and human, that we find our true role.

PART IV

MASTERY IN ACTION

THE MASTER CONSULTANT'S RELATIONSHIP TO SELF

CHAPTER 9

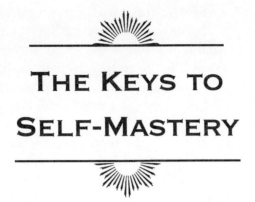

THE KEYS TO
SELF-MASTERY

The outward freedom that we shall attain will
only be in exact proportion to the inward
freedom to which we may have grown at a
given moment. And if this is a correct view of
freedom, our chief energy must be concentrated
on achieving reform from within.

—*Mohandas K. Gandhi*

UNTIL THIS POINT, we have focused on two of the three aspects of consulting mastery—the consultant's relationship to clients and relationship to knowledge. We now turn to the third and last relationship. I believe this one is most important—and the one from which every other aspect of consulting mastery depends. It is the consultant's relationship to self.

As I complete the writing of this chapter, I have just had a unique experience that points to the very essence of consulting mastery as it relates to the self. I am guiding one of my clients through a multi-year organizational transformation process. One of my responsibilities has been to help the client figure out how to measure its progress over time and use that information as feedback and as guidance for future development. As part of this, we have put together a measurement team that has been determining which variables to measure and how to measure them. They have decided to seek a consulting firm to work with the measurement team—one that is expert in designing organizational surveys. To get more acquainted with what is available in the way of survey consultants, they invited nine consulting firms to visit them to share how they approach this kind of work. I have taken part in almost all of these presentations since I will play some role in the survey design and feedback process.

Interestingly, almost all the firms offer the same technology, skill, and method in the survey feedback process. What differentiated them was the way they interacted in the meetings with us. Most tried to convince the team of their survey prowess, taking a sales-like approach. The two firms that rose to the top and made the final cut were different, however. Their bearing and their behavior stood out. Instead of trying to prove their ability, their attitude was one of integrity, partnership, and commitment to the client. They listened to the questions asked, they responded thoughtfully, they seemed genuine in their ability, and they were honest. Their spirit of partnership showed in their behavior. In contrast, while the others talked about the importance of partnership, they pushed their own agenda and expended a lot of energy trying to be impressive.

One consulting firm was particularly *unimpressive* in this regard—the top consultant led with a standard presentation designed to "wow" clients. He kept telling the team how his survey was better than all the rest. It could do things others could not. For example, he claimed that because of the brilliance of the design, the results were far more "actionable" than other surveys. He was also clever in adapting the two-page request the measurement team sent to all consultants into his presentation. Alas, his salesmanship came across as transparent and off-putting to the measurement team. In the end, his survey tool was no different than the others, except for the way the results of his surveys were displayed on a screen. Indeed, his firm could boast a flashier reporting system than the others. But the client wanted substance, not showy graphics. He was quickly rejected, not because his tools and process were lacking, but because he just didn't connect well to the team itself.

The two finalists who were chosen preferred genuine exploration, seeking to interact with the client team in a spirit of partnership. The qualities of their inner self shone through, while the others did not. Tools, techniques, and specialized knowledge are useful to the consultant, but by themselves they can't make the big difference clients seek. Instead of knowledge, the consultant's character—attitude, conduct, and bearing—makes the difference between good and great consulting.

Allow me to illustrate with a personal example from early in my career. The team-building session I was leading was rapidly deteriorating. In a panic, I called Mike McKeon, the consultant I referred to in Chapter 7, for help. "Mike," I said, "this session is terrible! These people just aren't open to looking at themselves. I've got a bunch of lawyers and economists who are *way* too analytical—they just don't get what I'm doing! They're intellectualizing the whole process and completely resistant to change. I'm really frustrated, and the team-building session is rapidly going south." I went on for a few minutes more, explaining all the things I thought I was doing well—and all the ways the participants were just not responding as they were "supposed to."

Mike listened patiently for a couple of minutes and then, with warmth in his tone, said something to me that will be forever etched in my brain. "Keith, you sound like you've passed judgment on the people in the room. Is there any chance that your judgment may be creating and feeding their resistance?"

His comment rattled me for a moment. Once I got my bearings, though, I reluctantly acknowledged that, indeed, I was feeling judgmental and shared openly some of the judgments I was holding. After hearing my thoughts, Mike simply suggested I get in touch with my compassion and respect for these people. It didn't take long for me to realize the wisdom of his suggestion. After a few more minutes of reflection, I began to regain respect and compassion for the participants, recognizing that, in their tendency to intellectualize things, they were actually a lot like me.

I returned from the break and continued the process. The team-building session slowly but surely metamorphosed from a psychological tug-of-war between the participants and myself to a process of give and take that proved very productive.

After the team-building session was over, I reflected on what had happened. It became clear to me that by viewing the client through judgmental eyes, I had set up the conditions for failure. My judgmental stance was felt by the participants in many communications that suggested I was right and they were wrong. Naturally, they resisted what I brought to the team-building process. While on paper everything may have been going according to plan, because of how I brought myself, I was like the conductor of a train heading for a wreck. As soon as I shifted my perspective from that of being judgmental to unconditional positive regard, I was able to get off that track and onto another. The tools and techniques I was using did not change; what changed was my *inner stance*; and that change made all the difference in the world.

Creating organizations and leading them is more than a mere cognitive process. It is also a matter of the heart. Great leaders of organizations understand their organizations as systems—as an interweaving set of forces that together create their results over time. Great leaders of organizations create conditions of trust and openness. Great leaders of organizations are role models. Great leaders of organizations build teams. Great leaders are intelligent strategists. You can't help the leaders of client organizations make this leap without making the same leap yourself. I'm reminded of the saying expressed in Chapter 7: "You can't take a client further than you have taken yourself." To help organizations and leaders become great, you must begin with your own heart.

We don't usually think of management consultants and "heart" in the same thought. But we need to. Too many recommendations of consultants come from the head. The heart goes, shall we say, unconsulted. There is a logic to this. Figuring out why an organization isn't functioning at its optimal level is easy. The hard part is to help it change. Masterful consultants believe that to help organizations truly change at the deepest level, their inner self matters a huge amount, and they develop it consciously and directly. They attend personal growth workshops, they participate in different modes of therapy, they meditate, and they invite feedback. They are lifelong learners of the inner landscape. They know that the most important component of consulting mastery is self-mastery. By self-mastery, I mean the ability to make conscious and wise choices, from an inner stance of self-confidence and self-knowledge.

Consultants who exhibit self-mastery are people who take charge of their own lives while encouraging others to do the same.

They take responsibility for their conditions and the conditions around them. Instead of seeing problems around them, they see opportunities. They work closely with their clients in ways that create opportunities where everyone can win. They have a powerful vision for themselves and for the clients they work with. Most importantly, they take responsibility for their own behavior and for their outcomes.

The following two quotes are from two consultants who echoed the thoughts of almost every other master consultant.

> To really help other people I am consulting I have to be congruent. I believe that we need to partner in the true sense of the word. If I believe that people ought to be clear about what their priorities are and be able to make choices consistent with those priorities, then I have to do the same. When they look at me, I want them to honestly say that I am the role model I am asking them to be. As consultants we have that obligation.

> I don't think about being a role model in my practice as much as I think about acting the way I want to act. I'm sure it turns out that I am a model, but it is not a conscious part of my practice. What I am always conscious of is following the process and being true to my principles.

This ability to live with integrity while helping others do the same did not come overnight for these consultants. It took years. They worked at it, and they keep working at it. To them, living with integrity is a challenge from which there is no respite. To them, mastering consulting and mastering self are one and the same. The clients I interviewed felt the same way. The qualities they mentioned most frequently of the best consultants they ever worked with were things like integrity, vulnerability, sensitivity, respect, and deep listening. This is the stuff of self-mastery, and while it is hard to "put one's finger on it," the feeling one gets from it is powerful and enduring. If consultants are makers of change, this sense of self is the engine of change. Because it is real, change becomes possible.

As I look into my own experience on the path of learning, and as I listen to elders whom I respect deeply, I believe there are three keys to self-mastery: being guided by an inner compass, self-knowledge, and self-acceptance. From these keys comes the experience of confidence, vulnerability, authenticity, commitment to learning, and ease of interaction. They produce the requisite qualities of consulting greatness, and they are all produced from within. Let's explore each key and its implications.

KEY ONE: BEING GUIDED BY AN INNER COMPASS

The core experience of people who exhibit self-mastery is one of having a clear internal compass—a clear sense of one's purpose, beliefs, values, and aims in life. To use a concept popularized years ago, they are inner directed, rather than outer directed.[1] When I feel deep in my bones that I am guided by an internal compass, I feel two things: first, a peaceful sense of self-control, and second, the absence of any need to control others.

By-products of this feeling include inner solidity (a sense of being OK and "together") and outer spaciousness (a sense of possibility with others rooted in deep mutual respect). People who experience themselves as inner directed have many choices in front of them, and know that they are the chooser, not others. People who are inner directed are highly resilient. Instead of seeing the conditions around them as affecting them, they see themselves as affecting those conditions. They have a sense of control of where they are going; they have a sense of responsibility for creating their career. As a result they naturally tend to be more successful and more satisfied with their work.

IT MATTERS NOT HOW STRAIT THE GATE,
HOW CHARGED WITH PUNISHMENTS THE SCROLL,
I AM THE MASTER OF MY FATE;
I AM THE CAPTAIN OF MY SOUL.
—FROM WILLIAM ERNEST HENLEY'S POEM
"INVICTUS"

Inner direction is an attitude masterful consultants claim in their lives, not something that is bestowed on them. It is not created by managers, by clients, by other people, or by one's family. It is created as a result of the consultant's internal commitment to extraordinary results and extraordinary experience in life. Doesn't this make sense? The more a person allows others to determine his fate, the more likely he becomes victim to their choices. They are the ones in charge of his life, not because they chose it, but because he did. And he probably did it unconsciously. We all do, from time to time.

Many people insist that they are inner directed, unaware of the subtle and unconscious ways they hand power over to others. For example, while you may believe you are in control of your own choices in a given situation, perhaps you are playing out an unconscious expectation of your parents. A consultant in a workshop I once led worked to make a lot of money as a consultant. He believed that money was a primary measure of success. Upon deeper scrutiny, he discovered he was fulfilling an expectation his father had of him, to be powerful and influential in life. He remembered how his father showered him with love when he was the best in his class, and withdrew approval when he was not. He also began to recognize the many ways his father had communicated to him that, to live a good life, one had to make a lot of money. These were his father's values, and honestly come by. Upon deeper examination, he realized that they were not *his* values, and that he was playing out a script for his life that his father had written; he was not his own author. So while he felt he was making choices for his consulting career, they weren't his own choices at all. They were his inner child's way of satisfying his father.

So many of the consultants I interviewed exuded a solid inner compass. As I interviewed them, I had the sense I was talking with people who knew who they were, what their purpose in life was, and what their path was. I felt moved to be in their presence, as they spoke with quiet, unassuming authority. The words of two reflected the feelings of many.

I have always stood back a little from becoming a loyalist in organizations in a blind way—of becoming the stereotypical organization man. A key element today in successful consulting involves looking at one's self as the location of authority as opposed to the location of authority being external.

I often ask myself if I am part of the problem or part of the solution. I ask myself if I am dealing with tough issues, facing them head on. The big question for me in my career is: how have I really been able to influence these systems? When you are more masterful, then you really do have influence. That comes out of knowing more of who you are, knowing what your work really is about—knowing the stance that you are taking and willing to take.

KEY TWO: SELF-KNOWLEDGE

Carl Jung, the great psychoanalyst and explorer of the human psyche, laid down the gauntlet for self-knowledge better than anyone I have known. He said:

> Nowhere are we closer to the sublime secret of all origination than in the recognition of our own selves, whom we always think we know already. Yet we know the immensities of space better than we know our own depths, where—even though we do not understand it—we can listen directly to the throb of creation itself.[2]

Jung was not the first to call us to look inside, just perhaps the most poignant. Etched into the stone walls of Apollo's temple at Delphi are written the words, "Know thyself." Socrates too, saw inner knowledge as the key to a whole and meaningful life. Each is calling for the same thing: *Seek inner knowledge first.*

Great consultants demonstrate outward effectiveness because they have a deep understanding and capability with their inner self. The most important aspect of their self-knowledge has to do with the distinction between acting from ego and from inner wisdom. When masterful consultants work with a client, they put their ego aside and let wisdom be their guide. Let's explore what I mean by *ego* and *wisdom.*

For the sake of simplicity and clarity, I am using the term *ego* here in a Buddhist way, to refer to the part of us that protects ourselves. The Buddhist view of ego is that it is the neurotic "self." Buddhists contend that we form beliefs about the world, and people within it, and that these beliefs then form judgments. We pigeonhole others and decide what we like and don't like, all through the subjective lens of the ego. Our ego sees the world in a way that helps us feel safe. It protects our own current views, causing us to believe we are right and others wrong. Ego raises individual selves up while simultaneously lowering others down. My ego wants me to believe I know better than others, and that I am infallible.

Wisdom, on the other hand, is the ability to see the world and take action within it, from a place of peace, self-solidity, compassion, and non-attachment to outcome. All wisdom teachings, from Zen Buddhism to Sufism to that of the Toltec tradition share the idea that inner peace and outer effectiveness go hand in hand. Inner peace ushers in a deeper sense of knowing. This is in direct contrast with the shallow sense of acquiring facts or information that our society tends to value. When we view the world from ego, we see through a distorted lens. From ego, my needs are driving how I see the world, and I do not know this, so I can see in no other way. When I see the world from inner wisdom, there is no personalized need present in my seeing, and so I am able to see and act more clearly.

Masterful consultants seek to understand themselves, to understand how ego plays such a central role in our functioning, and to learn instead to let their deeper wisdom be their guide. Masterful consultants quiet the inner stirring, and seek to act from inner knowing—the inner self.

When we encounter and experience the world from the lens of our inner self, we no longer need to act from ego. We recognize that ego causes us to inflate our ideas, our views, and our judgment. We recognize that the ego is no longer the center of identity, and its importance is reduced. In its place is an ability to see more fully, more openly, more wisely. Instead of allowing our ego to make choices in the service of the ego, such as buying an audacious car or home, we make choices in the service of humanity. In short, by connecting to and operating from inner self, we no longer need to prove our self-worth and our competence. Instead, we gain many benefits:

- A deeper understanding of our psyche and how it functions

- Better management of our psychological makeup

- Fewer psychological battles and fewer battles with others

- Greater inner resourcefulness, so we are able to act from stronger inner states

- Inner freedom, inner peace that comes from detachment

The journey toward self-mastery is a journey of self-knowledge that has no end. The more you know yourself, your motivations, needs, drives, and ways to draw on even deeper clarity and wiser action, the more effective you become. Not surprisingly, all the masterful consultants I interviewed, and all that I know, value this journey tremendously, perhaps more than anything else in their lives. Here are some of their words:

> There is always the potential to use my power as a consultant in ways that act out unresolved issues left over in my own development. That means the potential for abuse of clients is always present. This is a serious matter both in terms of effectiveness and in terms of the way I communicate about my openness to feedback. Intimidation, for example, is a power concept that is often present in most client situations. If I am not paying attention to myself, I won't know my involvement of intimidation on the part of other people. If I haven't dealt with my own issues of power, I risk hurting others.

> The "use of self" work occupies most of my current teaching, my work as a consultant, and as an educator. I'm always working on my use of self as a change agent, or as an agent of stability for that matter.

> The use of self actually says: Pay attention to what you're doing and what is happening as you interact with other people. . . .

Self is the part we have the most control over. Changing other people is an extraordinarily difficult path.

KEY THREE: SELF-ACCEPTANCE

All people on the journey toward self-mastery know that the process of learning is a never-ending process of self-acceptance. A simple truism is inherent in this process: The more you judge yourself, the harder it is to see yourself. The harder it is to see yourself, the less you know. The less you know about yourself, the more you take action driven by psychological needs or projections rather than from wisdom.

Self-acceptance means that I accept all of the forces inside of me, dark and light, shallow and wise. By acceptance I do not mean that I believe all these forces are good, for goodness and badness are merely judgments, and judgment moves me further from acceptance. By acceptance I see that all of these marvelous forces exist, and I accept that they are all natural parts of me. I seek to understand these inner forces and channel them in ways that serve people.

Masterful consultants who are guided by self-acceptance also naturally accept others as they are, without judgment. Through acceptance of self and others, they are able to act wisely. They talk not in terms of goodness or badness, but in terms of what works. Good and bad, right and wrong are absolute terms, ones that masterful consultants shy away from. To masterful consultants, there is no good or bad, there is only what works or doesn't in a given situation given one's goals. For example, when debriefing a meeting to discuss how well it went, masterful consultants will encourage a conversation about what worked well and what didn't instead of a conversation about good and bad. Things that didn't go well are treated as opportunities for learning. The participants in the meeting experience the consultant as nonjudgmental, and so they will participate in the process more fully, more freely.

Ron Tilden, one of the best consultants I know, uses this principle actively. He enters a meeting with a calm self-assurance derived from self-acceptance. Whenever I meet him, I find his countenance to be inviting, his manner fully at ease. I imagine that if clients feel the same, their hearts open and their trust level is high. Others

I have seen who exhibit mastery have the same effect. "I am just fine," suggests the stance borne out of self-acceptance, "and so are you. Now let's get to work."

These three factors: self-authority, self-knowledge, and self-acceptance, together allow the masterful consultant to effectively live by a set of principles. These principles form the basis of the character of masterful consultants, and guide them in whatever they do.

SELF-MASTERY AND THE MASTERFUL CONSULTANT'S CREDO

If it is true that all roads of the inner journey lead to the inner self, and that deep down we are all the same and all connected, then it is natural that all masterful consultants operate from a similar source and have a similar set of principles that guide their behavior. I call these principles *the masterful consultant's credo,* not to rigidify it, but to suggest that this set of universal values translates into consistent and effective action. The credo is often unspoken. Rather, it lives deep within each of the consultants I interviewed, and in each of the consultants that the clients I interviewed respect the most.

I also observe that when I act consistent with this set of principles, I am significantly more effective. In many cases, when I have been less successful as a consultant, I can trace a line back to having wavered from one or more of these. As discussed in Chapter 2, the four principles that make up the masterful consultant's credo are shown here again.

THE MASTERFUL CONSULTANT'S PRINCIPLES OF CONDUCT

1. ALWAYS TELL THE TRUTH, AT THE DEEPEST LEVELS
2. COMMIT TO LEARNING—FOR SELF AND FOR THE CLIENT
3. BRING MY WHOLE SELF IN FULL PARTNERSHIP
4. PLAY A BIG GAME

Self-mastery, through self-knowledge and self-acceptance, produces a natural way of being that results in greater success in the consulting process. It is a well-earned success, derived from years of work on developing one's inner self. Perhaps it is because it requires work that so few climb this mountain. Those who make the climb reap the rewards of greater success and inner contentment.

To understand how inner self-mastery translates into outer behavior, let's look at each principle of the credo more fully. The following four chapters deal with each principle and its implications for consulting mastery.

CHAPTER 10

HONESTY AT THE DEEPEST LEVEL

Truth is within ourselves.

—*Robert Browning*

IN THE YEAR 2002, a subtle, yet troubling event occurred in the consulting industry. Few in the outside world noticed it or paid attention to it, yet it marked a clear shift in the integrity of the consulting profession. The Association of Management Consulting Firms, the leading industry association, under pressure from its members, changed a piece of its code of ethics relative to integrity. As of 1969, the code of ethics read: "Not to serve clients under terms or conditions . . . which impair objectivity, independence, or integrity." As of 2002, it reads: ". . . immediately acknowledge any influences to objectivity . . ." In effect, the current code says a consultant can violate integrity, just as long as he or she acknowledges it. And indeed, that is how so many people in the field of consulting conduct themselves. Money or power becomes an attractive tonic, and actions that violate our integrity are perpetrated by almost everyone. We need look no further than the Enron debacle and Andersen Consulting's participation in it for evidence.

No different than any other profession, we face the struggle of doing the safe thing or the financially attractive thing versus doing the right thing. And all too often we choose the former. Masterful consultants choose the latter.

As I write the first draft of this chapter, I am struggling with a crucial issue in one of my client organizations. The situation is familiar, one I have faced many times in my career, as have all experienced consultants. The outcome of this situation is yet to be determined, since there is an action I know I must take, and have not yet taken. It speaks to the heart of what consulting with honesty is all about. I will share the situation with you now, not knowing how it will end. Later on, at the end of the chapter, I will share the outcome.

My work with one of my long-standing clients is reaching a plateau. I feel stuck. The senior team and the CEO of the company, Bill, are at odds with one another, and each is expecting me to fix the other. Bill is a very bright, highly authoritative-style leader, who has very effectively helped take the company from the startup phase, through an IPO, to being a growing company in a repressed economy. His direct reports see Bill as a bold decision maker and a knowledgeable leader. They also experience him as a micromanager, making too many detailed decisions himself and not empowering them to make key decisions.

Many times the CEO has asked me to coach some of his direct reports, wanting them to exhibit a more authoritative style. At present, I feel like a Ping-Pong ball between the two parties. Each wants to change the other. The net result is that while I have been modestly successful in helping both parties grow, the central disconnect between the two parties regarding leadership style still remains. So far I have not been successful in helping them address that central disconnect.

I've been aware of this disconnect since the time I began to work with the client. I know I have been avoiding the issue, fearful that it's a make-or-break issue fraught with potential landmines. Frankly, I've been afraid of going into the issue with them, failing, and losing my work with them. In the back of my mind I am also aware that I am the fourth in a series of consultants they have hired to work with the leadership of the company in helping it grow, and none of my predecessors have stuck with this client. I believe none of them were credible in Bill's eyes, and I have managed to work with him so far because I have earned his trust and respect, while helping his company grow. I know I must confront these issues.

I will now share with you my thoughts about honesty and its relationship to consulting mastery. Later I will return to the above saga and share with you what I did and how it turned out.

HONESTY IS NOT AN ABSOLUTE

Most of us think about honesty in a binary way, drawing a black and white line between truth and untruth. You either tell the truth or you don't. This decision, while it makes the situation very plain, sidesteps everyday reality, which is usually much more ambiguous, with many shades of gray.

Honesty may not really be a black and white issue. For instance, I can be outwardly honest and inwardly withholding— passively dishonest. Or I can be partly honest and partly lying, that is segmenting my honesty into parts. Or I may tell you honestly how I feel, yet not be aware of other feelings that are also present—a dishonesty that begins with self-deception or denial. And so on.

You, the reader, may also say to yourself, "I am a very honest person. I cannot remember the last time I lied." I encourage you, however, to challenge your own self-perception and consider the much more subtle and unconscious ways in which you (and I) are not honest, and explore those. If honesty is a continuum, then the question is not whether I am "honest" or not. The question is: How do I move toward greater and greater honesty with others and myself? Truth is a spectrum, and consulting mastery demands we march toward the light that is brightest.

MOMENTS OF TRUTH

Organizations face many moments of truth. Some that come to mind are:

- Confronting a difficult issue

- Finding the deeper cause of a problem

- Making a "bet the farm" decision

- Communicating fully to all people

A moment of truth is any crucial dilemma—when, at the fork in the road, the firm must choose which way to go. On one path are the deeper truths that must be spoken for the organization to progress. With this pathway comes fear and risk. On the other path is the possibility to shy away from truth and remain safe, comfortable, and stuck. Organizations that take the first fork consistently risk loss but have a greater upside for extraordinary performance. Organizations that take the second fork are safe, but are rarely industry leaders.

I recently witnessed a beautiful example of what I mean. I was facilitating a client meeting. The CEO and his senior executives were all there. They were faced with the possibility of losing their business and with a major decision that would potentially seal the fate of the company. Instead of shying away from the issues at hand, each executive, one at a time, spoke vulnerably and directly about the mistakes they made that got them to this point. A couple executives admitted they operated from fear as they held back information and even swept some dirt under the rug. Another admitted feeling shame over not having lived the core values she held dearly. No one blamed anyone in the meeting. It was simply a meeting during which each expressed nakedly and vulnerably multiple truths that got them in the pickle they were in. With some guidance, they then sought to unravel the mess. Not easy to do, but impossible without the truth on the table.

I have seen the beauty of countless acts of courage—grace under pressure. They are moments when fear is talking, and yet our wisdom knows that honesty is required.

In many ways, masterful consulting is a process of helping the client face multiple moments of truth and take that first fork. To do so requires that consultants be walking examples of courage, principally the courage to speak the truth. For me it is that simple. While of course there is so much more to masterful consulting, it is at the very least about choosing honesty over self-protection. In the end, the only thing that keeps us from being honest is the need to self-protect. Great consultants know this, and choose to see the bigger system as their responsibility and tell their truth, regardless of the personal impact on themselves. If we are to truly be committed to the client's well-being, even over our own, and if the client is the

---

FEAR, RISK, AND LIVING LIFE FULLY

A colleague of mine once told me she spent years searching for the key to effective communication and never found it. Instead, she discovered the devil. She said the devil is the part of us that wants to believe we can live life fully and be comfortable.

---

whole system, then speaking honestly, speaking our truth, is the only game in town.

HONESTY IN TWO AREAS

Telling the truth has two faces to it, each of which is important—telling the truth to others, and telling the truth to oneself. In the story I began telling above, I had both avoided telling Bill the truth about the impact of his leadership and avoided telling myself the truth about the impact of my avoidance.

HONESTY WITH OTHERS. The principle of honesty is simple. Tell the truth, no matter what. It doesn't mean tell every truth. It means tell the truth when the truth is meaningful. At any given moment, I may have a feeling, a judgment, a thought, etc. about a person or a situation. Telling these thoughts might be the truth, yet have no meaning. I have lots of thoughts. If I were to tell them all, always, I'd be a nonstop chatterbox. Many of my thoughts don't deserve to be spoken. But those thoughts that have meaning or purpose need to be spoken. If there is a rupture in my relationship with another person I care about, I need to speak the truth. If there is feedback to another that is part of the explicit coaching relationship I have established with that person, then this is a truth to be spoken. If I am asked my point of view because another person seeks my counsel, then my honest point of view is a truth to be spoken.

Honesty is not something you do. It is a *place* from which to act. It is not a decision, it comes from the gut. To understand this, one need look no further than what is required to be honest, especially when it matters. It matters when something is at risk. Therefore honesty—the kind that truly matters—requires courage.

Interestingly, at the root of the word courage is the French word *coeur,* which means *heart.* Honesty at its most brilliant is an act from the heart.

As in any principle, it is a choice, one that I make moment by moment. I believe there are risks to being honest, and risks to not. When confronting a difficult truth, we can sometimes get burned. Yet if we choose the safe route, we are always avoiding something. We are letting our fear or our ego guide us, rather than wisdom. The key is in finding ways to tell the truth, fully, and yet with compassion. When people understand that we care about them and about the relationship, then telling the truth is in the service of something deeper. The truth is in the service of the relationship, of them, and of learning.

Recently, Chris, a masterful consultant in her own right, had an opportunity to experience the dilemmas embedded in this choice. One of her favorite clients was quietly in the process of seeking to hire a new president. For a variety of reasons, the CEO felt strongly that the search for this person needed to be done without the knowledge of members of the company, with the exception of a small handful of people, including Chris, who were on the interviewing team.

The company had just hired a new head of Research and Development (we'll call him Ted), someone who would naturally report to the new president, once he or she was on board. The CEO asked Chris to meet with Ted, get to know him, and explore ways she might be able to support a smooth transition into his new role. In the course of conversation, Chris asked Ted his thoughts about the upcoming change in structure and the introduction of the new president. Ted's eyes lit up, reporting that he had not heard about this change, to which Chris quietly gasped in response, realizing immediately her gaffe. Ted pointed out with some consternation that he was not "in the loop." Chris told him she had thought he would have known and that she had promised the CEO to keep the information confidential and clearly she had made a mistake here in sharing the information with Ted so casually.

To protect Chris, Ted graciously offered to keep his newly found knowledge under wraps. By offering this, Chris now faced the dilemma of either telling the CEO that Ted now knows about the hire, thereby admitting her violation of confidentiality, or keeping it to herself, thereby sweeping the fact under the rug. It would also require that when informed through more appropriate channels, Ted would have to pretend to be learning about it for the first time— in other words, he would have to lie. Moreover, he would have to go about his business with the knowledge of the hiring, without letting the CEO know that he now knows.

[Before reading further and finding out what Chris did, you may want to take a moment and think about how you would handle the situation yourself.]

In thinking it through and weighing all the options, Chris knew that she needed to admit her mistake to the CEO. Her reasoning was threefold. First, she did not want to put Ted in a position to lie. Second, if she was to earn Ted's trust and continue to earn the trust of the company, lying or avoiding facing the consequences of a lie did not put her in a position of being trustworthy. Third, she had developed a very open, honest relationship with the CEO, and were she to withhold her error from him, she was participating in a process that was not worthy of his trust. While it was enticing to consider not telling the CEO—after all, he would never know—it felt right to tell him, and to do so immediately.

She went straight into the CEO's office with some fear that she had not only violated her agreement of confidentiality but also put her relationship with him at risk. After all, she was aware that quite possibly he might think that if she violated this agreement, what other agreements might she violate in the future? Like any masterful consultant, she took her fear in hand and let the CEO know that she had "spilled the beans." She pointed out that it was an unconscious act on her part, having made an assumption that was clearly not true.

The CEO responded with great generosity, pointing out that he had not even realized Ted did not know. "I thought all the VPs knew," he said, "and it was an oversight that Ted was not included in this group. I actually can't remember at this point who knows and who doesn't, so it's no big deal that you told him. Listen, Chris, your error was based on an assumption that was understandable—

Ted should have been in the loop. I really appreciate your honesty, and it is one of the reasons why I like to work with you. I have a lot of trust in you, and that doesn't come easily for me."

INTEGRITY IS NOT AN ACT.
IT IS A STATE OF BEING.

I believe Mark Twain once said something to the effect that being honest is easy because you don't have to remember things. It frees my mind when I make a commitment to honesty, all the time. I found the masterful consultants I interviewed to be remarkably without pretension, willing to discuss their successes as well as their failures. They reported instances where their honesty was crucial to their success and their lessons from the moments they held back their honesty out of self-protection. Along with the other principles embedded in the master consultant's credo, it was an often-mentioned source of their success.

> In the deepest levels of my being there is a sense of wanting to speak my truth and do it in a way that speaks to my values, to what I hold as important. It allows me to make tough choices when I feel like I need to take a stand. I try not to take work just for the money. That doesn't serve the client or me. I take the work because it's consistent with who I am.

> The key is to continue to grow my "being" in the work. That's what this work is all about. When there is fear there is also great energy. The key when one is feeling fear is to take this big breath and be clear in myself about how I need to move forward. When I'm in my being, I can speak the truth, regardless of the fear.

In addition to being honest, many spoke about their ability to cut to the chase. They believed, and I would confirm, that one of the predictors of great consulting is in the ability to be straight and clean or, in the words of one masterful consultant, to "cut through the crap."

I experience myself as very direct and at the same time always on the other person's side. That combination of being non-judgmental and very direct is very potent. I once said to a client, "I don't understand, you are ruining the company. Why are you doing this? Three previous consultants have told you the same thing. Let's talk about it." I said this in such a way that he felt my concern for him. He knew I wanted him to be successful, and that I knew he wanted to be successful. So I was free to ask him what is really going on.

What I bring is my ability to open things up. I'm willing to stay in the conflict and the pain. My daughter one time jokingly asked me, "How many people did you make cry today?" I get to the real issue. I bring a willingness to get to the real issues and not to use all our techniques and terminology to cover up and protect. Let's talk about it straight and with compassion.

Being straight also means being willing to leave the situation because it does not fit one's values or because it is the best thing to shake up the client system. One consultant I interviewed spoke about a situation where the client said that he wanted the consultant to help him "shove this stuff down people's throats. We have this time pressure, and we need to move fast." The consultant replied, "I'm worth whatever you're going to pay me, but I'm not going to do it under those conditions."

In response to further cajoling from the client, the consultant said to the client, "Sorry, I can't stand for that. That's not how it works for me." The client saw the consultant's immovability and acquiesced. So many of the consultants I interviewed felt that not only was it crucial that they be honest because of their own values but also to succeed with the client. In the words of one, "that's where our real work shows up."

Note: The client won't always acquiesce. Sometimes telling the truth results in the end of the relationship. But worse things can happen—like continuing work that is not consistent with your purpose, values, or soul. You can live without those clients.

The clients I interviewed all echoed the importance of honesty and integrity. The best consultants impressed them with their forthrightness. Many commented that the best consultant was always direct—never afraid to provoke strong emotions in others. Moreover, they were more than willing to call out senior people whose behavior or actions were problematic. Here's what one client had to say, in thinking about the best consultant he ever worked with:

> He was very willing to take risks with us. There were a lot of tears, anger and emotion and he wasn't the least bit afraid to provoke all that. Other consultants seem to be afraid—they back off. He took us there and kept us there. He wasn't too polite or too nice, and he talked to us in a way that wasn't politically correct. Instead, he got right to the heart of the matter.

Another said the same thing in different words, when reflecting on the three best consultants she ever worked with:

> All three were direct in the sense that they said what they thought; they didn't pull punches. They were not slick. Instead they were straightforward and matter-of-fact. They talked openly and candidly.

Reflecting back on their practice, some of the consultants I interviewed said the biggest mistake they ever made was to take work they shouldn't have taken, that didn't allow them to tell the truth. They spoke about this being an early lesson, one they took to heart, which was a key to later success. The following quote echoed the feelings of many.

> I can think of three of four times early on in my career where I really wish I'd said to a CEO: "Look, if you're not willing to deal with this issue, it's not worth my time or your money." Now I confront these kinds of issues. I will tell a client, "Hey, you say you're happy with what is happening. Well I'm not. We could do so much more."

In the end, the essence of honesty with others can be understood as the tension between telling the truth and avoiding the truth to protect oneself. Honesty is easy when there are no consequences, but it sends shivers through us when the consequences are grave. Great consulting has to do with the path less taken—the courage to tell the truth, even when there is potential for personal loss.

HONESTY WITH ONESELF. One cannot be honest with others without being honest with oneself. I believe that self-honesty is actually harder to come by than honesty with others. Sir Gawain, noted among Knights of the Round Table for his extraordinary integrity, teaches us an important lesson about honesty. See the complete story on the next page.

This story reveals the standards upon which society measures what is noble and great. Through the respect he earns from the Green Knight, Gawain demonstrates he exemplifies honesty. Yet Sir Gawain understands that the standard within is far more important than the standard without. He rejects the honor he did not truly deserve. He reveals to us that nobility comes not from our actions alone, but also from our inner framework.

In contrast to Sir Gawain, most of us prefer to turn a blind eye to our own patterns, particularly the myriad of ways we do not live consistently with our own standards of honesty and integrity. We lie to ourselves, perhaps far more often than we lie to others. Our ego plays a big role here; protecting us from seeing ourselves, and in so doing, creates a powerful chink in our own self-awareness and therefore mastery.

Perhaps an example from my own life will be instructive. I believe that I am a very open and flexible person, and I find it hard to see the ways I am rigid. My wife and teenage son have no such disability. For years they have been trying to give me feedback about how my inner rigidity affects them. Admitting the truth of their feedback to myself has been difficult and has flown in the face of my self-concept. Finally, many months ago, I had a moment of self-honesty. I began to admit how I may be far more rigid than I make myself out to be. The problem is that I am quite open intellectually but a lot less open emotionally. They were trying to tell me about the emotional rigidity, and I wouldn't let myself hear it.

As I let in the possibility that my rigidity may be more

SIR GAWAIN AND THE GREEN KNIGHT

In the midst of a lavish celebration of Christmas in Camelot, the home of King Arthur and his Knights of the Round Table, a giant stranger, adorned in green, bursts onto the scene. The stranger explains that he has come to this famously valiant court to play a Christmas game. Whoever agrees to play this game will be allowed to strike him with a battle-ax on the spot, in the middle of the room; in exchange, the green stranger will strike a return blow upon the volunteer a year and a day hence. To protect the honor of the Knights, Sir Gawain agrees. The stranger gives the battle-ax to Gawain, who cleaves off the Green Knight's head in one mighty blow. But miraculously the knight does not die, as the body of the Green Knight picks up his own severed head, which speaks to Gawain. The knight charges Gawain to meet him at the Green Chapel next New Year's morning, so that he may receive his exchange blow.

True to his word, the following year, Sir Gawain sets off on a long and arduous journey to meet his challenge. Just before he arrives near the Chapel, he is invited to stay at a castle nearby for a welcome rest. He meets the lord and the lady of the castle and is given safe harbor but in return for their hospitality, the lord of the castle enacts a bargain. Gawain is required to share with the lord any gifts he receives while the lord is away hunting and in return the lord will do the same with him.

Two nights in a row while the lord is away, the enchanting and beautiful lady of the castle attempts to seduce Gawain. Both nights Gawain does not succumb to her advances. Instead he accepts a token kiss on the cheek. Each time the next day, Gawain gifts the lord with the kiss without telling him the source, which was not a part of the bargain. On the third night, the lady tries to seduce him once more, but again he does not give in to her

emotional, I began to see the truth of their feedback. Now I am working on becoming more energetically flexible—more at ease in my body. This work is having a noticeable positive effect, particularly with my relationship with my son. He and I are becoming more playful with each other, and our relationship is warmer than it has ever been. While I have much more learning to do to get to a place in myself of the kind of inner fluidity I seek, I have penetrated the barrier of self-delusion, and with it has come greater capability as a father and a husband.

The same level of self-honesty works in my consulting practice. I am no different than anyone else in this respect. From self-honesty coupled with trust in my inner wisdom has come greater competence in my work with clients. This is not always the case

wiles. In respect, she offers him a kiss once more and a green sash as a token of her appreciation. He accepts and the next day gives the lord a kiss, but does not give him the sash, knowing that this would automatically reveal the source of the kiss. In so doing, he kept her honor and the honor of the lord, yet at the same time violated his bargain.

Finally the day of reckoning arrives, and Sir Gawain makes his way to the home of the Green Knight. The giant knight welcomes Gawain, praising him for maintaining his part of the agreement. He tells Gawain to place his head down on a tabletop to receive his destiny. As a man of honor, the terrified but resolute Gawain exposes his neck to receive the fated blow. The green giant feigns two blows to the head. On the third stroke, the green giant splits the skin on Gawain's neck but that is all the injury done. The giant explains to the surprised Gawain that he is in fact servant to the sorceress Morgan le Fay. Morgan engineered the entire game to challenge the valor of King Arthur and his knights.

Continuing the explanation, the giant points out that the two feinted ax strokes represent the first two days of the game when Gawain faithfully shared the gifts with the lord of the castle. But that third day, Gawain, having concealed the green sash from the lord, was punished by the slight scrape on his neck. "No more than this is deserved," said the giant, "for you, Sir Gawain, are the finest man I have ever known and your only failure stems from your love of life." To honor his valor, courage, and honesty, the giant urges Gawain to keep the gift of the sash that will protect him for the rest of his life. But Gawain is harsher on himself, cursing his cowardice and covetousness and rejects the gift of the green sash because, in spite of the honor bestowed upon him, Sir Gawain did not deem himself worthy.

with many consultants whose drive for money, status, or power causes them to be less than fully honest. Many consultants will prostitute themselves and justify their choices by saying it's about business. To some, that may be true. To masterful consultants, business and honesty cannot be separate. To them, it's just good business to be forthright and honest.

Masterful consultants are aware that the desire for money and power lives within all of us. To deny it is to be ruled by it. To own it results in the possibility of choosing integrity in the face of being pulled by fear or by hunger for money.

To many of the consultants I interviewed, choosing to be honest is an ongoing choice, not an automatic experience. Here are some of the words of the consultants I interviewed.

One of my major lessons as a consultant is to realize I am responsible for the intentional consequences of my behavior as well as the unintentional consequences. Generally, if something shows up on my work that doesn't sit well, I look at the unintentional consequences of my behavior—I look at both what I said or didn't say, what I did or didn't do. My pattern is to use these things that don't sit well as opportunities to get clearer about myself.

When I first started doing this work with managers, I didn't realize how many issues I had with people in positions of authority. There was a significant part of me that wanted to nail those bastards, and I was using the guise of being this sweet, understanding, caring consultant to do the nailing.

We [in this work] are always trying to "fix" people. There is a big part of me that wants to help people whether they want help or not. We are just as twisted as others. Our twisting often has to do with this need to help or our avoidance of conflict by having rules around us so we don't fight and get beat up as some of us did as kids. Or the need to be good so people won't see the bad side of us. Our shadows feed our entry and presence in this work just as much as others' shadows feed their work.

Note that this honesty does not come alone. It's a package deal and must come with self-compassion and compassion for others. Honesty with self-judgment is hard and painful and often results in the behavior of a pushme/pullyou, the mythical two-headed animal in the Dr. Doolittle stories. I want self-honesty but it comes with a bite when I am judgmental of self. The more the bite, the more my ego shies away from it. By contrast, when honesty is coupled with self-compassion, the learning from honesty goes down much more easily.

Indeed, one of my central experiences in talking with all of these consultants was their ease. They were comfortable in their body and so when they spoke about life's lessons, their words came naturally and easily.

While honesty is the inner stance from which masterful consultants take action, the action is not honesty alone but honesty coupled with enormous generosity of spirit. Consulting mastery, self-honesty, and compassion go hand in hand. I say compassion because when you mine the depths of your soul, without judgment, compassion for others naturally follows. I have found that the more I understand myself, and trust myself, and the more I accept my own foibles, the more I am compassionate with others. The more compassionate I am, the more I am able to be honest with others in a way they can hear me.

This conclusion was echoed in many ways as the masterful consultants I interviewed talked about the many instances they confronted difficult situations and came through successfully on the other side. Their success, I believe, was due to their ability to confront issues with care and compassion.

Ultimately, it all adds up to one's ability to "walk the talk." We talk a lot in the consulting business about walking the talk. But only a rare few incorporate it into their lives; the rest get confused by the potential for money and power. Said one consultant:

> Probably the most important thing that comes to mind about
> myself is living what I say, walking the talk, being a model.
> Putting my "being" first and having that be important in the
> conversation in the service of modeling it. . . . It may mean I
> have to go outside my comfort zone to maintain my own being
> so I can deliver the work from a place of authenticity and
> integrity in myself. When I manage that boundary well and
> still deliver service, I have a much deeper impact than just the
> content of my guidance.

AFTER DOING SOME SOUL-SEARCHING

It is now three weeks after I wrote what you just read. I have been reflecting upon my work with the client I spoke of at the beginning of the chapter. I was all too aware that I had been protecting myself by avoiding the issues. About two weeks ago I decided I needed to confront this issue head-on with Bill the CEO and share with him my thoughts about the dynamics between him and the senior team, and the consequences of these dynamics for the company as a whole. I decided that while I value my relationship with this client,

I have been a hindrance to their greater success by my own avoidance of this central disconnect between the senior members. So I set up a meeting with Bill and told him I believed there is a disconnect between him and his senior team. He agreed wholeheartedly and pointed to a myriad of ways "they just don't get it."

I listened openly to his point of view, then told him I thought it had some validity. At the same time I said he was not facing the other side of the issue, namely his style of leadership. "Bill, it is not just them. The rift has a lot to do with your style of leadership, too. Many of your senior people prefer a different style of leadership than yours and find some features of your style disempowering to them and to others."

Bill responded with anger and frustration. "I don't believe it. If I had stronger leaders, I would let go more. I just can't seem to trust them."

"I can appreciate that," I replied. "And yet there is still an issue for you to look at, and I am concerned that if you do not face this part of your own leadership, you will lose the company."

We went back and forth for about an hour, with Bill getting defensive on many points along the way. In each case, I responded with understanding, and at the same time, not letting him off the hook. At the end of the meeting, he decided that he wanted to have me facilitate a senior team offsite to get to the heart of the matter. We discussed what the offsite would look like and the importance of him being open to learning.

The offsite was quite successful and since then, I have had a series of difficult, and at the same time, extremely fruitful conversations with Bill and others. The issue is out in the open, and he is struggling mightily to adjust his style while, at the same time, remaining true to who he is. The company continues to use my counsel and guidance and we have confronted many difficult issues since. Bill has taken a number of steps to let go of his vise-like grip on the company and to encourage others to make decisions. At the same time, the tension between his style and the preferences of others remains present, although less so.

We are about to have another offsite to explore the issue more and find another level of learning and success. While the story isn't over, progress has been significant since the moment I chose honesty.

CHAPTER 11

DEEP LEARNING

The one important thing I have learned over the
years is the difference between taking one's work
seriously and taking one's self seriously. The first is
imperative and the second disastrous.

—Margot Fonteyn

ALMOST EVERY CONSULTANT SAYS he is committed to learning.
Instead, most put up fences to learning. Even more to the point,
expert consultants believe they make their living based on what
they know. To reveal what they don't know is the height of vulnerability and goes against every fiber of their being.

And yet, that is precisely what masterful consultants do—
they admit they don't know everything. They are committed not to
the process of knowing but to the process of inquiry. And they are
committed to the process of shared learning—their own and their
clients. Most importantly, they get that if they want to help develop
organizations that are great in their ability to create, discover, and
learn, they need to model the same, moment by moment. Whether
they know it or not, they live by the ancient Greek principle of *aretê*.
Roughly translated, the concept of *aretê* means virtue, but not virtue
in the modern moral sense of the term. In the ancient meaning,
virtue or *aretê* had to do with a respect for wholeness in life, a striving for excellence in becoming fully human. *Aretê* was a dominant
value in Greek life for hundreds of years, an ideal reflected in
Homer's epic poems, *The Iliad* and *The Odyssey*. *Aretê,* to the Greeks,

was only possible when one is striving, striving to become. More-over, it can never be attained, for those who think they have attained it have lost it, passing into egotistical pride.

The quest for learning is a characteristic that distinguishes great consultants from others, but it is not limited to them. We all are born with this fundamental drive. Both of my children have taught me how powerful the drive is. My son, when he was two and a half, used to ask incessantly "why." "We need to go now, Josh," we would say. "Why, Daddy?" "The water is cold at the beach this time of year." "Why, Mommy?" Thankfully we answered these questions, more often than not, with patience and understanding. Sometimes it was exasperating, as we would get the "whys" many times in a row. Our daughter, who has just turned two, keeps pointing to things she has seen before, but we have never talked about, and asks, "What's that?" Again, she is deeply curious.

I believe this kind of curiosity lives within us all. Somewhere, however, the drive to know replaces the drive to learn. Our ego becomes invested in knowing, not learning. This transition gets reinforced in our school systems where people get good grades and approval for the answers. They don't necessarily get good grades and approval for being inquisitive! Having a good answer is rewarded, while having a great question bumps the teacher off schedule. And yet, answers end inquiry, while questions open inquiry up—it is easy to see which is more valuable.

Similarly, we often shun feedback because we fear we might have made a mistake or not done it well. In shunning feedback, we reduce learning. I believe seeking feedback is a crucial part of con-sulting effectiveness, and yet our ego erects barriers against it.

Recently, I had a valuable positive experience in the lesson of being open to feedback. In the middle of working with an executive team, I had confronted one of the executives, Greg, about his ten-dency to discard other people's views and feelings. Unbeknownst to me, Greg had been silently stewing with anger toward me ever since. During a break, I noticed his body language indicated some-thing was off, and I asked him what was going on. Seething in quiet anger, he told me that he felt inappropriately challenged by me in front of the others, and felt unfairly judged. My immediate thought was to dismiss his reaction, having felt that not only was the meet-

178

ing quite successful, but that part of the success was due to this very same moment, where when confronted, it opened up the group to feel freer in communicating with one another in a direct and open manner. Instead of defending myself, I invited him to tell me more. In listening carefully, I realized that indeed I had been feeling judgment toward him, frustrated by my own inability to be heard by him. I admitted this feeling directly to Greg, and that, rather than dealing with him directly about it, I used the group's similar feeling to bolster my own resolve to raise it. I then shared that, at the time, while I had thought it wise to raise the issue with him in the group meeting itself, I could have found a way to confront the issue more graciously with him. "I think I blindsided you with this, and for that I apologize," I said. In hearing this, he relaxed a bit, and we discussed what I could do to ease his feelings of concern about how others saw him after I had confronted him. After the break I shared with the group this moment and how I felt I could have done it more effectively, the act of which seemed to be appreciated by all. Later, thankful for my openness, Greg sought me out to work with him more deeply on the very subject I confronted him on in the first place.

For masterful consultants, learning is not a decision or an action. It is a way of being. Learning is where they come from, not what they do. Here are the thoughts of two masterful consultants that capture this spirit:

> I often don't know what is right. My bias is to pay attention to who I am and who I am becoming and not deal with myself as done or finished or that I have it all together. The worst moments for me as a consultant are when I "know" what needs to be done here. My best are when I'm in a state of inquiry and I'm searching and learning.

> I don't present myself as having the answer. Instead I understand the process and the emotional components of stepping onto the unknown and make the appropriate experiments necessary to figure it out. I help my clients through a process of greater and greater clarity even though we don't have a guaranteed outcome.

If learning is an inner stance, then it knows no bounds. It belongs to everyone and every moment. It is part and parcel to everything masterful consultants do. They display it themselves and they encourage it in others. It shows up in many forms: by asking for and giving feedback, by reframing situations to encourage deeper discovery, and through inquiry that reveals deeper possibilities.

An article in *The New Yorker* a few years ago spoke directly to the relationship between learning, mistakes, and mastery. The author asked surgeons if they ever made a mistake. Those who said "no" were typically those who were considered rather mediocre in the profession. The masterful ones pointed out that they made mistakes every day.

In addition to the consultants I interviewed, clients often spoke about the value of inquiry and learning. They often referred to the depth of questions asked by the masterful consultant, and pointed out that coupled with being a great listener, their commitment to learning distinguished them from others. Said one client, "The best consultants were willing to learn and think about new ways of doing things, which allowed them to synergistically incorporate what they brought to the table from their prior experience with what they are learning with us. They saw work as an opportunity to learn more."

Because of this deep commitment to learning, masterful consultants naturally form circles of inquiry. They create arenas, conversations, interventions, and experiences all designed to maximize learning. One consultant put well what so many others said in different words:

> I make the assumption that on an individual, group, or organizational level, we are all learning beings. That's the wonderful thing about human consciousness. We are always learning. So I often ask myself: What is going on that this individual, group, or organization can't learn? This assumes they naturally have the expertise to learn, and that something may be blocking it. This challenges me to figure out why they can't use their own existing knowledge to their advantage. My job, then, is to remove the barriers to learning.

Another spoke about the importance of creating conditions for deep inquiry.

> When I design group interventions, I think about what are the questions I want them to think about and discuss with each other. I think about the structure I want to put around them so that they are more likely to engage with these questions deeply, so that whatever they produce will be valuable. I don't anticipate or care about what they come up with, as much as I care that they are engaged with the right questions.

Still a third spoke about the deeper problems embedded in organizations and the importance of learning.

> My work is not always to create solutions. I don't usually walk into an organization where the client has a specific problem they want solved. In this day and age of complexity in our world, organizations just don't "get fixed." The amount of speed of change and difficulty of change is not going to go away. It's not like change and complexity are problems the organization can solve. What makes the difference is the way that I show up to collaborate on the dilemmas that exist in the current work environment and the world we live in, such that we both better understand what choices and options we have to address them.

All the comments about learning and its central role in consulting mastery boiled down to one primary question: What are the conditions that we can establish with our clients that allow us to *learn our way* through the complex situations we are in? This commitment to learning differentiates masterful consultants from others I have known and worked with.

Moreover, it determines or defines success in the long run. Indeed, almost without exception, my successes are the result of the relationships I form within client organizations wherein learning can take place. My job really is to cultivate these relationships, to bring them to bloom. My failures are almost always the result of my own inability to grow these relationships.

In this sense, the client's commitment to learning becomes as important as the consultant's. Because so many problems in business and in organizational life are knotty and bewildering, a learning attitude on the part of client and consultant is necessary for success. But the dynamic is circular. A client is not likely to learn from a consultant with no learning ethic. A "know-it-all" consultant is much more likely to match up with a "save me" client—a prescription for zero learning on both ends.

Truth be told, when my work as a consultant was not successful, I could almost always tell right from the start that the individuals in the client organization were not entering our relationship from an attitude of inquiry. Instead, they sought validation for their own approach to leadership, or they sought a savior. Neither invites inquiry. Early on in my career, instead of confronting what I felt, or turning down the work knowing that the relationship had little possibility for success, I just took the work—and watched with dismay as a useless outcome took shape. Now, I shy away from work where I don't sense the client will join me in a spirit of inquiry.

Learning and Accountability

Accountability is a term that is bantered around a lot these days. Sometimes it means to be accountable for results. This isn't the meaning I am referring to. I am referring to a spirit of responsibility that says that I recognize that what transpires is a result of *my* actions or *my* lack of actions. I see that my actions matter. Interestingly, the word *accountability* has in its roots the word "count." It implies to stand up and be counted.

**The ancient Roman Senate operated
from the principle of accountability.
When a vote was to be taken, Senators were
asked to stand up and be counted.**

Accountability is an attitude, not a point of fact. We can argue till the cows come home whether or not in fact I am accountable. But this argument misses the point. When I have the attitude that I am accountable, learning and possibility spring forward.

The attitude of holding oneself accountable is the opposite of feeling like a victim. When I view myself as a victim, I focus on the actions of others and how they "counted." I don't "count" my actions as relevant. Accountability breeds learning. Holding the point of view of a victim breeds blame, and learning is lost among the finger-pointing.

Masterful consultants see their accountability in all aspects of the consulting situation. When their work does not produce the outcomes they seek, they look no further than themselves. They look inside and seek the answers for failure. Moreover, they look deeper than their behavior. They look to understand how their inner stance caused their behaviors, which in turn, contributed to the results. In this way accountability and learning go hand in hand. One masterful consultant said it best when she said: "One of the most liberating things I discovered several years ago was that when something goes wrong, just say, 'I blew it. This is not what I wanted to happen, I'm sorry it happened and let's try to do something else.' One of the most powerful ways to alter a relationship is to be a learner, instead of being defensive."

In my life, the principle of accountability, more than any other, has been a principle that deeply affects my success. I remember many moments where I blamed others for things that happened. The tendency to blame others is just one more way my ego defends myself. In my attempt to protect me from blameworthiness, I make myself small. By blaming others, I am saying, "I don't count." Once I saw the positive power of seeing my accountability, my learning and my success improved astronomically. Let me illustrate the power and potential of accountability.

I once was part of a small consulting firm that had a good reputation among its small set of clients. It also was vulnerable in that its largest client represented over 50% of its revenues. This particular client was led by a CEO who was difficult to work with. She was noted for her tendency to blame others, to be pushy and arrogant, and to lack an openness to learning. At the same time, she valued what we did in principle, and paid a lot of money to have us work with her company.

The lead consultant in our firm working with this client (the only one who had developed a positive relationship with the CEO) asked me to lead an offsite for the senior staff. She was actually at her wit's end, having no other choice among our consulting ranks. The CEO had spit all the rest of our consultants out, including the president of our firm.

After a couple of spotty and unproductive interactions with the CEO and one rather clumsy strategy session with her senior team who were altogether uninterested in dealing directly with some key team issues, I took my place at the end of a long line of consultants from our firm—five in all—who got the boot. A couple of months later, we got a call from the CEO telling us she was not renewing our contract to work with her. Basically, in one brutal decision, we lost half of our future revenues. I was distraught and felt I was to blame.

The Managing Partner of our firm convened a meeting to discuss our work with the client. You can imagine that this might have been a tough meeting, particularly for me. Well, it was the opposite. Our Managing Partner stood up and spoke to the six consultants, all of whom had worked with the client. Rather than blame me for what amounted to the final straw, he said the following: "I want you all to know that I feel 100% responsible for our failure with this client. I worked with the CEO three years ago and didn't do the job. I wasn't at my best, and my own weaknesses as a consultant kept popping up. She fired me then, and I knew then and there that this wasn't a good client to work with. Instead of pulling out of the account altogether, I enrolled many of you to try to work with the client, each of whom, with one exception, had the same problems I had. It was a bad decision. We should have pulled out of the account when we knew she wasn't a good client, taken our losses and moved on. Instead, I saw dollar signs and denied my own feelings in the matter. I also did not defend each of you when you were fired from the account in kind. Instead, I privately hoped it would work out. As a result, I did not stand behind my partners the way I needed to."

I was almost in tears as the burden of blame for losing the account was lifted from me. I thanked him for his honesty and courage in taking responsibility for the situation, and told him he was not alone. I then stood up, and following his lead, pointed to the ways I had not done a good job and because of me, the whole firm was paying the price.

One by one the other consultants took responsibility in kind. We then agreed that the biggest mistake we all made was having one client be too much of our revenue source, and that this led us to feel financially vulnerable and less able to make the kinds of bold decisions we need to make in order to be effective as consultants. I view the actions of our Managing Partner as accountability at its best for he showed how accountability has the potential to beget more accountability. It wasn't easy—he took the obvious risk that others would pile on and blame him. But he understood something critical. With an accountable inner stance, learning—which is ultimately more important than keeping any single client—can take place. At the same time, blame always begets more blame, and learning is squelched in the process. Masterful consultants understand this well as they model and live accountably.

LEARNING AND THE SPIRIT OF INQUIRY

Adopting an inner stance of learning is more than moving from an attitude of "I know" to one of "I don't know." It's more than accountability, too. At its best, it begets a spirit of inquiry. An intense desire to discover forms the core of learning for consulting mastery. I have found something very interesting when I bring this desire to my clients. They join me. Their curiosity is sparked, too. They want in on the excitement. I let my clients know that if they choose to work with me, I will rarely if ever offer answers. I point out that if answers could be plucked from the lowest branch, they would have plucked them already. Moreover, I don't know their business that well, who am I to pretend to know what they need? Instead, I come with questions and ask them to join me in a spirit of inquiry. Those who are hoping for a savior don't like to hear this, because it means they have to take full responsibility for their situation and engage in the uncertainty that inquiry requires. Those who are attracted to the prospect of learning and figuring it out together offer their hand and say, "Let's get going."

During the course of consulting, I often ask questions designed to have them look at a situation from multiple angles. I ask them to offer hypotheses rather than opinions. I invite them to test their assumptions. I invite them to adopt opposing views. Through all this, eventually a light shines through the darkness and a path for growth is revealed. What drives the process is willingness, a confidence that arises from curiosity.

All this requires that I be able to hold my inner stance of learning solidly, and that I meet the challenge of my clients in a spirit of humility. This doesn't mean we forgo decisions, that we become meek and passive. To the contrary. I find that the decisions borne out of this spirit of inquiry are often far more effective. They stand on a foundation of deep understanding. The clients therefore trust their own decisions and are more likely to implement them. Figure 11-1 shows the contrast between an expert attitude and that of a masterful consultant.

With one exception, the consultants I interviewed displayed an abundant amount of inquisitiveness, even though all were extraordinarily successful. I felt their sense of ease as I explored issues. They shared their point of view without being dogmatic about it. At the same time, they seemed grounded in their knowledge, convinced of their own ability to help others grow. This confidence, topped with a scoop of humility, was evident in their bearing

Expert Consultant	Masterful consultant
Gives advice	Asks great questions
Attached to being right	Committed to learning
Focused on proving themselves	Focused on client discovery
Analytically driven	Driven by head and heart
Takes an "I know" stance	Takes a stance of "I don't know but I believe we can figure it out together."

FIGURE 11-1   ADVICE VERSUS INQUIRY

and in what they spoke about. Here are a few of the many examples where their humility and inquisitiveness shone through.

> What makes me effective is that I work to keep my ego from getting in the way. I don't expend much energy trying to pretend or trying to convey an image. I feel honored that you say I am one of the best, but I don't think of myself that way. I'm quite good, but I'm a very flawed individual.

> I don't want to be seen as the savior. The minute people put us on a pedestal, trouble is not far behind.

> We need to be able to apply to ourselves what we are asking clients to do for themselves—be learners.

> You need to have humility. Mother Teresa was revered because she was able to do great things in a humble way and that's the kind of greatness that sticks.

Far more than any other factor, learning and all of its manifestations were referred to as a key to the success of the consultants I interviewed. Most felt they were successful not because of their brilliance but because of their inquisitiveness. Moreover, they saw mistakes as opportunities, not problems. "All defects," said quality guru Joseph Juran, "are gold in the mine. We mine them by learning from them."[1] One consultant put it eloquently as she said, "the goal is not necessarily to be mistake free, but rather to assume that we are going to make mistakes along the way. The key to mastery is to understand what to do after the mistake."

In the final analysis, learning is all about listening. Not the surface level listening we are all accustomed to. It is about listening for deeper patterns—to see what others may fail to see. One masterful consultant I met years ago referred to this often as he spoke about the importance of "listening generously." I have grown to love that phrase as I seek to learn how to be an ever more generous listener to my clients, my family, my friends, and to the music in my soul.

Few have said it better than Lao-Tzu, the Chinese sage who lived twenty-five centuries ago:

It was as though he listened
And such listening as his enfolds us in a silence
In which at last we begin to hear
What we are meant to be

CHAPTER 12

Bring Your Whole Self, in Full Partnership

Everyone carries a shadow, and the less it is
embodied in the individual's conscious life,
the blacker and denser it is.

—*C. G. Jung*

A QUOTE BY A RABBI from the second century, cited by one of the
consultants I interviewed, speaks to the central issue of this chapter.
"God does not expect us to be perfect. There are enough angels in
heaven. He only expects us to be fully human."

As suggested earlier, many consultants have a tendency to
believe that one key to success is to be perfect. Masterful consultants
believe it is better to be whole. By whole I mean bringing your
whole self to the client situation: your intellect, emotions, and spiritual self. The masterful consultant comes to the client as a learning
being, as a person in motion, as one on a journey. She knows she is
far from perfect, and as someone who embraces wholeness, she does
not strive for perfection, for she knows it as a devilish temptation.
Being perfect means: *no mistakes.* Being whole means she shares her
mistakes in the spirit of learning. Being perfect means she knows
everything that needs to be known to add value. Being whole means
she knows little, and yet is able to guide the process of learning so

that we can know much. Being perfect means that she shows only those parts that make her look good. Being whole means she shows all of who she is, her best parts and her shadow side as well. Being perfect means she becomes invulnerable. Being whole means she shares herself vulnerably.

The paradox of mastery is simple. Mastery doesn't exist to masterful consultants. It is an illusion, just as perfection is illusion. There is no such thing as full mastery, for if we got there, we would have to deny our whole selves. Paradoxically, mastery means not trying to be masterful. It means letting myself be whole, warts and all.

This chapter, more than any other, speaks to what is the best of me personally and what is also my growing edge. One of my best qualities as a consultant is my willingness to share openly who I am and to be vulnerable. This has made me accessible to my clients and enabled me to become both a trusted guide and a trusted friend. At the same time, I have spent most of my life seeking perfection, and only in the past few years have I realized that it was an illusion all along.

Growing up, I felt great demands on me to be perfect. I don't recall being praised for my good-heartedness or hard work. I vividly recall the many times I was scorned or criticized for my failings. This was the water within which I swam, and I knew no other. So over time, I felt (quite unconsciously I might add) that in order to be loved, or in order to avoid criticism, I had to be perfect. This conviction spawned a noisy creature living inside me, a huge inner critic, whom I have been trying to tame ever since. One of the most telling moments in my life was the day I received my doctorate from Harvard. My mother was present and with tears in her eyes she told me how proud she was. I cried too, appreciating the sweetness of the moment for both of us. And then it dawned on me that I had never felt her be proud of me in my whole life. She may have indeed felt pride before, but I never knew. I mostly felt I was never quite enough.

My father was likewise a taskmaster, rarely if ever expressing appreciation or offering positive feedback, often pointing out my flaws. During my formative years, both of my parents were perfectionists in their own right and enormous achievers. I honor their toughness and hard work. But I believe that such a family environment was ripe to produce more than excellence. It produced a need for perfection and so with it I became intense and ill at ease. Thankfully, I saw this in me a few years ago and instead of trying to rid myself of the negativity of perfectionism, I have been seeking to affirm wholeness in my life. Through poetry, quiet self-reflection, couples therapy and an encouraging wife, greater fluidity and warmth are growing inside of me.

The relationship between wholeness and consulting mastery is crucial to our overall thesis. In many ways, the quest for wholeness and the quest for consulting mastery are the same thing. Mastery without wholeness—it can't happen. Moreover, wholeness ties into so many other parts of consulting mastery. The more whole a consultant is, the more she is able to be honest, to play a big game, and to take a learning stance in life. The more whole she is, the more she establishes effective co-creative partnerships with clients. And the more whole she is, the more effective her relationship to knowledge.

For many of the consultants I interviewed, wholeness translated into being genuine—in the sense of allowing others to see all of who they are. It means to show fully oneself, and not hide parts that are perhaps unsavory. Here is what a couple of masterful consultants had to say on the subject.

> I tend to hit more on the human side, even with the biggest shots I've ever worked with. If you hit on the human side, and let your real personhood shine through, sometimes they let theirs shine through as well. People in leadership positions don't often allow their personhood to shine through. I try to make it comfortable and safe for them by modeling that behavior—by just being genuine.

> I think the most important things I bring are kind of intangible. They have to do with a relationship I form between myself and my clients, an authenticity. It has to do with creating a relationship that could last the rest of our lives.

Wholeness, and the self-knowledge that comes with it, contributes to consulting mastery in three distinct ways:

- To be a better model for learning by embracing one's shadow

- To become a better barometer for what is happening in client organizations

- To be a clearer observer

EMBRACING THE SHADOW

Many observers of the human psyche, from Greek philosophers to Jungian analysts, point out that we all have a shadow side of our selves. To many, the shadow is the part of our self that we tend to not want to see. It is that which is disowned. The shadow self is different for different people. To the extent that I tend to be uncomfortable with anger and have judgments about it, I disown my anger, and so it is a big part of my shadow self. To other people who are comfortable feeling and expressing anger, their anger is not part of their shadow. Theirs could be their tenderness, or their sense of fragility or idealism. The nature of the shadow self is that since it is disowned, it goes underground, yet acts to influence our behavior and our choices. The more underground it is, the less able we are to control it, and therefore it controls us. Carl Jung spoke about this phenomenon in one of his brilliant essays on the subject of shadow.

> It is a frightening thought that man also has a shadow side to him, consisting not just of little weaknesses and foibles, but of a positively demonic dynamism. The individual seldom knows anything of this; to him, as an individual, it is incredible that he should ever in any circumstances go beyond himself. But let these harmless creatures form a mass, and there emerges a raging monster; and each individual is only one tiny cell in the monster's body, so that for better or worse he must accompany it on its bloody rampages and even assist it to the utmost. Having a dark suspicion of these grim possibilities, man turns a blind eye to the shadow-side of human nature. Blindly he strives against the salutary dogma of original sin, which is yet so prodigiously true. Yes, he even hesitates to admit the conflict of which he is so painfully aware.[1]

We disown our shadow precisely because we judge it wrong and fear it. It is dark to us for it contains so much that we mere humans can't face. Too often, we view the darkness in our psyche as unacceptable or evil, and in so doing, we move further away from being able to comprehend it and manage it. There can be no light without darkness, no passion without exploring and releasing the depths of our unconscious self. Wonder and beauty and all our future possibilities also lie hidden in the darkness, and far too often we confuse the shadow with evil. When we start to automatically dismiss something as evil when in fact it is merely outside our normal experience, we move further away from it, and it controls us, defines us, and eventually crushes us.

Carl Jung told a story that illustrates this well. He said he met a distinguished man, a Quaker, who could not imagine that he had ever done anything wrong in his life. "And do you know what happened to his children?" Jung asked. "The son became a thief, and the daughter a prostitute. Because the father would not take on his shadow, his share in the imperfection of human nature, his children were compelled to live out the dark side which he had ignored."[2] To deny one's shadow invites trouble. To embrace it invites learning.

There is no deep personal change that doesn't begin in the darkness of the human soul. We first have to discover an entrance into the darkness, and then we have to light a tiny candle in the dark, so that we can search for our future self. Finally we have to join with it. And that takes resourcefulness, and patience, and most of all courage.

**THE PATH TO CONSULTING MASTERY
ALWAYS INVOLVES ENTERING THE SHADOW.
ONE CANNOT ATTAIN MASTERY WITHOUT
EMBRACING THAT WHICH HAS BEEN DISOWNED.**

One of the keys to effective consulting is the ability to manage all of one's different selves. Bringing my whole self means all of me—lightness and shadow. The more I am able to be gentle with my self, the less judgment I have about my self, particularly my shadow self, the more capacity I have to learn, grow, and effectively be in the world.

So many of the consultants I interviewed spoke about their process of growth as a consultant, and connected that process to embracing who they are, shadow and all. When darker aspects of their personality or their behavior show up, they are light about it, and so they move more fluidly and gracefully, ever the learner. One consultant I interviewed spoke elegantly on the subject.

> Another thing I bring is my acceptance of my own shadow side. When I'm at my best I can look my shadow in the eye and embrace it and recognize how important it is in the power I have in the world. You have to bring shadow out to realize its power. I've had more accomplishment in my life not from the things I run away from, but the things I've feared and run toward. That has to do with shadow. I don't use the word "shadow" with clients. Instead I help them reach into parts of themselves that they are afraid of acknowledging—parts of themselves they've seen as weaknesses—usually personal. I tell stories about myself in that realm and that draws stories out of them.

This "owning" of our shadow sides acts as a model for clients. So much of what does not work in team, interpersonal, or organizational situations has to do with darker aspects of our psyche. So much of the tendency to control, to berate, to judge, to diminish, and to avoid has to do with disowned aspects of the leadership of organizations. Remember the principle: A consultant cannot take the organization farther than he has taken himself. This principle is all too true when dealing with the darker aspects of organizational life. Stamping them out does not work. This is akin to trying to rid oneself of important parts of our psyche. These parts just go underground and control us.

Instead, the key to growing ourselves as healthy consultants and healthy organizations is, in part, helping to learn about our darker features, and to rise above them, rather than rid ourselves of them. The shadow sides of individuals and organizations cannot be sucked into a box and disposed of, like ghosts in the movie *Ghost-*

busters. They have to be acknowledged, and allowed to be, as part of our natural selves. It means admitting that we're messy inside.

Masterful consultants understand this well, and instead of hiding from the shadow, they embrace it, and in so doing, they embrace an epigram of Jung's: "Ninety percent of the shadow is pure gold."

A BETTER BAROMETER

Wholeness has to do with being aware of my whole self, moment by moment. At any given moment, I am thinking, I am feeling, and I am connected to spirit—to all that flows between us and among us. The more whole I am, the more aware I am. Great consultants use this awareness as a source of information to understand what is happening in the client organization at any given point in time. They use their feelings as a barometer. In order to do so, they must be present. Here is what one masterful consultant had to say on the subject:

> People have the experience that I am very much *with them.*
> Without ego. It has to do with being informed by something
> greater than myself. It goes beyond my education. It goes
> beyond models and theories—really, sensing the opportunity
> in the moment to be of service in some way. To see something,
> to notice something, to reflect something back to the client.

It all has to do with being present, in the moment. Let me give you an example of what I mean.

Recently I was with a senior management team, leading an offsite, the primary purpose of which was to help the team identify crucial leadership challenges in the company. About a fourth of the way into the meeting, one of the members (we'll call him Bob) started pontificating about some issue, and the rest of the members went silent. What had once been a fluid interchange almost immediately became stilted. I noticed myself starting to feel turned off by this person, hyper-aware of a highly judgmental stance Bob seemed to be taking. Indeed, I started to feel emotionally protective of myself in his presence, and I sensed that others were feeling the same.

Trusting that my own desire to pull back from this person was a barometer of the feelings of other members of the group, I simply made an observation and asked what others were feeling. I said, "I notice the group has gotten silent and I am wondering what is going on." This gentle intervention was taken as an invitation to surface feelings, and one group member pointed out she felt Bob was off-base in his judgments and she was taken aback by them. Others offered that they felt the same, and a healthy dialogue ensued that both gave Bob some feedback as well as clarified what was okay and not okay to say and do in the group.

I cannot be an effective barometer if I am shut off from my thoughts, feelings, and spiritual condition. So many of us are aware of our thoughts, but are caught by them, unaware that other thoughts may be equally valid. So many of us deny our feelings, believing they have no role in the workplace. And so many of us are cut off from our spiritual condition, not knowing how to give credence to that which is so hard to define or grasp. Yet the ability to know our thoughts and to exercise fluidity, the ability to be aware of our feelings, and to use them as a guide, and the ability to recognize our connection to all things is what differentiates masterful consultants from others.

A CLEAR WITNESS

So much of what masterful consultants do has to do with holding up a mirror to their clients so the clients can see more clearly. Sometimes this means asking clients to reflect back on their experience. Sometimes it means offering an observation. In either case, the masterful consultant is seeing something the client is not seeing. To do this well requires that the consultant does her best to observe what is going on, without bias or judgment—in other words, to see clearly.

Robert Heinlein wrote the classic science fiction book, *Stranger in a Strange Land*.[3] Heinlein tells the story of Valentine Michael Smith, orphaned progeny of the first manned expedition to Mars, who has been raised by Martians and brought back to Earth by a second human expedition. Still a young man, Smith looks at everything on our planet through the innocent eyes of a child, and faces the job of learning how to be a human being. Throughout the book we learn about Valentine's planet, where among other things, are people known as "Fair Witnesses."

A Fair Witness is a professional observer—a person with complete memory and keen observational skills, admitted to testify in court about any factual aspect of a situation. A Fair Witness is trained from an early age to simply describe people, situations, and events, without bias, predisposition, or judgment. In addition to perfect recall, a Fair Witness will never render any opinion about what he observed, nor infer anything that he did not actually see or hear. The concept of Fair Witness is illustrated in Heinlein's book by Jubal, one of Valentine's friends, who asked Ann (a Fair Witness) what color the house on the hillside was. Ann's response was, "It's white on this side, Jubal." Note that she did not say the house is white, for she could not see the other side and made no assumption of anything she could not see. In Valentine's world, members of the Fair Witness Guild are highly respected professionals and are held to extremely high standards of integrity.

We know that it is impossible for a human being on this planet to reliably be a fair witness. We can't be objective, for human beings are riddled with subjectivity. We are meaning-making machines by design. Yet the more we are able to own our subjectivity—to recognize our values, our biases, and our predispositions—the more clearly we can see, without them controlling what we see. In other words, the more we acknowledge the lenses through which we see the world, the more we can keep them from skewing our vision and can draw closer to becoming a clear witness in our client's world. Masterful consultants do this all the time in numerous ways including participating in learning processes designed to illuminate biases and unfounded assumptions, seeking feedback from others, looking deeply into their own character, psychotherapy and any of a number of means to become more open and accepting. They go to the root of subjectivity to find its ego and other causes. In so doing, they become more objective and a better agent for learning and change.

So often, clients call upon us for this particular added value. Our ability to bring all of ourselves, and to distinguish observation from interpretation, is crucial to this need. Clients assume that we are objective because we are not a part of their system. Such an assumption is false for we are all too human. The best consultants, however, hone their ability to be more objective by embracing all of who they are, and in being skillful in putting aside their assumptions, biases, and predispositions so they can see more clearly.

In short, bringing one's whole self makes one a better consultant and a better human being. We make an indelible impression on our clients not from what we do, but from who we are. One consultant I interviewed said it best. "What people most remember about masterful consultants is not what they say, for what they say is long gone from people's memory. What remains enduring is how the masterful consultant makes them feel. How we make each other feel is what's most important of all."

CHAPTER 13

PLAYING A
BIG GAME

What most of us mean by competition:
"It's not enough that I win, I also have
to make certain that you lose."

—Harvey Robbins & Michael Finley[1]

DECADES AGO, THOMAS SZASZ, the great observer of human illness
and well-being, said that what people really need from life is not
wealth or comfort, but a game worth playing.[2] Too often we engage
in ordinary games, where there are winners and losers, and where
the outcomes satisfy the ego but not the soul. In contrast, masterful
consultants seek to play a big game, where their clients and the
world at large are uplifted and renewed, and where greater results
can be achieved. To illustrate, I turn to a different arena.

A couple of years ago, Sports Center on ESPN ran a story that
was extraordinary and spoke volumes about what human beings are
capable of. The story was about Jake Porter, a senior at Northwest
High School in southern Ohio, who has fragile X syndrome, a common form of inherited mental retardation. He loved football and
loved being a part of his high school football team. Although he was
handicapped and unable to play, Jake practiced with the team, went
to games with the team, and did everything he could to support the
team as their team manager. Jake always suited up, for he was a part
of the team. But he didn't care if he ever played, and never expected

to. Just being around the team, and being around the game, gave him deep satisfaction. And he was legendary throughout his hometown and other teams in the team's conference for his positive attitude toward life, an inspiration to many.

On an important game with Waverly, a conference rival, Northwest was behind 42–0. Jake's team had the ball with only a few seconds left on the clock. They were on Waverly's 49-yard line and needed a miracle to break the impending shutout.

The opposing team's coach, Derek DeWitt, called a time-out and met with Jake's coach with an inspired idea: to have Jake run the ball so that he would have a chance to play. The idea of Jake coming into the game had been hatched the week before in a meeting between the opposing coaches, but the plan was for Jake to down the ball, not run it. It was too dangerous to Jake for a real play to take place. The idea of letting him score a touchdown had not been the plan. At first, Jake's coach, Dave Frantz, refused, concerned that Jake would get hurt, but soon came to realize that the idea allowed the boys on both teams to play a bigger game than the football game, and trusted that the boys on both teams would know what to do. With the clock still stopped, Frantz went quickly to the sideline and put Jake in the game. "Give the ball to Jake and let him run with it," he said to the quarterback. "Trust me." At the same time, DeWitt informed his own team of the play.

What unfolded was a thing of beauty, unrehearsed, and certainly not choreographed. Waverly went into the huddle. The quarterback called the play. It was a handoff to Jake, the new tailback. The other members of the team nodded in understanding. They saw immediately their opportunity to give a gift to Jake, whose courage and devotion to the team had gifted them for years.

Jake took the handoff and seemed confused, not knowing what to do at first. Soon, he collected his wits, and as an opening in the Waverly's line of scrimmage showed itself, he started to trot toward Waverly's end zone, guided in part by the Waverly team members themselves who pointed the way. Clearly, losing the shutout meant little to the Waverly team who had provided the opening. Supporting Jake meant everything in the world. The boy held onto the ball as if life itself depended on him not fumbling and crossed the end zone to break the shutout.

Everyone on both teams congratulated Jake while the people in the stands cheered like they had never cheered before. There was not a dry eye in the stands. They were not only cheering for Jake, but for the coaches and the football players for recognizing a game bigger than the game on the field. They had just witnessed the human species at its best.

During the interviews on ESPN, who only later had caught wind of the event, Jake talked about what the moment meant to him. He understood that the other team had helped him to the goal line, but that was OK. He played—that was all that mattered. And he accepted a gift of love from the other boys that he would never forget as long as he lived. His mother was interviewed, too. With tears in her eyes, she said that it was the biggest gift her son could have ever received, and she felt thankful beyond words.

This story is about a game that transcended the competition of a football game. Football was the event listed on the program. But life is what took place on the field.

This story, while not about consulting, has a lot to do with consulting. Masterful consultants seek to play a bigger game than others. They are committed to a game where everyone wins. When faced with a conflict among others, they seek to reframe the situation so that a larger, deeper, more enduring possibility may be discovered. When faced with either/or problems, they seek both/and solutions.

Some say that playing a game where everyone wins goes against human nature—that nature is "dog-eat-dog," and so are we. "The natural way of things is survival of the fittest," they say, and they believe it wholeheartedly, even if they are describing social Darwinism, not Darwin's actual theory of evolution. They also point out how our whole economy is founded on the value of natural competition. In a free enterprise system, where competition is encouraged, we all win because the cream rises to the top, and progress unfolds. Others argue that it is also our nature to be cooperative, and that all species cooperate with one another. I do not share either point of view. Instead I am interested in whether we can actually influence either nature.

In other words, we can take two points of view about human nature. The first perspective is that our nature is fixed, and that the survival instinct and the need to compete are so deeply etched in our human functioning that to deny them is to deny nature. This view also acknowledges that our need to cooperate is also present, but when push comes to shove, competition wins out.

The second view is that indeed we are blessed with two natures, and of course, much more. We are indeed "naturally" competitive in many spheres, from sports to business and social life. But we are also "naturally" cooperative in these same spheres.

Instead of seeing human nature as fixed, this view would say that it is within our capability as a species to guide our own unfolding. If it is true that both live within us, then the question is not, what is human nature? The question is: what nature do we want to encourage? The more we seek a world where everyone wins, the more we create organizations, societies, and a planet that can thrive. This is the attitude of masterful consultants, and to them, it is the only game in town worth playing.

SEEING A BIGGER PICTURE

To masterful consultants, "playing a big game" doesn't just mean playing a game where everyone has the potential of winning. Masterful consultants also seek to understand the larger dynamics and to shift the whole system to a higher plane. They help their clients move from either/or thinking to both/and thinking. They live from an attitude of abundance rather than one of scarcity. They tend to be spacious in their view of people and events rather than judgmental. And above all, they are committed to serving the whole organization and indeed all of society, not just serving themselves. Playing a big game is what David McClelland referred to when he spoke about the positive face of power—which he called Socialized Power.[3]

Much of the cause of any organization's "stuckness" has to do with their narrow perspective. Playing a small game more often than not drives the narrow perspective. We often see this in industry, where a company sets one team against another to solve a problem. Tracy Kidder wrote about such an incident in his book, *The Soul of a New Machine*.[4]

Kidder described the creation of a new microcomputer developed by Data General in the early 80s. At Data General, Ed DeCastro, founder and CEO of the company, pitted two teams of comput-er developers against one another. The winning team (the one developing the most elegant prototype) would have its design implemented by the company. In the end, one team won out, described in dramatic fashion in the book. One might argue that this is the application of competition at its best. I would argue to the contrary.

I had the interesting opportunity to work at Data General and to consult to both teams six years after the events described by Kid-der's book. The winning team never developed another leading edge computer, although they continued to be the driving force for each new generation of computers. The "losing" team had been devastat-ed by the act of putting so much effort toward no outcome. Morale had been low for all the years since, and turnover rampant. The rest of the company saw that team as "losers" as well, describing them in much the way one would describe a minor league team. We calculat-ed the loss for the company as well over $150 million.

In organizations, more often than not, when competitive urges are sparked, business units tend to demonize one another in their bid to survive—forgetting that the real victory is succeeding as a company, and that together, the two teams may have the knowl-edge that neither team has on its own. Witness the leaders who complain that workers need to take more initiative—even while these same leaders do everything possible (micromanaging, infor-mation withholding, clobbering people when they make mistakes) to remove the possibility of initiative. Witness all the companies who look at their competitors with disdain and ridicule, only to get their lunch handed to them three years down the road, as a new market opens up, or a new technology changes everything.

Consultants who come in with a narrow perspective also par-ticipate in these dynamics, sometimes without being aware of it. They offer solutions within the beliefs and rules they were taught, and then wonder why the solutions didn't work. Einstein once said, "We cannot solve today's problems with the same level of thinking that created them." The same is true in organizations. Sometimes, a company's crying need is not to bash or humiliate other companies in its industry, but to create new space for itself there. New thinking is the answer here, not tribal bloodletting.

FROM SEPARATE TO CONNECTED

One consultant in our firm says he can't stand false dichotomies—views of life where we can see only differences and fail to recognize connections. White/black, right/wrong, either/or, good/bad—this is how we describe the world we live in, but it's not necessarily how the world actually is. We engage in narrow, limited thinking all the time. We see our ideas and ourselves as being pitted against one another. If you open your vision widely, you see that much of our world view is a false dichotomy. I can't count the number of times I have observed two people deadlocked over who is right and who is wrong, and broken the deadlock by asking a simple question: "In what way might both of you be right?"

So much of the destruction on this planet is driven by false dichotomies. "I'm right, you're wrong" gets played out in the classroom and on the battlefield, in the home and in the workplace. What if the problem was not "them," but the inner stance we take. If this is true, then the biggest added value we can provide as consultants is to help our clients see more expansively, and from that seeing, make fresh choices.

The Buddha said that the source of all suffering is attachment. I believe he was referring not just to things, but to our beliefs as well, the way we want to see the world. When we recognize that our opinions and beliefs about right and wrong are just points of view, and that other points of view may enhance our understanding, we shift from a narrow perspective to a broader one. Notice the feeling inside of you when you hold something as a point of view—when you own your statements as driven by a perspective and that other perspectives may be valid or useful. You move away from attachment toward exploration.

The interesting question then becomes: What do we like so much about narrow thinking? I believe that looking at our ego reveals part of the mystery. Our ego's primary function is to protect our self. It believes that we are separate individuals. The more we see ourselves as separate, and the more ego acts to protect our separate self, the more narrow our perspective becomes. We protect our beliefs, our opinions, our views, and our ways of living. In this protection, we reaffirm separateness. We see others' views, opinions, beliefs, and ways of living as competitors, as threats, and so we seek to change others or make them wrong. In this view, we reaffirm separateness.

What if the experience of separateness was at the heart of our narrow thinking, and that the awareness of connection creates the opening for broader solutions—for playing a bigger game? I was witness recently to an example of what can happen when we "get" that we are connected.

My wife and I and a handful of friends were eating dinner outside at a local café, on our way to seeing my son perform in a local musical theatre. In the corner of my eye I saw a woman coming toward us in a wheelchair. She came right up to our table and she was clearly troubled, tears in her eyes. She was unable to speak but used a computer monitor on her wheelchair that enabled her to communicate. I wanted to help her but was unsure what to do. My wife, on the other hand, was swift to act. She sat down next to her and held her disfigured hand, and stroked her arm, and asked, "What do you need?"

The woman, amidst deep heaving sobs, pecked out on her keyboard that her hired helper had just quit, that she couldn't feed herself, and she had no way of getting back home. My wife tenderly began feeding her from her own plate. The rest of us watched, transfixed without a word. After helping the woman complete her dinner, my wife asked the troubled woman if there was anyone else who could help her get home. Then the woman typed out her father's phone number, which my wife dialed on her cell phone. The woman then beckoned me to come closer, which I did. She held my hand, and typed in the words, "Bless you." I could tell that she was not thanking me for my actions, but thanking me for my wife's kindness.

After her father arrived and picked the woman up, we all discussed what had just transpired. We all commented that we were unsure what to do, while my wife knew intuitively exactly how to respond. My wife's tender response marked a significant moment in all our lives and taught us that reaching out in compassion requires no communication—just the feeling of love and awareness that we are all connected in the great circle of life. And just to add intrigue to the whole story, the next day I shared this story with my brother who then told me that he had helped a woman in need two weeks prior in much the same way. Remarkably, after describing the woman to him, it turns out it was the same woman he had helped.

COMMITMENT TO MAKING A BIGGER DIFFERENCE

In addition to seeing more expansively, playing a big game also means asking deeper questions, ones whose answers have the potential for making a bigger difference. Like these masterful consultants, I yearn to make a bigger difference. And I know I am not alone. Consultants who care about their craft ache to have a bigger impact on their clients, some even on the world as a whole. It's not satisfying to take home a big paycheck when we know deep in our bones that the client didn't truly change. Spiffier window dressing, without real change within the organization, does not satisfy the conscientious consultant. It plagues the soul.

To make a big difference, questions need to be asked, such as:

- How can I show up with a client in such a way that I profoundly impact who they are and how they operate?

- How can I form the type of relationship that becomes truly transformational?

- How can I influence others such that their work and their lives are more effective and more whole?

- How do I better influence organizations to become more fluid, more effective, and more fulfilling to be a part of?

These are not superficial questions. They ask how the consultant can shift organizations in powerful ways and effect "deep change." Too often we are taught a bag of tricks to help organizations change, an endless number of exercises, models, frameworks, and processes. Few of these techniques, however, penetrate the fundamental patterns in organizations that seem impervious to change.

Consultants who manage to change these patterns do so not with a set of better tools, but with a greater attention to their inner selves. They bring mystery to the process of consulting, and with it, greater mastery. They seek to ask the challenging questions and to do so in a way that prompts inquisitiveness rather than defensiveness. They wrestle with the sources of light and shadow that lurk beneath the surface of an organization's dynamic and encourage their clients to do the same. They help organizations unglue themselves from their patterns and form new, more effective ones. To do this, they see their work in the broadest possible context. They see themselves as acting in service to others. Here, the words of one echoed the feelings of so many I interviewed.

> I see my work as a path through life—as a way of discovering myself while serving others. The importance of that has to do with putting work in a larger life perspective. I often forget this perspective but I'm at my best when I remember it, when I remember my life has a larger purpose. My work has to do with service in the world, by contributing in some way to the evolution of mankind. Apart from this sense of purpose, everything else is just methodology—trying to figure out how to live my purpose. It happens to be the case that I serve others through consulting. It could be donut-making. Work with my clients validates the pursuit of my life's purpose—that of contributing to others.

From time to time, in working with clients, I play them a movie that plants an indelible image in people's minds of what it means to play a bigger game. The movie is called *Powers of 10*.[5] The first image shows a man lying down in a park in the city of Chicago. Picture the camera moving up into the sky at a rapid speed, and that speed increasing tenfold every 10 seconds. After a few seconds you see the whole park. After a few more, you see the city of Chicago. After a few more, you see most of the United States through the camera's eye. Seconds later, the camera's lens exposes us to the whole Earth. Less than a minute later, we see the solar system, then our galaxy, and eventually the constellation of galaxies that make up the known universe.

This breathtaking image is then reversed, the camera lens moving rapidly downward until it once again reaches the man lying down in the park. Rather than moving outward, it now moves inward, at a similar rate, onto the man's skin, into a pore, into the cellular structure, down into the molecules, atoms, and subatomic particles.

The discussion of the movie invariably triggers a central insight. *What one sees depends on the lens one uses.* The wider the lens, the more one can see, and the more one can see how we are all connected. If we are all connected, then the only sensible game to play is one that encompasses the needs of us all on the planet. The principal reason organizations fail in their efforts has to do with the vantage point from which they view the problem. It is rarely skill or knowledge they lack. It is a deeper or broader understanding that often eludes them.

Put simply, one of the greatest added values a consultant can provide is a wider lens. Archimedes, one of the great Greek scientists, said in 220 BC, "Give me a place to stand and a lever long enough and I will move the world." I believe the place to stand is far away.

**WITH THE BIG PICTURE CLEARLY IN VIEW,
THEN AND ONLY THEN DOES ONE HAVE THE LEVERAGE
TO MAKE THIS WORLD OF OURS BUDGE.**

Let's look at two consulting situations and explore what playing a big game might look like. For each, I will describe a real client situation and ask you to think how you might respond from a larger perspective than the client's. Then I will explain what the consultant did. There is no right or wrong answer—false dichotomy, remember? Rather, this process illustrates what playing a big game means in the context of consulting—as well as to stretch your thinking on the subject.

SITUATION ONE

Fred and Shanna are often at odds with one another. He is the COO and she the head of R&D. The company, Metamark, Inc., developed specialized semiconductor chips for multiple applications and the company is growing. They soon reached a point where they sought help in their working relationship. Emma, the consultant, interviewed each and discovered the following:

FRED'S VIEW. Fred sees Shanna as stretching way beyond the appropriate extensions of the current line of Metamark products. She has spent too much money from his point of view in dallying in product areas for which there is no clear market. For the products they are developing, she often seems to view manufacturing as a separate organization. He feels she acts as if a product can be developed, then thrown over some big wall for manufacturing to deal with.

SHANNA'S VIEW. Shanna is frustrated with Fred's conservative attitude. She sees him as fearful of change and overly protective of the manufacturing organization. She has invited manufacturing to join R&D's planning sessions many times, but whenever they come, they are naysayers. She eventually felt they were hampering her team's ability to think expansively and offer state-of-the-art chip designs. So she decided it wasn't worth the effort. The company CEO gave her orders to "stretch the boundaries" in R&D and that is what she intends to do.

OK. Take a moment and think about how you would handle this situation.

_____

_____

_____

_____

_____

_____

_____

WHAT EMMA DID. Emma, the consultant, felt that there were bigger issues here than just the tussle between Fred and Shanna. She felt that to focus on the two of them missed a larger, more important point. She sensed in talking with them that there were many factors influencing their conflict, including lack of role clarity for Shanna, lack of clear strategic direction for the company, and maybe some confusion in the market itself. Emma suggested that she gather more information about the company as a whole and how it might be influencing the situation. Following this research, she called a meeting with the CEO, the VP of marketing, Fred, and Shanna to discuss the broader issues underlying Fred and Shanna's struggles.

Many issues arose, the greatest of which was the lack of strategic clarity for Metamark. Emma agreed to facilitate a session designed to achieve greater focus for the company and greater clarity of strategic direction. After a successful series of meetings, she sat down with Fred and Shanna and easily worked through some of the interpersonal issues that had marked their relationship to date. That was the easy part; it was seeing the big picture that eluded them.

SITUATION TWO

The Board of PeachCare was at a crossroads. The company had not grown for two years and was losing market share to a competitor that was aggressively moving into many of its key markets. The competitor was using ruthless pricing tactics to get a foothold and making promises PeachCare knew couldn't be sustained. Some Board members thought they should consider buying the competitor before it was too late. Others thought they should entertain being bought by another company in their market space and use their combined size to squash the upstart's efforts. The CEO felt that both of these were overreactions to a situation that would burn out on its own. But the Board was unable to resolve the differences, and so they sought guidance from a strategy consultant.

Brad was called in to assess the situation and provide strategic guidance. He interviewed each of the Board members, and each had a compelling case to support his or her point of view. Brad also learned that each view was driven by the honest desire to be responsive to the stakeholders they represented. A couple of Board members were part of Venture Capital Companies and sought a fairly rapid exit strategy. The Venture Capital Companies had decided that PeachCare was no longer a good investment for the long run and wanted to get out. Three other Board members were tied to more secure investment funds, and leaving soon would not botch their investment expectations. The CEO was 63 years old and did not have another "major play" in him.

Take a moment and think about how you would handle the situation. Write down your thoughts here.

_____

_____

_____

_____

_____

_____

Brad was stymied by the situation. He felt the Board was at a standstill, and was unsure how to handle it. He sought guidance from one of his mentors, a masterful consultant who asked some questions that got Brad to explore different options. The questions his shadow consultant asked were:

- What options are not yet being considered that might break the logjam?

- What knowledge do they have about customers and how they are responding to the competitor?

- What perspectives are not being considered that need to be considered?

- How might the needs of all of the Board members be served in this situation?

- What might industry analysts have to say on the subject?

These questions helped Brad recognize there were things neither he nor the Board knew enough about. Without any certainty as to the best strategic direction, Brad suggested that he facilitate an offsite with those involved to explore and gain some altitude on the situation. He suggested that not only the Board be involved in the offsite, but also customers, a couple of industry analysts, select members of the management team, and a group who were part of the health care industry, but not direct competitors. The purpose of the offsite wasn't to decide anything but to explore industry trends, to learn what was being called for by customers, and to gain greater understanding of emerging needs in the current market.

The offsite proved to have far greater impact than anticipated, as all present learned so much about the market and how Peach-Care was positioned in it that none of the original ideas were reintroduced. Instead, PeachCare decided to focus on an aspect of the market not yet well developed and bypass the competitive situation altogether. This proved to be crucial, and in two years they had forayed into new territories themselves and were now back on a relatively steep growth path.

Each of the approaches described above were not necessarily the right ones, although each proved to be effective. What defines them is the expansive view that each of the consultants took and how they encouraged the clients to do the same. The solution to many problems cannot be found within a narrow framework of thinking. Masterful consultants know this and spend far more energy helping people broaden their view than solving immediate problems.

PART V

ATTAINING
MASTERY

CHAPTER 14

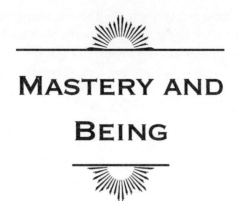

MASTERY AND

BEING

Much learning does not teach understanding.

—*Lao-Tzu*

THE JOURNEY TOWARD CONSULTING MASTERY is a journey toward oneself. It has been suggested that much psychological illness can be attributed to lack of self-awareness. Indeed, almost all of psychotherapy is designed to help one attain greater self-awareness in the service of healing. The same is true of mastery. The deeper one goes, the more one knows, the more mastery is available. Abraham Maslow and countless others have strongly suggested the direct relationship between optimal psychological health and effectiveness. Clearly, healthy human functioning has a verifiable relationship with each of the following:

- Clearer perception of reality

- Openness to experience

- Spontaneity and expressiveness

- Creativity

- Ability to be both abstract and concrete

- Self-confidence

- Honesty[1]

Each of these is directly related to consulting mastery. Everything you have read so far is a testimony to this. So the journey toward consulting mastery is a journey of self-discovery. To deepen this exploration, let's step back for a moment and define what we mean by "mastery."

MASTERY

Webster's New Dictionary tells us that the word "master" means: "someone regarded as great in his field, who serves as inspiration to later generations; a person of consummate skill in an art, technique, etc." Mastery implies greatness, brilliance, exceptional proficiency, and command of an art form, a profession, or a situation. It's a term that eludes precise definition. It is something that one feels or observes, and therefore is subject to human interpretation. Yet, at the same time, we know it when we see it.[2]

In any profession, when we see "mastery" we are typically observing seemingly effortless action, what the Italians call *sprezzatura*. Its beauty can be mesmerizing. A sense of flow, ease, and enchantment is embodied in any state of mastery. And it is because of this that we seek it, much as we seek peace inside ourselves.

This state of grace comes with great practice, and it is because we don't see the practice behind it, we say that the person exhibiting mastery must be a "natural."

Witness the great tennis player whose strokes seem so fluid that she appears to dance around the court with enormous ease. Her powerful backhand, the kind that eludes so many frustrated weekend players, comes easy to her. And indeed it is, but it wasn't always. It came from thousands and thousands of hours of trained and repeated action, honing the microscopic adjustments that are invisible to the untrained eye. The result seems natural only because it was built on a foundation of practice, which eventually became indelibly etched in the player's muscle memory. The backhand seems natural because the tennis master has long ago let go of technique and now hits the ball without thought.

Few people reach this state of mastery in tennis, and few reach it in their profession. It requires dedication, enormous practice, disciplined attention, ability, and the right learning environment. Mastery exists in rarefied air, yet at the same time it is available to us all in some arena in our lives. While we may not have the genes to become a master tennis player, we have the genes to become a master *something*—perhaps a musician, a poet, a sculptor, a chef, or an accountant. But in almost all cases, it requires hard work.

We give the term "master" to those that reach the pinnacle of their profession. We give it to the ones who do their work so well that we are transfixed, in awe of the beauty of extraordinary performance. We feel inspired by mastery, sometimes even transformed. Such is the case of people who are masters of the consulting profession. Who among us has not witnessed a great consultant in action and said to himself, "Wow, I wish I could have done that. That was masterful."

I remember the first time I saw a masterful consultant in action. I had just graduated from college and was part of a team of people responsible for putting together plans for creating a new Department of Social Services in the State of Massachusetts. One day we were engaged in an all-day meeting to begin planning a new state-of-the-art management information system. An information technology consultant was brought in to help guide the project. Many were doubtful about the value of bringing in a consultant; introducing a new MIS system seemed like a straightforward proposition. The head of the project never rebuked these doubts. He simply asked the team to be open to new ideas. Most reluctantly agreed.

We sat around a large conference room table in a simply furnished room typical of state bureaucracies—functional, no frills. The consultant entered, right on time. I was first struck by his looks. In contrast to my expectations, he appeared, well, a bit disheveled. His hair was unkempt, his belly poked out of his shirt a bit, and his clothes were rather casual. His whole presentation reminded me of that famous fictional detective, Colombo.

He began the meeting in an unexpected way. Instead of asking us typical questions like "Tell me what kind of system you have in mind," or "Tell me the problems you want to solve with the new information system," he said: "So, tell me your dreams for the new department." With that, he took us immediately out of our heads and into our hearts. There was a hesitancy to talk, at first, but with each new, probing question from the consultant, we got into the spirit of exploration more fully. Often, he punctuated our thoughts with his own excitement. "That's great," or "wonderful," or "yes, yes, yes!" he would say.

Little by little, a litany of thoughts, feelings, and ideas emerged, some of which had never come up in prior conversations. After about an hour, a buzz of excitement about the project had clearly replaced the initial humdrum feeling. Through each simple question he asked and the exploration that followed, the symphony of ideas grew and reached a crescendo by mid-morning.

Then, through a set of simple yet profound questions, he helped us explore how the new management information system might serve our vision. His ability to ask questions that helped us relate that vision to practical reality was extraordinary. By the end of the day, not only had we fashioned the parameters of a new information system, we were excited about the prospect of bringing it into fruition. Whatever cloak of doubt people had felt earlier had been lifted and replaced by the promise of possibility.

Many readers might respond somewhat cynically at this point, and say this was just good consulting. Wasn't he just helping us get our vision and purpose clear before defining the project goals? Isn't that what good consulting is all about? All true. Consider, however: first, the excitement that resulted from his process was really significant; second, his own infectious enthusiasm and nimble ability to grab us and keep us engaged were essential in generating that excitement; third, we felt that *we* owned the information system plan when we were done, not him; and, fourth, this was the mid-70s, and the concept of "vision" was not yet even part of the business idiom.

This consultant was ahead of his time. He brought us to places in our imagination where few information technology consultants dared go. More importantly, it planted a seed of possibility inside of me that had never existed before. I don't remember the consultant's name. But I will never forget the flame he ignited inside me.

Why does mastery matter so much? Because it points to what is possible in life. It calls us to stretch and deepen ourselves. It can even transform us, letting us see what we could not see before. If you buy the notion that learning is a fundamental human need, then the desire for mastery, and the journey that it requires, are central to our fulfillment as humans.[3]

Tiger Woods, who has taken golf to a whole new level, illustrates this point beautifully. Even the best professional golfers marvel at what he can do with the golf club. They say that he has taught them things they did not know. They have been inspired by his mastery. Yet golfers and fans often do not see what truly differentiates him from others. It is not his skill or technique. Witness the many younger golfers who drive the ball even farther, whose strokes are more fluid. What differentiates Tiger Woods from others is his heart. It is his drive (no pun intended), his will, his equanimity under pressure, and his belief in himself. More than any other golfer of his generation, he is determined to be the best.

Regardless of the profession, the remarkable achievements of any individual are the direct result of hard work and consistent attention over long periods of time. No different than athletes, artists, and leaders, the master consultant earns his place through concerted effort.

Part of what makes mastery elusive is that it is a journey without a final destination. It is all process. Moreover, it is highly subjective—relative to the observer. You may say that all the golfers on the PGA tour are masters, and by most measures they are. At the same time, most of them see Tiger Woods as a master beyond their current skill level. I've seen this on the tennis court, where I managed to achieve a degree of mastery as a four-year letterman in college and a ranked, championship-level amateur. A good amateur might look at my strokes with admiration; yet to my eye, there is much that is not masterful. I can see so many ways I still have to learn. To me, it is the tennis pros who seem masterful, clearly beyond my capability.

Mastery, then, appears to exist ever beyond oneself. The very act of achieving it, at some level, reveals the next level of possibility, a level one might not have been able to see in less advanced stages. As a result, people who are viewed as a "master" by others seldom view themselves that way; they are looking for the next stage of their own development, the next higher precipice on their journey. A light story may be revealing here.

Two monks were walking together down a path. They see a group of monks up ahead. One says, "Hey, that looks like a bunch of masters. Let's see if they will walk with us so we may drink from the fountain of their wisdom." The other monk says, "Those are not masters, just a bunch of monks like you and me." "How do you know?" asks the one. "Watch, I'll show you," the other replies and calls ahead: "Masters, masters, wait for us." The monks ahead stop and wait. "You see," said the second monk. "They clearly are not masters at all."

With only two exceptions, the carefully selected interviewees in my study never claimed they were masters. Many even seemed uncomfortable with being considered a "master." A few pointedly balked at the term. Their humility in the face of success prevents them from ever admitting to themselves, let alone anyone else, that they are masters. They simply see themselves as good consultants, working hard to be true to their principles, act with integrity, and continue to be the best "vessel" they can be for positive growth and change.

A ZEN PROVERB SAYS: "BEFORE ENLIGHTENMENT, CHOP WOOD. AFTER ENLIGHTENMENT, CHOP WOOD." IN THIS SPIRIT, CONSULTING MASTERS FEEL THEY ARE ON A JOURNEY TO GROW IN THEIR ABILITY TO DO GOOD WORK IN THE WORLD, AND TO MAKE A DIFFERENCE. NOTHING MORE, NOTHING LESS.

Although unwilling to admit it, masterful they are, for they consistently (if not always) produce greater positive outcomes in their client organizations than others, and they consistently leave their clients feeling stronger and more capable. When asked, they told me that what makes the difference for them is not any particular knowledge they might have. It is the quality of their "being." Of course, they didn't say so in so many words. Their innate humility wouldn't allow them to compare the quality of their being to anyone else's. Yet when they talk about their success, everything they say has to do with that one thing: their being ("where they come from") when they take actions. In this sense "mastery" and "being" are intertwined.

BEING

Being is an elusive concept. It cannot be objectified. One cannot touch it, smell it, taste it, or see it. Moreover, because so many branches of science, psychology and philosophy deal with the concept of being, it has been defined in a variety of ways. For example, Martin Heidegger, the 20th century philosopher, refers to being as a fundamental state of existence in the world. He was interested in the "is-ness" of being. He also believed that living an "authentic life" had something to do with discovering and expressing one's natural state of being. Looking at being from a slightly different angle, many eastern philosophies refer to being as the innermost core of one's self, that which is connected to all things. Each of these views clearly has merit, as do so many more.

While many have wrestled with the concept of being, we need a concrete definition. When I refer to one's *being,* I am simply referring to where one's consciousness is located at any given moment. My consciousness, in this case, has to do with the content of my thoughts and my awareness. It is where I come from when I take action. When a friend is troubled by my angry expression and says, "Hey, Keith, take a look at where you're coming from," she is asking me to look at my attitude with regard to that particular situation, or at the thoughts that produce the anger. She wants me to see where my anger derives.

At any moment, I can come from any of a number of places in my inner being. Sometimes I am in touch with my core self and feel connected to all things. Sometimes I am the wounded child of my deeper self and act petulantly. Sometimes I express myself through my outgoing personality and am playful. In every case, my behavior is driven by some part of my inner being.

Defining one's being with precision helps us appreciate the thoughts that distinguish masterful consultants from others, and to understand where these thoughts derive. Indeed, looking closely at the process by which we think and act becomes a powerful teaching tool. It is insufficient to suggest to an eager consultant-in-training to adopt a certain being. This instruction is too elusive, like asking a novice tennis player to "be more fluid." It doesn't work that way! It is often more instructive to suggest that the developing consultant adopt a particular thought process. This is something that can be more easily received and acted upon. Eventually, repeated thought processes begin to shape—or reshape—one's being.

Here's a brief example. A colleague recently was invited to a senior executive staff meeting in a new consulting situation. It was hard for her. In addition to garden-variety performance anxiety, she was aware of a deeper distress. She was working much too hard to impress the client with her abilities. This desire to impress was driven by worries that she might not be fully accepted, part of a deeper issue she had with rejection—a repeated life concern that shaped her overall *inner stance* in life.

Because she wanted to impress, she spent a lot of time and energy thinking about what would dazzle the client, what would show them how bright she was. The possibility that she might be rejected also weighed on her. These thoughts produced actions that came across as showy, pushy, strained, and unnatural. In the end, instead of impressing the client, she had the opposite effect. The client experienced her as needy, disconnected from the group, and not confident. During the meeting, the client's feelings and perceptions were not immediately obvious to her. Yet afterwards, as the members of the executive team discussed their feelings, they reported to each other that they felt she did not belong in the culture of the business and were concerned that she was not the "right fit" for them.

While initially unaware of why the client decided not to work with her, the reasons became much clearer when she later reflected upon her *inner stance*. She realized that she had not felt quite right within herself when making her presentation. Had she felt solid, truly connected to who she was—to her deeper capabilities—and had she trusted herself fully, she would have felt much less of a need to impress. She would have known she was perfectly fine just as she was, naturally. Had she been in a more solid *inner stance,* in other words, she would have more likely been successful. I know her as a marvelous consultant. What came out, however, was less than that.

If I were to coach her on how she could have been more effective, I probably would not have said something like "Trust yourself, you'll be fine." Although generally true, this does not help her know the factors that prevented her from trusting herself, nor does it guide her on where or how to come from a solid capable place in her being throughout the meeting. Instead, my coaching would have more likely gone down a path that looks more like the following:

a. How were you feeling going into the meeting?

b. How were you feeling throughout the meeting?

c. What thoughts were driving these feelings?

d. Where do those thoughts come from?

e. What alternative thoughts would have been more productive?

f. What mindset or belief would best produce those thoughts?

g. How can you best stay in that mindset throughout the meeting?

This process helps her locate more precisely the *inner stance* that will help her become more effective. Although I might offer suggestions along the way, the nature of the inquiry invites her to get clearer for herself and assumes that she already has the knowledge and ability to come from a solid place inside herself. This is often the case.

I believe almost all great consultants go through the same process of asking similar questions. Their self-reflection is designed to help them discover and learn ways they can be even more effective by being more solid in themselves or in their being. The term *centered* has all to do with this same notion, and being centered, calm, and relaxed is the goal so that you can bring your best to any given situation.

HEALTHY BEING AND MASTERY ARE INSEPARABLE.

Lest we get too far astray, let's ask the obvious question. Why look at one's *inner stance* to understand masterful consulting? Why not look at one's actions? The answer is simple. Since different people have different styles and exhibit different external behaviors, it's very difficult to put one's finger on an external reason why some consultants are masterful while others are only so-so. The answer isn't found in behavior, personality, or interpersonal style. I have met many great consultants in my day. Some are charismatic, others are shy. Some get right to the point, while others are subtle and suggestive. Some even have behavioral patterns that are slightly off-putting, such as a tendency to repeat themselves (one of my flaws—and might I add, thank goodness for editors), or *umm*-ing and *uh*-ing in every sentence. Masterful consultants come in every shape, size, gender, race, personality, and style.

So the commonalities among masterful consultants are not found in their behavior (although some behavior patterns or personalities work better with certain clients than others); nor do they lie in the consultants' knowledge. I have personally witnessed consultants employing a remarkable variety of theories about organizational effectiveness, from simple four-box models,* to highly elegant, complex depictions of organizational life.

WHAT MATTERS MOST, WHAT ULTIMATELY MAKES THE "BIG DIFFERENCE," IS THE QUALITY OF BEING AT THE CONSULTANT'S CORE.

But ultimately theory, knowledge, technique, or actions aren't what matters most. A famous aphorism in the Bhagavad Gita, the ancient Hindu guide for living, tells us: "Established in being, perform action." This phrase teaches us the key to mastery: To be great, tune your inner stance first, and then take skillful action. Have you ever met people who impressed you immediately, not with anything they *said*, but with how they *were*? Later, you saw

---

* If I only had a dollar for every four-box model I've seen!

them in action and it confirmed your feeling. More likely than not, they are guided by this very aphorism. They focus on their inner stance, knowing that skillful action follows naturally.

MY EARLY TRAINING ON MY BEING

For six years, from the time I was 31 until I was 37 years old, I got the best training I could ever imagine in the power of looking at the quality of my being. It came at the hands of my mentor at the time, Mike McKeon, one of the best consultants I know. Mike had been a senior consultant at a consulting firm committed to organizational transformation that I had joined in the late 80s, and for three years was my manager and mentor in the area of "being."

Later, I left the firm, and he eventually joined me as my partner in creating a new firm, that has since become Avista Consulting Group. The training I received as a result of working with Mike was profound in its implications, and at the same time powerfully simple. Whenever I returned from a consulting engagement to debrief, he would ask me how the work turned out. I would tell him the outcome, and then he would ask, "What was your state of being?" After months and then years of these simple questions, I became proficient at shining a light on my "being" and seeing the direct relationship to the consulting outcome. These "debriefs" were always revealing, for they caused me to take accountability for the results of my work.

Early on in my training, however, they were also painful, for when the work did not turn out well it forced me to "own" the outcome, completely. Many a time I wanted to squirm away from these debriefs when the work didn't go as well as I would like. I wanted to blame the circumstances, blame the client, blame the setup, or chalk it all up to bad timing. Yet Mike never let me squirm out of taking responsibility, and for this I am eternally grateful.

I don't mean to imply that one's inner stance is more important than skillful action. It is not. Great internal health without effective action is as empty as effective action without purpose. The two are inextricably intertwined ("established in being, perform action"). What I am saying is that relative to skillful action, the road to mastery is established in one's inner stance.

CHAPTER 15

THE ROAD TO CONSULTING MASTERY

He who looks outside, dreams; he who looks inside, awakens.

—Carl Jung

Mastery in any endeavor is not given. It is earned. It is the birthright of all people yet requires that we go on a journey and face terrible demons within ourselves, to arrive whole. Almost all heroic myths that depict a long and arduous journey are stories of an inner journey toward consciousness, and the attainment of mastery requires such a journey.[1] I am reminded of a story told among the Buhera Ba Rowzi people of Zimbabwe, passed down through their oral history from generation to generation, that speaks to the courage and internal commitment necessary for self-mastery and for consulting greatness. It is both an ancient story, and yet, like all archetypal stories, it speaks to a universal truth about courage and integrity. The story is about Mella, a young girl facing an eternal challenge, and the choices she made along the way. Like many myths, the story is best interpreted as a parable or even as a dream, the external events of the story understood as the dynamics unfolding in one's psyche.

MELLA AND THE PYTHON HEALER

As Mella's father, the chieftain of the tribe, lies unconscious on a mat in their humble home, facing death, Mella, heavy in her heart, realized she must seek help from the terrifying Python Healer, who lives deep in the jungle. All the other efforts to revive her father had been in vain.

Her journey took four days and nights, through unfamiliar groves and across powerful streams. Finally she arrived at dusk at the entrance to the cave. Mustering her courage, she called out to the hollow of the cave, "I am Mella, sent to you by Bomu Rambi. I have come to ask your help, for my father has lain ill for many moons and his weakness is the weakness of my people."

After waiting in silence for what seemed like an eternity, she saw a pair of eyes in the dim moonlight and heard a frightening voice "The bravest have fled in terror from my door. Does such a small girl have no fear that I might strangle you and leave your bones about my cave?"

"I do have fear, but my love for my father is even stronger," replied Mella. "My father has done no wrong, yet neither the Nganga healers nor the spirits of the ancestors can heal him. I beg you for help, if any can be given."

"Your love is more powerful than your fear?" the Python Healer questioned. "Would you turn your back and let me crawl close to you then?" Though terrified, Mella turned her back, the pride of her people and her love for her father giving her strength.

The Python Healer, now close at hand asked, "Would you let me twine myself about you as if to eat you?" Terrified even more, Mella allowed the Python to wind itself about her upper body, with only small openings between the coils through which to see and breathe. The Python Healer instructed Mella to begin the long walk home.

Exhausted from carrying such a heavy load, she arrived at the edges of her village with the Python Healer still coiled around her.

When the villagers saw the monstrous creature walk into a clearing, they ran for their

Understood as a parable of our psyche, this story has enormous richness in its implications for consulting. For me, among other things, this is a story of courage and choice, to explore and face one's inner fears. It is a story of the eternal struggle between ego (greed) and selflessness (courage and wisdom). It also a story about the journey toward self-awareness, a journey that requires one to

arrows and spears, but Mella called aloud, "It is I, Mella, inside the Python healer! Do us no harm for I have traveled far to bring healing to my father." Bewildered, they put down their weapons as she walked through the door of her home. Once inside, the Python Healer uncoiled itself and slithered to the foot of her dying father's mat.

From a small pouch that hung about its neck, Mella took the healing bark as the Healer had instructed her. From the small deer horn that hung about its neck, Mella took the muchonga oil as well. Following his instructions, she made a fire that sent the vapors of the healing bark floating into the upper reaches of their hut, while the Python Healer recited holy chants of the Buhera Ba Rowzi people. Then, to her amazement, Mella's father arose from his deathbed, stood erect, and began talking, something he had not done for many moons.

His work done, the Python Healer once again coiled himself around Mella's body to begin the journey home. After returning to his cave, the Python showed her a room laden with pots of gold and silver, ivory and precious jewels, riches beyond her belief. Generously, he offered, "Take what you wish, for your courage and love should be rewarded."

Mella was both honored and embarrassed, for in her eyes, it was he who should be rewarded. In a whisper, she replied, "It is your choice, not mine." From a wicker basket, the python took a golden chain into its mouth, upon whose links hung a golden crescent of the moon, the sacred image of the Buhera Ba Rowzi tribe.

Upon returning home, Mella told her family of the treasure of the cave, proudly showing the golden Ndoro she had earned as a gift. Upon hearing her story, greed entered the hearts of her brothers who began to plot the python's murder in order to steal his riches. Overhearing the scheme, Mella ran quickly to the python to warn the Python Healer of her brothers' plans. When the brothers arrived, they were greeted by bursts of hot, unpleasant smoke and thunderous roars, and they fled in terror.

Later, when her father died, the people of the village appointed Mella as their leader, honoring her courage, honesty, and love. Throughout her many years, Mella led them with wisdom and grace, often visiting the Python Healer for help.[2]

travel the inner recesses of one's own unconscious, represented by the Python Healer and his cave.

Those who enter the cave, facing their fears of the shadow, may eventually partake of its riches. Not everyone takes this journey, and it must be done with open heart and integrity. In the end, Mella shows us the power of holding an inner stance that is pure and giving. Her story teaches us that mastery comes not from skill, but from finding a deep place within, from which to choose and act. The place is found through an inner journey toward a more solid state of being, and once found the choice becomes clear.

The outcome of the journey within is profound and universal as it relates to consulting mastery. People who have attained a high degree of inner mastery feel and relate to the world in the following ways:

* They know who they are.

* They see themselves as unique.

* They take full responsibility for their feelings.

* The act genuinely.

* They are open and receptive to others.

* They are flexible internally and externally.

* They are fluid, spontaneous, and natural.

* They are present—"in the moment."

* They include others easily.

All of these factors relate to trust, and trust is at the core of all relationships and at the core of consulting mastery.

FROM BEING TO ACTION

Alas, to say just "develop a healthy state of being" is not enough. One must also take action and do the inner work that mastery requires. Moreover, that action must be pure. An Italian saying speaks directly to the heart of the issue: *Tra il dire e il fare, ce in mezzo il mare*. Translated, this means, "There is an ocean between saying and doing." Masterful consultants spend a lifetime swimming that ocean, bridging the gap between being and action. It is the work of consultants eager to become great in their craft.

The story of King Midas is instructive here. Like many, King Midas believed that if he were only rich, he would then be happy. So he made a pact with the gods that everything he touched would turn to gold. Not a bad deal, he thought. However, the deal ends in misery as the food in his mouth and the wine on his palate turned to gold before he could swallow them, and his daughter turned to gold as he went to embrace her. Fortunately he had the wisdom to undo his mistake and begged the gods to take his gift away. Amused and observant that he was genuine in his learning, they did so, as he vowed to seek riches in the simpler things in life. This parable echoes through the ages as we continue to want the fruits without the labor. It is in the labor of the inner journey that true riches derive.

I know at least four ways to help one achieve mastery in the consulting business. The first is highlighted by so many of the stories I share about my own lessons on my own journey, namely, *keep paying attention to how your inner stance affects your actions.* When you do something that is less than stellar, look at your inner stance and explore how you might have changed it to be even more effective. When you do a piece of work that is extraordinary, look to find what about your inner stance contributed to success. The second way is to *work closely with others who already are masterful.* Get a mentor to provide you with guidance. The third way is to *tune your inner stance* before each piece of work you do. Ask yourself: how do I need to "be" in this interaction or intervention such that the outcome is maximized. The fourth way, and by far the most crucial, is to *see the process of becoming masterful as a lifelong journey.*

I will speak to each of these in turn.

PAY ATTENTION TO YOUR INNER STANCE

A masterful consultant's inner stance yields masterful actions, which in turn produce the highest levels of success. Success is not simply a completed project. Success in consulting mastery has to do with achieving the outcomes and leaving the client more capable and healthier. The complete model is shown in Figure 15-1.

Just as Mike McKeon used to ask me how my inner stance was, ask yourself the same question. I find it helpful to ask it in a spacious and exploratory manner, such as: How might my inner stance have contributed to these results? Then look in each of the three relationships for your answers. Usually, it will be more than

Masterful Inner Stance	Masterful Actions	Masterful Results

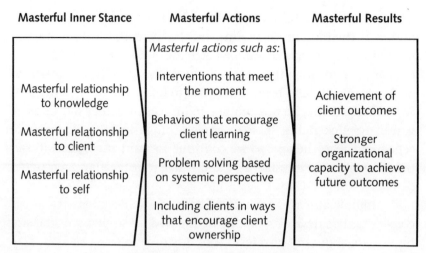

| Masterful relationship to knowledge

Masterful relationship to client

Masterful relationship to self | *Masterful actions such as:*

Interventions that meet the moment

Behaviors that encourage client learning

Problem solving based on systemic perspective

Including clients in ways that encourage client ownership | Achievement of client outcomes

Stronger organizational capacity to achieve future outcomes |

FIGURE 15-1   THE MASTERY MODEL

one. You will find some feature in the relationship to knowledge, client, or self, or some combination of all three. They are always present in any consulting situation, and therefore available for introspection.

In paying attention to your inner stance, one crucial principle makes all the difference: Your focus on your inner stance must be done with openness and without self-judgment. When self-judgment is introduced into the process of introspection, more often than not, pain or hubris is not far behind. When we fail and feel self-judgment, we feel pain. Our ego will want to protect us from that pain, and therefore we will likely avoid looking inside ourselves deeply for learning. When we succeed and feel self-judgment, we feel hubris. This reinforces a bloated ego. Neither pain nor hubris contributes to our ability to learn. In learning to be masterful, it is best to treat each as opportunities for learning. Nothing more, nothing less.

SEEK A MENTOR TO GUIDE YOU

I said it before, and I will say it again here. I am only where I am as a result of some very powerful mentors who showed me the way. I have had three mentors in my consulting career and many great teachers. Early on in my career, Bill Torbert was an outstanding guide. He introduced me to the importance of one's "being," and I am ever indebted to him for having introduced me to the state of inquiry necessary to be effective as a consultant. Mike McKeon was my mentor, guide, partner, and friend for many years before his premature death from cancer. More than anything, he taught me to trust myself and to let go of judgment toward self and others. Ron Tilden has been a wonderful guide and friend for the past 12 years. About every two months we meet and explore life and consulting together, and I always leave feeling enriched by his presence and loving guidance. More recently, David Bradford has played a profound role in supporting my growth as a leader and the growth of our consulting firm.

From all that I learned from each of these mentors, the most important thing is that almost all of my time with them focused on my inner stance. I can only remember two times of the hundreds of interactions I had with them where we ever discussed tools, techniques, instruments, or models. My journey of discovery focused almost exclusively on the inner aspects of consulting—and for this I am forever grateful. Whenever I asked "How to?" they responded with "Where are you coming from?" Whenever I asked, "What should I do?" they responded with "What needs to drive your choices?" They never supplied pat answers. Instead, their questions help me see differently and find the answers from deep within. That is the power of a good mentor, and there is no substitute for it.

TUNE YOUR INNER STANCE

We began this book with a simple notion. Your inner stance drives your thoughts. Your thoughts drive your behavior. Your behavior in turn drives your results. The secret to consulting mastery then, begins with a well-tuned instrument—a well-tuned inner self. In the long run, the key to tuning your instrument is clear—keep developing your self, through personal growth workshops, therapy, spiritual pursuits, and the like. In the short run, the answer is less clear. There are so many ways we get off track. My experience tells me that the best way to develop mastery is to think thoughts that masterful consultants think.

Start with an image of yourself as a masterful consultant—a vision so to speak. Such imaging has huge potency. Rainer Maria Rilke, the 19th century poet, put it well when he said, "You must give birth to your images. They are the future waiting to be born." The kinds of images you might want to form revolve around the following:

- How I see myself as a consultant in the future

- The clients I will work with

- The kind of work I will be doing

- My code of conduct as a consultant

- The impact that I will have.

Forming an image at the broadest level acts as a magnet for you. The more you hold that image, and the more you refer to it, the more it becomes you. At the more micro level, before each piece of work you do, think about how you want to be in the meeting. Often, before I go into a crucial meeting, I will tune my inner self by relaxing, reflecting, and imagining how I want to be and what I want to create in the meeting.

QUESTIONS TO HELP YOU TUNE YOUR INSTRUMENT —YOUR BEING

1. What is the outcome I want to create for this meeting?

2. How do I need or want to be in this meeting so that a successful outcome occurs?

   What thoughts do I need to have?

   What feelings do I need to have?

   What attitudes do I need to adopt?

3. How do I want others to be in this meeting?

4. What will I need to do and be in order to encourage others to be the same way?

THE LIFELONG JOURNEY

In the final analysis, mastery is not a destination, nor is it a thing you do. Instead it is a journey of a lifetime that knows no ending point. While the ideas and examples in this book point the way, the best way to develop your inner stance is through a lifelong journey of self-exploration, self-awareness, and self-discovery. Many traditions offer powerful guidance including Taoism, Buddhism, The Gurdjieff Work, Christian and Jewish Teachings that focus on Meditation and Prayer, Toltec Training, Jungian Psychotherapy, Personal Growth Workshops, and so many others. These traditions offer guidance toward self-mastery, and there is no substitute for ongoing inner work. All of them operate from the basic premise that our inner stance guides our thoughts, and from our thoughts, all else follows.

THE THOUGHT MANIFESTS AS THE WORD;
THE WORD MANIFESTS AS THE DEED;
THE DEED DEVELOPS INTO HABIT;
AND THE HABIT HARDENS INTO CHARACTER;
SO WATCH THE THOUGHT AND ITS WAYS WITH CARE;
AND LET IT SPRING FROM LOVE
BORN OUT OF CONCERN FOR ALL BEINGS.

AS THE SHADOW FOLLOWS THE BODY,
AS WE THINK, SO WE BECOME.

FROM THE DHAMMAPADA
(THE SAYINGS OF THE BUDDHA)

All of the masterful consultants I know have been on the journey for a long time. They know that the source of their effectiveness and the deepening of their self-awareness are one and the same. They have each engaged in activities, practices, and disciplines designed to examine their thoughts, feelings, and beliefs and find ways of being in the world that are more resourceful, capable, and ultimately satisfying.

No singular roadmap exists for the journey toward mastery. One consultant I know has participated in many personal growth workshops as a key part of his learning. Another favors psychotherapy coupled with a religious devotion. Still a third seeks self-discovery through movement, art, and poetry. Many great consultants I know use these vehicles simultaneously. Regardless of your preference, if you choose this path, over time, the journey toward mastery will inevitably lead you to a deeper relationship with yourself. It will lead you also toward much greater deftness in working with clients. Masterful consultants rarely use blunt instruments. Like the experienced diamond cutter, they know where to apply a little force to have a great impact. This is the masterful way, and one not journeyed by many. While the road is paved by a few, the rewards are ever the greater. The famous parable, "The Rainmaker," by C. G. Jung speaks to what I mean.

THE RAINMAKER

There was a great drought. For months there had not been a drop of rain and the situation became catastrophic. The Catholics made processions; the Protestants made prayers; and the Chinese burned joss sticks and shot off guns to frighten away the demons of the drought, but with no result. Finally the Chinese said: "We will fetch the rainmaker." And from another province a dried-up old man appeared. The only thing he asked for was a quiet little house somewhere, and there he locked himself up for three days. On the fourth day the clouds gathered and there was a great snow storm at the time of year when no snow was expected, an unusual amount, and the town was so full of rumors about the wonderful rainmaker that Richard Wilhelm went to ask the man how he did it.

In true European fashion he said: "They call you the rainmaker. Will you tell me how you made the snow?" And the little Chinese man said: "I did not make the snow; I am not responsible." "But what have you done these three days?" "Oh, I can explain that. I come from another country where things are in order. Here, they are out of order; they are not as they should be by the ordinance of heaven. Therefore, the whole country is not in Tao, and I also am not in the natural order of things because I am in a disordered country. So I had to wait three days until I was back in Tao and then naturally the rain came."[3]

Masterful consultants are rainmakers in their own right. The rain they make is not money, of course. It is making a difference in people's work lives. They know all too well that the journey toward mastery is an inward journey. You cannot see it in their actions. But you can feel it in their souls.

THE INTERVIEWS
AND THEIR IMPACT

THE ORIGINAL CONCEPTION OF THIS BOOK did not include interviews. Some colleagues wisely suggested, and I readily agreed, that interviewing people considered contemporary masters of our craft would give both weight and credibility to my thoughts, and even more importantly, offer insights beyond my own experience. How right they were! I have learned through my interviews more than I could have offered on my own, and have been inspired by their wisdom, for it points to many ways I can continue to grow myself as a consultant.

Going one step further, I also decided to interview people in positions of authority in organizations about what they seek, value, and appreciate in a consultant. I was particularly interested in their view of the best consultant they have ever worked with. In the end, I interviewed 14 masterful consultants and 10 clients to add to and deepen my own perspective on consulting mastery.

My Approach to Selecting Masterful Consultants to be Interviewed

The process of identifying participants to interview was itself a learning process for me. I began by asking many highly respected and well-connected colleagues whom they consider a masterful consultant in our field. Each colleague gave me a list of people. At first, I took this at face value and believed that, if my respected colleagues believed these people were masterful, they must have something on the ball. However, in probing further, I discovered that this was not necessarily the case. I began to ask, how do you know these people are masterful? Almost in all cases their answer was the same. "Well, I know them by reputation. These people are known throughout our field as being great." Again I probed further. "How do you know, I asked?" Almost all answers sounded like the following: "Well, I heard about them. I heard they do a good job." Seldom did my colleagues observe these consultants consulting in the flesh.

From this experience, I began to make a distinction in my own mind of the difference between reputation and actual ability. Were they the same, or was there a difference? Were there people who were distinguished by reputation who may not necessarily be models of mastery? Are there people who are extraordinary practitioners who are seldom known by others? I was eager to answer these questions for myself, so I kept the process of selection alive.

I began to share my original "masters by reputation" list with others whom I considered to be "in the know." In all too many cases another colleague would say, "Oh my goodness, I did work with that guy and he was a nightmare." Or, "She was so arrogant, she pissed the client off." Or "He was a lot weaker than I ever expected." So the reputation of many of the consultants on my initial list, while initially strong, quickly sagged when subjected to close scrutiny.

This phenomenon suggests a clear difference between people we believe are effective and people who in our experience actually are effective. Many of the folks with a reputation in the consulting field have developed that reputation because at some time they may have done great work, or they are great conceptual thinkers. They think about our work and the process of their craft in a way that's compelling to fellow consultants. However, many of the pioneers in the consulting field are not pioneers because of the quality of their consulting. They are pioneers because of the quality of their thinking and their writing. They have offered new and different ways of exploring the process of consulting and have helped shape our understanding.

Since being a masterful practitioner and a master conceptualizer are not the same thing, I needed to get a bit more rigorous in my approach than going by reputation. In other words, my question had to shift. My question was no longer "Who do you believe is a masterful consultant?" My question became "Who have you directly experienced as a masterful consultant?"

To help gauge this question a bit more precisely, I chose my interview pool by defining a set of criteria and then asking many of my colleagues to nominate people who directly fit this set of criteria:

a. The person had a long-standing practice.

b. The person's work consistently and repeatedly had a positive and enduring impact on whole organizations.

c. Clients consistently call the person back, time and time again.

d. The nominator had to have seen the person in action.

e. The nominator considered the person to be the best he or she had ever worked with and seen in action.

The nominators that I chose were also consultants who were among the best I had worked with, and who I considered masterful as consultants themselves. My belief was that people who do great work consistently know great work when they see it. Put differently, they have a sufficient standard of excellence that for them to say: "This is the best person I have ever seen in action," says a whole lot. That alone was probably enough to make it onto my "masterful consultant" list.

Many nominees were mentioned more than once. This became a litmus test of sorts. If nominated by more than one person, this suggests, to a modest degree, that nominations were somewhat less influenced by an individual nominator's bias or personality preference.

THE INTERVIEW PROCESS. The interview process was designed to be wide open to begin with and let the interviewee tell me about his or her own thoughts about consulting. I wanted them, unrestrained or unguided by me, to tell me about what is important to them in being a consultant.

Then I probed more deeply to focus on the qualities of their inner stance that made the difference in their eyes. If, along the way, the interviewee did not touch upon the following questions, I left room at the end to be sure I captured their thoughts. Their answers to these, and my own experience, formed the thesis for this book.

1. What is the role of a consultant in helping clients grow and change?

2. When you excel as a consultant in that role, what qualities are you exhibiting that make a difference?

3. What characteristics or qualities distinguish your consulting from ordinary consultants?

4. When you have made mistakes in the past or were less effective than you believed capable, what factors may have contributed?

5. When you contemplate being a role model for our clients, what comes to mind? What does it mean to you?

6. What do you believe about the ownership of the change process?

7. What quality of relationship do you seek to establish with clients?

Interviews typically took about two hours and were rich with anecdotes, self-reflection, and deep inquiry.

Client Interviews

In addition to interviewing contemporary masters, I sought the input of organizations that use consultants readily. For this part of the inquiry, I sought to interview executives in or from organizations who used consultants often, and who could easily discern the difference between a great consultant and a good one. The kinds of questions I asked these executives were:

1. Name the best consultant you have ever worked with (one who positively impacted the whole organization in an enduring way).

2. Tell me about the approach that the consultant took—his or her style, thinking, the quality of his character, etc.

3. How is this approach, style, thinking, and quality of character similar or different from that of others you did not select as the best?

Answers to these questions and the follow-up probing enabled me to discern the client perspective on masterful consulting.

In the end, while I did conduct some research on the subject, the ideas expressed here are both personal and universal. They formed through my 25 years of work as a consultant and were reinforced, challenged, and reexamined by the interviews themselves. At the same time, the ideas do not belong to me. The way I express them certainly does, but many of the concepts embedded in the book are timeless, shared throughout the ages among all people who choose to be in a helping profession.

Notes

Introduction

1. See, for example, H. Mintzberg, *The Rise and Fall of Strategic Planning* (New York: The Free Press, 1994); J. Micklethwait & A. Wooldridge, *The Witch Doctors: Making Sense of the Management Gurus* (New York: Random House, 1996); J. O'Shea & C. Madigan, *Dangerous Company: Consultants and the Businesses They Save and Ruin* (New York: Times Books, 1997); and M. Kihn, *House of Lies* (New York: Warner Books, 2005).

2. "Firms Bidding More to Win Less," *Consulting News*, vol. 32, issue 8, 2002.

3. "What You Need to Know to Survive the Recovery," *Consultants News*, vol. 34, issue 6, 2004.

4. *Consultants News*, vol. 34, issue 6, 2004, www.Consulting-Central.com.

5. N. Nohria & J. D. Berkeley, "Whatever Happened to the Take-Charge Manager?" *Harvard Business Review*, Jan–Feb 1994, pp. 128–137.

6. "The Cracks in Quality," *Economist*, April 18, 1992.

7. R. Schaffer, *High-Impact Consulting: How Clients and Consultants Can Work Together to Achieve Extraordinary Results* (San Francisco: Jossey-Bass, 2002), p. 9.

8. Exceptions include P. Block, *Flawless Consulting: A Guide to Getting Your Expertise Used*, 2nd ed. (San Francisco: Jossey-Bass/Pfeiffer, 2000); G. Bellman, *The Consultant's Calling: Bringing Who You Are to What You Do* (San Francisco: Jossey-Bass, 1990); and D. Maister, C. Green & R. Galford, *The Trusted Advisor* (New York: The Free Press, 2000).

9. A notable exception is Robert Schaffer's recent book *High-Impact Consulting* (cited in Note 7), which chronicles the flaws of many of the practices that underlie most high-profile consulting firms.

10. Antoine de Saint-Exupéry, *The Little Prince* (New York: Harcourt, Brace & World, 1943), p. 87.

CHAPTER 1

1. Chris Argyris's many books speak well about how the explicit and tacit goals and strategies drive people's behavior. These distinctions have influenced my thinking.

2. Curt Schleier, "Consulting Innovator Marvin Bower: His Vision Made McKinsey and Co. a Pioneer," *Investor's Business Daily*, Nov 9, 2000.

CHAPTER 2

1. R. Bly, ed., *The Soul Is Here for Its Own Joy: Sacred Poems from Many Cultures* (New York: HarperCollins, 1995), pp. xvii–xviii.

2. A. Einstein, *Ideas and Opinions* (New York: Crown Publishers, 1954; reprinted by Gramercy, 1988).

3. These principles are laid out in C. Argyris, *Intervention Theory and Method: A Behavioral Science View* (Reading, MA: Addison-Wesley, 1970) and have been a guide to many great consultants ever since.

4. For an excellent description of the value of contracting around all aspects of the client-consultant relationship, see M. Weisbord, "The Organization Development Contract," *The OD Practitioner*, vol. 5, issue 2, 1973, pp. 1–4.

CHAPTER 3

1. For an excellent treatise on the importance of well-defined goals in a consulting situation, see R. Schaffer, *High-Impact Consulting: How Clients and Consultants Can Work Together to Achieve Extraordinary Results* (San Francisco: Jossey-Bass, 2002).

2. After the initial car sale, many car dealers will try to convince a customer to buy a number of options including the wax job necessary to protect the paint. I am told that this "full wax job" is short of useless, inexpensive for the car dealership to apply, and very costly for the customer. The proposal is made at a time when the customer often thinks, why wouldn't I want to protect the investment I just made, thus preying upon the customer's vulnerability.

3. B. L. Toffler, *Final Accounting: Ambition, Greed, and the Fall of Arthur Andersen* (New York: Broadway Books, 2003).

4. D. A. Blackmon, "Familiar Refrain: Consultant's Advice on Diversity Was Anything But Diverse—For Big Fees, Powers Perrin Gave Many of Its Clients Nearly Identical Reports—Nissan Westinghouse Balked," *Wall Street Journal*, March 11, 1997, p. A1.

5. M. Lindfield, "Reflections on the Natural Art of Consulting," *Consulting to Management*, vol. 13, no. 2, 2002.

6. W. Bynner, *The Way of Life According to Lao Tzu* (New York: Capricorn Books, 1962).

Chapter 4

1. D. Katz & R. Kahn, *The Social Psychology of Organizations* (New York: John Wiley, 1978); P. Senge, *The Fifth Discipline: The Art and Practice of the Learning Organization* (New York: Doubleday/Currency, 1990); M. Wheatley, *Leadership and the New Science: Discovering Order in a Chaotic World* (San Francisco: Berrett-Koehler, 1999).

Chapter 5

1. I am grateful to Frank Basler for pointing this out to me.

Chapter 6

1. E. Schein, *DEC Is Dead, Long Live DEC: The Lasting Legacy of Digital Equipment Corporation* (San Francisco: Berrett-Koehler, 2003), pp. 173–174.

2. G. Bellman, *The Consultant's Calling: Bringing Who You Are to What You Do* (San Francisco: Berrett-Koehler, 1990).

3. K. Lewin, in *Field Theory in Social Science: Selected Theoretical Papers*, edited by O. Cartwright (New York: Harper & Row, 1951), p. 169.

4. G. Bateson, *Steps to an Ecology of Mind* (New York: Ballantine, 1972), p. 449.

5. A. Szent-Gyorgyi, in *The Scientist Speculates*, edited by I. Good (New York: Basic Books, 1962).

Chapter 8

1. R. Moore & D. Gillette. *King, Warrior, Magician, Lover: discovering the archetypes of the mature masculine.* (San Francisco: Harper Collins, 1990) pp. 100–101.

2. Much of this analysis was borrowed from J. O'Shea & C. Madigan, C. *Dangerous Company: management consultants and the businesses they save and ruin* (New York: Times Books, 1997).

3. J. O'Shea & C. Madigan, C. *Dangerous Company: management consultants and the businesses they save and ruin* (New York: Times Books, 1997) p. 136.

4. J. O'Shea & C. Madigan, C. *Dangerous Company: management consultants and the businesses they save and ruin* (New York: Times Books, 1997) p. 141.

5. J. O'Shea & C. Madigan, C. *Dangerous Company: management consultants and the businesses they save and ruin* (New York: Times Books, 1997) p. 144.

6. R. M. Rilke, *Letters to a Young Poet*, translated by Stephen Mitchell (New York: Random House, 1984).

CHAPTER 9

1. D. Riesman. *The Lonely Crowd*. (New Haven: Yale University Press, 1950).

2. C. G. Jung. "Analytical Psychology and Weltanshauung" in Collected Works 8: *The Structure and Dynamics of the Psyche*. (Princeton, NJ: Princeton University Press, 1970) p. 737.

CHAPTER 11

1. J. Juran, *Quality Control Handbook* (New York: McGraw-Hill, 1951).

CHAPTER 12

1. C. G. Jung, "On the Psychology of the Unconscious," in Collected Works 7: *Two Essays on Analytical Psychology*. (Princeton, NJ: Princeton University Press, 1970) p. 35.

2. A. I. Allenby, describing a conversation with C. G. Jung, in *C. G. Jung Speaking: Interviews and Encounters*, edited by W. McGuire and R. F. C. Hull (Princeton, NJ: Princeton University Press, Bollingen Series, 1977), p. 158.

3. R. A. Heinlein, *Stranger in a Strange Land* (New York: Putnam, 1961).

CHAPTER 13

1. H. Robbins & M. Finley, *TransCompetition* (New York: McGraw-Hill, 1998).

2. T. S. Szasz, *The Myth of Mental Illness* (New York: Hoeber-Harper, 1961).

3. D. McClelland, *Power: The Inner Experience* (New York: John Wiley, 1976).

4. T. Kidder, *The Soul of a New Machine* (Boston: Little, Brown, 1981).

5. C. Eames & R. Eames, *Powers of 10* (1968, 9 minutes). Available on DVD: *The Films of Charles & Ray Eames,* Volume 1 (Image Entertainment, 2000).

CHAPTER 14

1. A. Maslow, *Toward a Psychology of Being.* (New York: D. Van Nostrand Company, 1968) pg. 157.

2. For a lucid and compelling exploration of the concept and practice of mastery in any profession, see G. Leonard, *Mastery: the keys to success and long-term fulfillment.* (New York: Penguin Books, 1991).

3. Paul Lawrence and Nitin Nohria, in a compelling examination of the most basic and deepest levels of human drive, identify the drive to learn as one of the four key drives that define human beings. The others are the drives

to acquire, to bond, and to defend. P. R. Lawrence & N. Nohria *Driven: how human nature shapes our choices*. (San Francisco: Jossey-Bass, 2002).

CHAPTER 15

1. J. Campbell powerfully makes this point in *The Hero with a Thousand Faces* (Princeton, NJ: Princeton University Press, Bollingen series, 1949).

2. Adapted from *Ancient Mirrors of Womanhood: A Treasury of Goddess and Heroine Lore From Around the World* by M. Stone (Boston: Beacon Press, 1979), pp. 153–157.

3. C. G. Jung, *The Nature Writings of C. G. Jung* (Berkeley, CA: North Atlantic Books, 2002).

INDEX

ABOUT THE AUTHOR

Keith Merron is the founder and Managing Partner of Avista Consulting Group, an organizational consulting and leadership development firm dedicated to helping organizations with bold visions achieve sustainable high performance and industry leadership. He has more than 23 years of experience assisting executives and managers in business, government, and education. In partnership with his clients, he has successfully conducted over twenty-five large-system cultural, technical, and systems change efforts. His work has positively impacted Hewlett-Packard, Freddie Mac, AmeriGroup Corporation, MedCath, Wang Laboratories, General Public Utilities, WorldCorp, Endocare, CSAA, the National Institute of Standards and Technology, and the Healthcare Financial Management Association, as well as over 200 other companies and organizations.

Keith received his doctorate from Harvard University and is the author of *Riding the Wave: Designing Your Organization for Enduring Success,* published by Van Nostrand Reinhold in 1995.

Your Signature Path
Gaining New Perspectives on Life and Work

Geoffrey M. Bellman

Your Signature Path explores the uniqueness of the mark each of us makes in the world. Bestselling author Geoffrey M. Bellman offers thought-provoking insights and practical tools for evaluating who you are, what you are doing, and where you want your path to lead.

Hardcover • ISBN 1-57675-004-3
Item #50043-415 $24.95

Audio, 2 cassettes • ISBN 1-57453-071-2 • Item #30712-415 $17.95

True Partnership
Revolutionary Thinking About Relating to Others

Carl Zaiss

In this book, an international business consultant discusses the four mistaken beliefs that keep people from building productive and satisfying relationships: seeing themselves as separate and autonomous, relating to others through power and authority, having an either/or mentality, and seeing the world as fixed and predetermined.

Paperback • ISBN 1-57675-166-X • Item #5166X-415 $15.95

Performance Consulting
Moving Beyond Training

Dana Gaines Robinson and
James C. Robinson

Performance Consulting provides a conceptual framework and many how-to's for moving from the role of a traditional trainer to that of a performance consultant. Dozens of useful tools, illustrative exercises, and a case study that threads through the book show how the techniques described are applied in an organizational setting.

Paperback • ISBN 1-881052-84-2 • Item #52842-415 $29.95
Hardcover • ISBN 1-881052-30-3 • Item #52303-415 $34.95

Berrett-Koehler Publishers
PO Box 565, Williston, VT 05495-9900
Call toll-free! **800-929-2929** 7 am-9 pm EST

Or fax your order to 1-802-864-7626
For fastest service order online: **www.bkconnection.com**

Stewardship
Choosing Service Over Self-Interest
Peter Block

Peter Block shows how to recreate our workplaces by replacing self-interest, dependency, and control with service, responsibility, and partnership. In this revolutionary book, he demonstrates how a far-reaching redistribution of power, privilege, and wealth will radically change all areas of organizational governance, and shows why this is our best hope to enable democracy to thrive, our spiritual and ethical values to be lived out, and economic success to be sustained.

Paperback • ISBN 1-881052-86-9 • Item #52869-415 $19.95

Hardcover • ISBN 1-881052-28-1 • Item #52281-415 $24.95

The Power of Purpose
Creating Meaning in Your Life and Work
Richard J. Leider

Concise and easy to read, and including numerous stories of people living on purpose, *The Power of Purpose* is a remarkable tool to help you find your calling, an original guide to discovering the work you love to do.

Paperback • ISBN 1-57675-322-4
Item#53224-415 $14.95

Audio • 2 cassettes/3 hours • ISBN 1-57453-215-4 Item #32154 $17.95

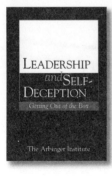

Leadership and Self-Deception
Getting Out of the Box
The Arbinger Institute

Leadership and Self-Deception reveals that there are only two ways for leaders to be: the source of leadership problems or the source of leadership success. The authors examine this surprising truth, identify self-deception as the underlying cause of leadership failure, and show how any leader can overcome self-deception to become a consistent catalyst of success.

Hardcover • ISBN 1-57675-094-9 • Item #50949 $22.00

Paperback • ISBN 1-57675-174-0 • Item #51740 $14.95

Berrett-Koehler Publishers
PO Box 565, Williston, VT 05495-9900
Call toll-free! **800-929-2929** 7 am-9 pm EST

Or fax your order to 1-802-864-7626
For fastest service order online: **www.bkconnection.com**

Berrett-Koehler books are available at quantity discounts for orders of 10 or more copies.

Consulting Mastery
How the Best Make the Biggest Difference
Keith Merron

Hardcover
ISBN 978-1-57675-320-0
(or 1-57675-320-4)
Item #93200-415
$34.95

To find out about discounts for orders of 10 or more copies for individuals, corporations, institutions, and organizations, please call us toll-free at (800) 929-2929.

To find out about our discount programs for resellers, please contact our Special Sales department at
(415) 288-0260; Fax: (415) 362-2512.
Or email us at bkpub@bkpub.com.

Subscribe to our free e-newsletter!
To find out about what's happening at Berrett-Koehler and to receive announcements of our new books, special offers, free excerpts, and much more, subscribe to our free monthly e-newsletter at www.bkconnection.com.

Berrett-Koehler Publishers
PO Box 565, Williston, VT 05495-9900
Call toll-free! **800-929-2929** 7 am-9 pm EST

Or fax your order to 1-802-864-7626
For fastest service order online: **www.bkconnection.com**